PENGUIN BOOKS

LAST DAYS IN OLD EUROPE

'Richard Bassett is no ordinary journalist
musician with a doctorate in architect
gourmet whose appetite is not li
is a dedicated observer of peop
escapes … The book includes cu
others, Shirley Temple, alongside w   Czech
riot police. There are poignant vign   rbachev
and Dubček, some Schloss-hopping,   s visit to the
officers' mess of the Queen's Dragoon G   as at Wolfenbüttel.
Whatever may be happening around him, Bassett at no point
loses his taste for the recondite, and this amiable tour is never
less than entertaining' Adam Zamoyski, *Literary Review*

'As Soviet rule in central Europe collapsed in the late 1980s,
newsworthy events, thrilling and poignant, abounded. Many
were enriched by the diffident, elegant presence of Richard
Bassett. By his own admission, he was not a hardened
hack … But charm, brains and a cultural hinterland work
quite well too, as the author's journalism then, and this
memoir now, demonstrate' Edward Lucas, *Financial Times*

'This enjoyable Baedeker-meets-Brideshead memoir of Central
Europe in the Eighties by a former correspondent for *The Times*
starts out being not so much of its era as yearning for an even
earlier one … Vivacious elderly contessas and jovial princes
people Bassett's narrative … he is deft at eliciting otherwise
unheard information' Julian Evans, *Daily Telegraph*

'Bassett wears his erudition without false modesty. As an art
historian, he describes approaching Venice by sea as a "magical
transition from Whistler to Canaletto"; his ear for the subtleties
of linguistic identity and class allow him to comment on different
types of Austrian accent. He attends the Opera Ball but notes
that it has become too *bürgerlich* for the true Austrian
aristocracy to attend' Clovis Meath Baker, *Standpoint*

'Full of insights about the death of two empires, the
Habsburg and the Soviet. In the age of nostalgia we have now
entered, when to so many people almost everywhere the past
seems so golden, it strikes a remarkably topical chord … short,
funny vignettes, filled with irony and eccentric characters'
Victor Sebestyen, *Evening Standard*

'If Oscar Wilde was correct that "history is gossip", then Bassett serves up a delicious cocktail of the very best kind – polite, learned, and insightful, merely leavened with touches of history and geopolitics, making one thirsty for more . . . A memoir can breathe life into history, and this is indeed Bassett's achievement as he breathes new life into shattered kingdoms, their now-mouldering cast of characters, and all of the fascinating stories that would otherwise vanish with them.' Kevin J. McNamara

ABOUT THE AUTHOR

After reading Law and the History of Art at Cambridge, Richard Bassett set out for Central Europe and in 1983 became principal horn of the National Slovene Opera House in Ljubljana. In 1985 he was appointed Central European and then Eastern European correspondent for *The Times*. His previous books include *A Guide to Central Europe* (1987), *Hitler's Spy Chief: The Wilhelm Canaris Mystery* (2005) and *For God and Kaiser: The Imperial Austrian Army, 1619–1918* (2015). He is a Bye-Fellow of Christ's College, Cambridge, and Visiting Professor at the Central Europe University of Budapest. He is currently working on a biography of the Empress Maria Theresa.

RICHARD BASSETT

Last Days in Old Europe

Trieste '79, Vienna '85, Prague '89

PENGUIN BOOKS

PENGUIN BOOKS

UK | USA | Canada | Ireland | Australia
India | New Zealand | South Africa

Penguin Books is part of the Penguin Random House group of companies
whose addresses can be found at global.penguinrandomhouse.com

First published by Allen Lane 2019
Published in Penguin Books 2020
002

Copyright © Richard Bassett, 2019

The moral right of the author has been asserted

Typeset by Jouve (UK), Milton Keynes
Printed and bound in Great Britain by Clays Ltd, Elcograf S.p.A.

A CIP catalogue record for this book is available from the British Library

ISBN: 978-0-141-97999-1

www.greenpenguin.co.uk

MIX
Paper from
responsible sources
FSC
www.fsc.org
FSC® C018179

Penguin Random House is committed to a
sustainable future for our business, our readers
and our planet. This book is made from Forest
Stewardship Council® certified paper.

In memory of Cornelia Kirpicsenko-Meran
(geb. Gräfin Meran)
1963–2013

and

Reinhold Gayer-Ehrenberg
1950–2018

nunc Scio quid sit amor: nudis in cotibus illum
aut Rhodope aut Tmaros . . .

Donau in Oesterreich
Mich umwohnet mit glänzendem Aug'
Das Volk der Fajaken;
Immer ist's Sonntag, es dreht immer
Am Herd sich der Spiess

(Danube in Austria
With their gleaming eyes I am surrounded by
The people of the Phaeacians
For whom the roast-spit ever turns
And for whom it is always Sunday)
                                        Friedrich Schiller, *Xenien* (1797)

Contents

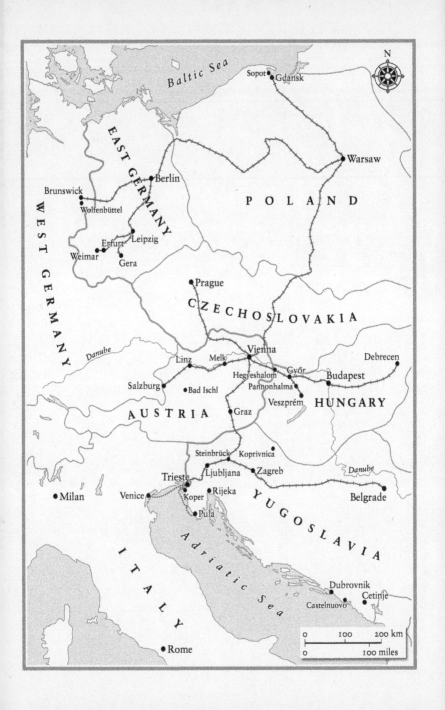

Acknowledgements

This book could not have been written without the kind support and friendship over many years of the people I encountered in Central Europe. Forty-year-old diaries and a fading memory are modest foundations on which to bring personalities back to life, but it was the presence of those personalities in Trieste, Vienna, Warsaw and Prague which made life along and behind the Iron Curtain so memorable and enriching, and I hope I have described them faithfully in these pages. If I have succeeded in conveying the excitement and reward which arises from chance encounters across different generations, then this book will have succeeded in its purpose.

In Vienna, Christopher Wentworth-Stanley, the *Tischherr* of the English *Stammtisch* (regulars' table) in Hawelka's, played over several decades a much underestimated role in bringing Austrians and English travellers abroad together. In Trieste, Mietta Shamblin discharged the same duty, while in Prague, Victoria Reilly-Spičkova and her husband Daniel generously put their handsome villa at the disposal of many other equally fulfilled *incontri*. I am also grateful to Frank Giles, one of the *Sunday Times*'s most distinguished editors, for reminding me of the circumstances in which a *Times* foreign correspondent was expected to operate nearly half a century ago. These parameters formed part of an unspoken tradition dutifully and conscientiously discharged by an ever-courteous *Times* Foreign Desk, then under the capable leadership of Ivan Barnes, a prince among foreign editors.

Given that it was proficiency in playing the French horn which allowed me to first live in and develop my knowledge of Central Europe, it gives me great pleasure to thank here the three horn teachers of my youth: first and foremost, Dr William Salaman, but also his occasional, inspiring successors, Jeffrey Bryant and Timothy Brown.

Fifty years later, I have become convinced that much professional achievement, academic or literary, is easily dwarfed by the discipline and diligence needed for the mastery of a musical instrument.

During the early 1980s I was fortunate to enjoy the company in Central Europe of Caroline Mauduit, a gifted watercolourist who frequently reminded me that the visual can complement the literary. In Cambridge I must mention my High Table colleague and friend Michael Perlman, an Honorary Fellow of Christ's College. I am indebted to him for his help in tracing in his native Brazil the remarkable story of HM Consul-General Robert Smallbones, whose name I first encountered in Trieste in 1979.

I owe a particular debt to Stuart Proffitt, for encouraging me to attempt to describe the eccentricities of life in Cold War Europe for a generation unfamiliar with that world and bringing his forensic skills to bear on the text. He and his colleagues, including Donald Futers and Ben Sinyor, have polished my prose, removing with tact and precision innumerable infelicities of style and content.

Part of the first section of this book first saw the light of day as a Christmas essay, 'Trieste '79', published privately by John Sandoe Books for their customers in 2013. A year later, translated by Ada Cerne, it was published also in Italian by the Umberto Saba bookshop of Trieste. I am therefore indebted to Johnny and Boojum de Falbe and Mario Cerne for acting as publishing midwives to this entire project.

Finally I should thank my wife, Emma-Louise, and our children Edmund and Beatrice, who have at times bravely entered the alternative cosmos which was (and is) life in *Mitteleuropa*.

Salzburg, 18 June 2018

The View from the Molo Audace

Trieste–Zagreb–Ljubljana–Graz

There are many shades of sky-blue. In my experience, the most intoxicating is the one which fills the Adriatic sky around Trieste each January after a few days of the Bora wind. The air has a clarity which I have seen equalled only in the highlands of Tibet. From the Molo Audace, simple slabs of Istrian stone stretching out to sea like a pier from the Triestine Riva, the peaks of the Alps, faintly pink, can be glimpsed nearly 70 miles away to the west beyond the lagoons. To the east, the Istrian peninsula, lazy and shimmering in the sunlight, stretches like some reclining voluptuary towards the hazy and distant lands of the Quarnero. It is cold in this bright sunlight but the colours are so vivid one scarcely feels it. 'Come to Trieste,' James Joyce once wrote to a friend, 'and you will see sun.'

It was on such a day in January 1979 that the 'Simplon-Orient Express' dropped me at the foot of the old Südbahn Terminus after rattling down the cliffs beyond Duino. I was young, tall and thin, conforming to the continental European view of the English stereotype at the time. A heavy midnight-blue barathea coat with wide double-breasted lapels, and an impatient air with the bureaucracy of the luggage carriage, no doubt confirmed the image. Although I had been travelling for more than thirty hours, luggage (sent in advance in those convenient days) was one simple large suitcase. Opening the case the officials found that it contained little to arouse their interest. A pair of pyjamas, some second-hand shirts and collars, a pair of corduroy trousers and a duck-egg green paperback copy of Stephen Spender's memoirs all failed to attract their attention.

In some places, it seems that the circumstances of travel never change. The train will always more or less be a quarter of an hour late, the officials will always be indifferent. Indeed, I might have chosen any time in the previous twenty-five years to effect this arrival in Trieste and I would have been greeted by the same picture of perennial stillness. Trieste had been quiet since the early 1960s. Its status as a minor port of Italy, much disputed by Marshal Tito's Communist Yugoslavia in the immediate aftermath of the Second World War, had finally been stabilized by an international treaty four years earlier. The Cold War had sealed it from its hinterland and this once great metropolitan port had become, in practice, an enormous museum – a museum with very few visitors.

I had studied the map of Trieste from an old Baedeker of the Eastern Alps bought for a pound from John Ruston's wonderful anti-quarian bookshop, Commin's, a few minutes' walk from our house in Bournemouth. Although none of the names seemed to be correct I had managed to find my destination within half an hour of walking from the station. The British School, Via Torrebianca, had placed a small advertisement in *The Times* asking for an 'English teacher'. Glimpsed from a dark cold windswept avenue on the south coast a few weeks before Christmas, the very name 'Trieste' appeared to conjure up romance and a chance to escape from a peculiarly English parochialism. An exchange of telegrams a month later and the post was secured. It was, friends assured me, entirely the consequence of a good degree from Cambridge.

But it appealed because it was not my first visit to the city. Six months earlier, the train had taken me from Ljubljana to Trieste and then, as now, the Bora had just died down to reveal a horizon of breathtaking clarity. Filled with enthusiasm and energy I asked a heavily made-up lady in the tourist office where I might stay and she told me of a small hotel near the Amphitheatre. Mietta Shamblin was elegant and middle-aged, keen to practise her rather archaic English and correct my halting Italian. She offered to ring them to ask if they had a room, noting *en passant* that Trieste was a very welcoming place for strangers. Thanks to Signora Shamblin, for whom nothing was too much trouble, this proved to be the case. With its soft im-perial Viennese architecture, the bright light, the superb coffee, the abundant evidence of different peoples and creeds and a wealth of old

Imperial and Royal civilization,* it was almost as if the essence of the Habsburg Empire had been bottled into this one place for preservation for future generations so that the stranger might pass along its streets thinking, 'Ah yes. This must be what an Imperial Austrian city was *really* like.' So the advertisement in *The Times* that wintry afternoon on the Hampshire coast had fallen on fertile ground. It offered me a chance to renew an exciting new acquaintance, learn another language and deepen my knowledge of a fascinating city. To a twenty-two-year-old, these seemed to be happy prospects.

The next day, as I entered a tobacconist's shop just off the main square to buy some postage stamps, a lady with spectacles attached by wires around her neck took one look at me and hailed me with a familiar greeting. There had been no exchange of addresses six months earlier but Mietta had not forgotten the young Englishman and I could never have forgotten her enthusiastic warmth.

'What are you doing now? Come with me.' Mietta grabbed my arm. Chattering merrily about the power of coincidence, she briskly escorted me to the small canal which stretched from the solemn neo-classical Church of San Antonio near by towards the sea. It was another dazzlingly sunny day. As we marched along the Ponte Rosso, I remembered the difference between the 'tourist' and the 'traveller' which the amiable and owlish Senior Tutor at Christ's, Gorley Putt, had been fond of pointing out. The former was a prisoner of superficialities, forever condemned to be ripped off and abused; the latter penetrated below the surface and could be relied upon to 'understand' the places he visited (in those days at Cambridge it was, sadly, usually 'he'). The key to this was of course rapport with 'the locals'. If you knew the inhabitants in a foreign city you were halfway to understanding how it worked.

'I want you to meet some friends', Mietta said. Halfway along the canal, a small unpretentious door led to the Bar Danubio. It was a modest place, very unlike the grander cafés glimpsed in Vienna or Graz or even elsewhere in Trieste. Later I would discover the opulent

* Imperial and Royal: from 1867 the Dual Monarchy of the Empire of Austria and the Kingdom of Hungary.

Caffè Specchi, on the Piazza Unità, and the Stella Polaris with its ornate columns, all of them distinct in atmosphere and style from the Bar Danubio. Mietta ushered me into a space whose walls were a fading cream unadorned save, very high up, for a small black and white photograph of Trieste taken from the nearby clifftop at some indeterminate date between 1860 and 1960.

There could not have been more than half a dozen tables in the quiet, austere room. Three were occupied. Behind a large coffee-machine, the waiter was intently studying the newspaper's cryptic daily 'Rebus'. Conversation, if there had once been any, had stopped. As though we had entered a library, everyone seemed to be in a state of mild concentration, examining the printed word.

'This is the poetess Lina Galli,' intoned Mietta with a flourish. I saw a grey-haired old lady with a large silver medallion round her neck. The poetess looked up from her newspaper and smiled 'Piacere.' Before I could engage her, Mietta pulled me to one side towards a second table, where an old man with heavily lidded eyes gazed up unshaven from another newspaper. 'And this is the writer Giorgio Voghera ... and his friend Piero Kern.' Voghera smiled benignly. Kern, who seemed in his mid-fifties, streaks of red in his hair, responded in short, deceptively languid phrases: 'So you are English? Have you read *King Solomon's Mines*?' Without waiting for a response Kern replied enigmatically: 'So ... the palaver is over.' He pronounced the word in the Hungarian manner with an accent on the first syllable and returned to his paper.

At the third table an old woman with a handsome profile sat gazing at the 'Rebus' quiz. 'And this', said Mietta with faintly recalibrated enthusiasm, 'is my aunt, Myrta Fulignot, the widow of the famous painter Guido Fulignot.' Myrta smiled with dark inscrutable eyes. I had not, alas, heard of this great painter, but I nonetheless found Mrs Fulignot easier to converse with than the other denizens of the Danubio. She spoke German with an Austrian accent and asked if I enjoyed playing *Pritsch* (bridge). Though I did not know it, that bright morning in this sparsely furnished space, and notwithstanding an average age difference of more than half a century, I had made friends for life.

My duties at the school were light. Every day after the morning's teaching, on Myrta's advice I would go to a little restaurant, the Casa

Maria near the Greek Orthodox Church, where a kind, portly woman offered a simple pasta and salad washed down with a quarter bottle of Merlot from the Gorizia hills a few miles away. Despite its plainness, this humble trattoria was far from cramped and we ate in comfort under vaulted ceilings. On the walls, a portrait of Emperor Franz Josef gazed down. The old Emperor had visited Trieste in 1882 to be greeted in the Habsburg tradition with demonstrations and bombs. In death, and more than a half-century after the end of Habsburg rule in Trieste, Cecco Beppe (a contraction of 'Francesco Giuseppe' but also meaning Blind Josef), as the Italians had called him, was venerated in cafés and trattorias across the city.

There were about a dozen guests each day at Maria's. One table attracted attention immediately because it was laid out every weekday for four respectable-looking men in their late fifties, each dressed in a dark tweed jacket, tie and flannel trousers. Each place was set with its individual miniature bottle of wine. These men were such regular lunchers they merited their own personal napkins, rolled into pewter rings. I would learn later that these anonymous bureaucrats were modest 'men of the Generali', the great insurance company headquartered in Trieste, whose careful underwriting in Habsburg days had stretched to every corner of the Austrian Empire. The firm had been so prevalent in writing policies for the bourgeoisie of the empire that one could generally discover whether someone had been an Austro-Hungarian citizen by asking whether they or their family had ever been insured by the Generali.

The four men were convivial but they never raised their voices nor stooped to conspiratorial whispers. Each consumed his individual quarter-litre of Tocai Friulano or Refosco without fuss or criticism. Until this time in my life, I had placed a high value on energy and dynamism, but I could now see that here was something faintly enviable: a simple bureaucratic life, undisturbed by problems or challenges that might interfere with the routine of lunch with a few colleagues. These were not men who would ever confuse movement with progress. As I watched them leave promptly each day at ten to two, to head back to their offices or perhaps to a siesta, seemingly untroubled by worries, I was unaware that I was witnessing a middle-class *douceur de vivre* on the brink of extinction in Europe.

Voghera had worked most of his life at the Generali. I had not then read his autobiographical masterpiece *Il direttore generale*, about the personalities of the Generali insurance company in the 1920s (let alone his celebrated *Anonimo triestino: Il segreto*), but it was clear that, within the confines of the city, his reputation was high. Despite his overall air of untidiness, it was equally obvious that long years of service in the Generali had afforded Voghera the luxury of early retirement. He had enough material comfort to write. Had he opted for the more intellectual life his brilliance merited and become a university professor, like his protégé Claudio Magris, author of the acclaimed *Danubio*, he could not have enjoyed such freedom. Magris's spare frame and intense expression could occasionally be glimpsed across the marble tables of the nearby Caffè Tommaseo.

At first, Voghera was inscrutable. Though he never offered the slightest protest, I often felt I was disturbing his peace and calm with my foolish questions about Trieste. Gradually, as my Italian improved, we moved away from conversing in German and he became far more garrulous. On the topic of Trieste's railways (an object of unceasing fascination) he explained in painstaking detail how there had been three routes to Trieste under the Austrians and that one, running past the lake of Bohinj, had been especially beautiful *dal punto di vista panoramico*. The Pontebba Bahn, the Staatsbahn, the glorious Südbahn and the engineering feats associated with them were all described with the exactitude of a learned specialist, though railways never featured in his books: those dealt with altogether more profound psychological themes.

Voghera seemed to be knowledgeable about everything. There was no escaping the fact that he had been an exceptionally gifted child. The opening lines of *Il segreto* summed up perfectly his intellect and dry wit: 'Non c'è alcun dubbio: io fui un bambino precoce. Se mi dovessi basare su quel poco che ho letto di psicologia infantile, dovrei concludere che fui proprio un fenomeno' (There was not the slightest doubt: I was a precocious child. On the basis of what little I have read of child psychology, I am forced to conclude that I was really a phenomenon').

To encourage my Italian, he urged me to use the most complicated words I could find 'as these are more or less the same usually in every language'. When I announced one day that I was going to visit Cividale, he gave me a short lecture on the civilization of the Lombards. When I was off to Milan for the weekend, he cautioned me against the impenetrability of the local dialect and urged me to visit the courtyards of the town palaces in the centre of the city, to enjoy their secret treasures of vegetation and architecture. Occasionally Kern would add to Voghera's advice, though on the whole he seemed indifferent to the thrills of travel, exuding an air of a weary *uomo degli affari*, always keen to get to the bank before it closed, or complaining of the cost and the delay in transferring money from Brazil where he had spent the war and where it seemed (though he never alluded to this directly) he still had business interests. Kern's grandmother had married the father of Gustav Mahler. They had been 'teachers in a school in Bohemia'.

When, with the fussiness of youth, I had corrected him by pointing out it was Moravia not Bohemia, Kern observed in a deadpan voice, 'Ma Lei è pedante nel corrigermi su queste piccole cose' (But he is a pedant to correct me on these little details). Yet if he asked you some question about an obscure book and you failed to answer correctly, his refrain, delivered equally unemotionally, was 'Ma la sua ignoranza è spaventosa' (Your ignorance is terrifying).

Very occasionally, we were joined in the Bar Danubio by a striking figure, complete with Homburg and red curls, who would introduce a histrionic energy into the café previously absent. Salmona was a Hebrew scholar and clearly a man of great learning. For my benefit he spoke in a loud fractured German, rich in grammatical errors and an exaggerated use of the plural pronoun which one morning finally provoked Voghera to exasperation. Turning his penetrating gaze on this highly accomplished intellectual he gave him a petulant look and said, 'Schauen Sie Salmona, mit diesem "Euch" kommt man nirgends hin!' (Look, Salmona, with this use of 'Euch' you cannot get anywhere).

Other guests at the Bar Danubio were less cerebral. In particular Myrta knew some beautiful women who struck me as the apogee of Adriatic beauty and utterly unlike the female company I had known at school or university. First there was Signora Corbidge, a Greek woman in her early thirties, with classically shaped eyes and hair. Then there was Mrs Jacobs, a blonde and elegant half-English woman with sparkling countenance and a wonderful smile. It seemed perfectly normal in Trieste that these sophisticated women should patronize a run-down bar in an unfashionable quarter of the city.

Myrta lived in some style in a set of rooms above the canal in the old Palazzo Scaramanga opposite the Serbian Church whose great blue dome was visible from the windows of her salon. On the walls hung paintings by her former husband, a mixture of fashionable portraits of society women and nudes of intense sensuality, whose haunting eyes gazed down on me. A white and black top hat, made of Venetian glass, stood upside down on the table. It served as a vase, and was filled with orchids. Gradually, I grew to know each of these paintings, but it would be many months before Myrta confided that they were all studies of her, nearly half a century earlier. Myrta, as she had made clear at our first meeting, was a keen *Pritsch* player. The game, then as now, was a passport into civilized company and it was not long before I was introduced into the Circolo del Bridge which met each week in fine high-ceilinged rooms in the Palace of the Old Stock Exchange. Consuls (mostly honorary) gathered there each week to exchange the odd piece of political or commercial gossip between rubbers. The Circolo was open to all, but its membership was mostly made up of mentally agile octogenarians.

Through an old friend in Graz, I had an introduction to one of these – Geoffrey Banfield, a highly decorated Imperial Austrian air ace and the Honorary French Consul. It was a sign of the rich multinational fabric of the old Austrian Empire that his name was quintessentially English. His friends called him Gottfried, Goffredo or Geoffrey, depending on their mother tongue. Banfield appeared impervious to these distinctions, clearly revelling in the linguistic riches of the empire whose devoted and most highly decorated officer he had once been and half a dozen of whose languages and dialects he spoke fluently.

I was invited to visit him on yet another of those sunny bright January mornings in his office near the Riva at the headquarters of the Tripcovich shipping company. Those who visit the Scuola di San Giorgio degli Schiavoni in Venice will see in the dark ground-floor room, beneath the great series of Carpaccio paintings, the name of a sixteenth-century Captain Tripcovich commemorated in one of the wooden stalls. The Tripcovichs, like the better-known Cosulichs, were Triestine shipping aristocracy: they had all originally hailed from the small island of Lussin Piccolo in the Quarnero. Banfield had married a descendant of this intrepid family in the Brompton Oratory in 1920.

Escorted up a grand staircase by a liveried porter, I was ushered into the *Barone*'s anteroom. His secretary, another elegant lady, sensed my lack of fluency in Italian and spoke to me in French. While I waited outside Banfield's office, she looked at me intently and asked what I was reading. It turned out that she had never heard of Stephen Spender.

'Have you read any Proust?' she asked. I cannot now remember what I replied, but it obviously exhausted my limited understanding of modern French. She showed me a copy of *L'École des femmes* by Molière and urged me to read it, saying I should find it 'full of insights'. In later years I came across many personal assistants to important men who acted like gargoyles on drawbridges guarding a castle. This lady, in contrast, was utterly charming. I promised her I would read Molière. A few seconds later, I was shown into a large office with three windows overlooking the Adriatic. Below an old steam locomotive chugged slowly along the Riva towards the port.

I was not sure what this hero of the Great War would be like. In 1915, at the age of twenty-five, Banfield had been given command of the newly established Trieste naval air station. At first his command had consisted of two flying-boats and one machine gun but by 1918 he was commanding a squadron of twenty-four planes which daily faced an enemy three times as numerous. As the Great War developed, the Gulf of Trieste became the fulcrum of Italian attacks and it was largely due to Banfield and his fellow pilots that their opponents in the Entente, despite their overwhelming superiority in numbers, never enjoyed undisputed access to Trieste's airspace. He had conducted daring rescues of wounded colleagues, fought brave dogfights against countless enemy planes and had even disabled a British submarine. When I met him, six decades later, in 1979, he was the last former Imperial Austrian officer alive to have been decorated personally by Emperor Franz Josef. In 1917 he had also been awarded the empire's highest award of chivalry, the Order of Maria Theresa, by Franz Josef's successor, the last Habsburg Emperor Charles. This decoration automatically conferred the title of Freiherr of the Empire, elevating the handsome pilot in his twenties to the junior ranks of the Austrian aristocracy.

The man opposite me seemed smaller than I had expected, but his silver-grey hair framed a face still strong and handsome with penetrating blue eyes. In so many ways he appeared English, yet his face was softened by smiling Austrian lips and an aquiline nose. He was the lowest of low keys, diffident and charming. One hand waved me to a chair while another pulled out a deep drawer in his desk from which emerged two glasses and a bottle of Stock brandy. The distillery, in those days still run by the formidable Baroness Stock, was less than two miles away along the coast.

'Mr Bassett. Can I offer you something to drink?' It was shortly before nine in the morning. Banfield's English was faultless. He enjoyed flitting effortlessly into Italian and occasionally into the Triestine dialect whose dry open vowels were becoming familiar to me: 'xe un bel zità' (it's a beautiful city) as he pointed with one hand towards the Riva below. But he also spoke the Viennese dialect of the aristocracy with its clipped past participles and drawling French adjectives. Things were either *mi-se-raabel* or *ak-zep-taabel*. After discussing the imperial naval engagements in 1915, he moved the conversation to England where he had worked as a draughtsman for Vickers Armstrong in Newcastle in the 1920s. The English industrial unrest and social dislocation which prevailed in the late 1970s struck him as the inevitable consequence of a failure to adapt to 'modern conditions'. How calm Trieste appeared compared to the England of power cuts and trade union anarchy which I had left a few weeks earlier! He was confident the English would learn from their mistakes although it would require a change of approach. 'I remember during my days working for Vickers in Newcastle that when I pointed out certain things could be done more quickly or more easily, the refrain always was: "My dear Geoffrey, we are going to do it this way, because we have always done it this way."' Thus our conversation meandered over industry, finance, geopolitics, before settling on the Emperor Franz Josef. Here Banfield's expression became serious.

Two months before his death in 1916, the old Habsburg Emperor – who by that point had reigned for nearly sixty-eight years – had spent more than an hour talking alone to Banfield, eager to hear all

THE VIEW FROM THE MOLO AUDACE

about the 'war in the air'. His parting words to the young pilot had been 'See to it that you come through this war alive, my dear Banfield. Austria will need men and pilots like you after the war.' Even more than his later encounter with the Emperor Charles, this was, Banfield confided, the most vivid memory of his entire career and the one that had left the deepest imprint.

Although he had clearly been a hero and without doubt one of the most skilful pilots of the entire war, after 1918 Banfield never sat in the cockpit of an aeroplane again. Had the war in the air with its ceaseless combat and killing disillusioned him? I formulated the question with exaggerated obliqueness and received the answer it deserved: 'Some more brandy, Mr Bassett?'

Wandering back along the Riva, past the faded, peeling stucco of Caffè Tommaseo, I sat down in one of the chairs that overlooked the sea and the Molo Audace and ordered a *caffè latte* (what in the rest of Italy is called a *cappuccino*). Boats rarely moor alongside the Molo these days, but in 1914 the scene was very different. Photographs show the bustling Molo San Carlo, as the Austrians named it, loading and disgorging passengers and luggage to accompany the busy traffic between Trieste and Dalmatia under a bright sun and cloudless sky. The Molo is Trieste's most poignant and yet understated monument to its once glorious past. No individual is commemorated. No name is inscribed. Only a fine bronze wheel records the landing of the Italians here in November 1918, but there is no hint of earlier poignant memories. It was impossible not to feel the spirit of the place, even before reading the melancholy recollections of Countess Lanjus, the lady-in-waiting of Franz Ferdinand's wife's.*

In late June 1914, a launch had taken the Archduke Franz Ferdinand from here to the waiting warship *Viribus Unitis* and the fateful journey to Sarajevo. Less than a week later, on 2 July, another launch had brought him and his wife Sophie back in coffins. After a brief benediction by the massed ranks of Trieste's clergy, the coffins were set in front of a large detachment of sailors arrayed in two solemn lines. Then, bedecked in imperial naval battle ensigns, and with a full naval and military escort, they were brought to the Südbahn

* *Dal Belvedere di Vienna a Sarajevo*, ed. Eugenio Bucciol (Trieste, 2015).

railway station a mile and a half away. Immediately behind the coffins walked the only woman to have been in the Archduke's immediate entourage, Countess Wilma Lanjus, who had been in the car directly behind the imperial couple in Sarajevo that tragic morning.

As she walked behind the coffins under a 'baking sun' and a 'merciless' Triestine sky, she later recalled, 'The streets were lined with thousands of mourning Triestini, but in their loyalty to the Habsburg Monarchy I did not hear a single noise from anyone as we walked along. Not a sound. For almost an hour there reigned a *silenzio assoluto*.'

I walked on to the Molo, retracing Countess Lanjus's footsteps, gazing out to sea and pondering the timeless view before turning back. As I rejoined the Riva my eye was caught by a poster in the elaborate red and cream livery applied to all publications emanating from the Teatro Verdi, and my mood changed. It gaily announced a performance of *La sonnambula* by Bellini to be given the following day.

A discreet office near the main entrance to the Teatro sold me an inexpensive ticket for high up in the amphitheatre, and the next evening I queued to climb the five flights of stairs to reach my seat. The house was packed, and the obbligato of the principal horn, my own instrument, was dazzling. The average age of the audience seemed to be in the seventies, but they came noisily alive after the soprano's brilliant aria in the last scene, just as it might have been a hundred years earlier when the theatre was a focus for Italian nationalism.

As spring approached, I realized I needed to find new quarters. Myrta immediately came to the rescue with a suggestion that we visit her friend *die Gräfin Korwin*, who lived on the second floor of a city palazzo on the Via XXX Ottobre. In Trieste, as in many other Italian cities, streets rejoiced in dates sacred to the Italian Risorgimento. Besides the XXX Ottobre (commemorating the 1918 plebiscite in favour of an Italian Fiume), there was the Viale XX Settembre (commemorating the seizure of the Porta Pia in Rome in 1870), the Riva III Novembre (the day Trieste was taken by the Italians in 1918) and many others. All reinforced the convictions of those Italians who felt that Trieste as well as being a great former Habsburg metropolis could also be *la città più italiana d'Italia* (the most Italian city of Italy).

XXX Ottobre ran from the Pantheon-inspired Church of San Antonio in a straight line towards the railway station, exemplifying neo-classical planning. It was not a distinguished street, although it did house the most celebrated chocolatier of the city, a Hungarian gentleman of the old school whose premises appeared unchanged since Habsburg days. Imperial naval officers had once filled La Bonboniera to queue for elaborate boxes of chocolate for their wives and daughters, but by now the place was normally empty. Instead, an elderly lady offered a languid 'Buongiorno', as one entered, and an even more adagio 'a Lei' in response to any farewells uttered on leaving. In between these two expressions she neither looked up from the counter where she was reading a book nor demonstrated the faintest inclination to engage with her customers.

Countess Korwin agreed to see us after lunch a few days later. As Myrta and I ascended the staircase, a voice echoed down telling us to mount the steps unhurriedly. 'Only take your time.' I dimly made out the source of this encouragement, a small fine head smiling benevolently down. As we reached the third floor, I heard a phrase I would hear often when I lived in Central Europe: 'English? How nice.' I looked across the landing to see a lady in her late seventies with a kind and compassionate face. Her arms were folded across a dark cardigan. Two black eyes were gazing at me intently.

A brass plaque with the name Colomba de Korwin in faint Jugendstil letters still adorned the door. Inside, not much seemed to have changed since imperial times. A kitchen of Balkan primitiveness with an old gas oven occupied one little corner; in a small room with a window on to a wall, tin bowls were stacked up beside a bath. Chaos was kept in check by phalanxes of wooden furniture, dark and heavy in the neo-Renaissance style so beloved of the old imperial aristocracy. I had often encountered this furniture in Graz, accompanied by the seductive smell of freshly applied wax polish.

'You know how difficult it is these days to find . . . *Personal*.' This last word the Gräfin pronounced in the Austrian upper-class nasal manner as 'Perr-so-naal'. A 'temporary' shortage of servants was responsible for the untidiness. Myrta and I smilingly acquiesced in this happy fiction which the manners of old Austria made easy to accept. Generally in Central Europe, even today, there is a studied reluctance to transmit unwelcome facts in anything but the most flattering light.

Myrta explained that Blanka, as I would soon come to call her, had experienced both the best and the worst of life. Fêted as a great beauty in the 1930s – James Stewart had invited her to Hollywood – she had married first an Italian prince and then, on his sudden death, become involved with the Finance Minister to King Zog of the Albanians. The arrival of the Communists in Tirana towards the end of the 1939–45 war had brought incarceration and torture. Years later in Albania, after Blanka had died, I was given a photograph of her taken by the Albanian authorities when she was released from prison, emaciated and exhausted. When I first met her the scars of her treatment were still faintly discernible, but they had been neutralized by a beatific smile and a general expression of intelligence and the faint hauteur which was second nature to that generation of European nobility.

After polite discussion of amusing superficialities, I gently moved the conversation to practical matters. Would she mind if I practised the French horn? 'Ach, of course. How nice. I love ze Corn.' Myrta emptied the cup of Turkish coffee we had been served, made her excuses and left us to agree the formalities. My room was generous with a single long window on to the street. Opposite there stood an old palazzo of the Josephine era, complete with Biedermeier columns and a grand pediment whose dignity was compromised only by a flashing neon sign on the *piano nobile* perkily announcing 'Club Mexico'. The furniture was simple and none of it looked more recent than 1910. In front of the mirror which rose solemnly from a marble commode, there was a fine Jugendstil white marble statue of a lady with all the femme-fatale features of others I had seen in Prague. A pair of doors led into the salon from which two windows opened on to a small stone balcony. On the far side of the salon, also linked by a connecting door, was the Contessa's bedroom.

In these musty rooms with their dark furniture and mirrors I would live for the best part of a year, occasionally teaching English to a beautiful Slovene girl from across the road, occasionally writing and sometimes playing the horn. Each day, I conversed in Italian, English, French or German with the Contessa. She came to personify for me more and more all the qualities of the Habsburg world: perseverance, courage, detachment and, perhaps above all, a sense of the absurd married to an inflexible observation of the rules of etiquette. However much we laughed together and became friends, the formal *Sie* was never once surrendered to the informal *Du*.

The tradition of imperial service ran strongly through Blanka's veins. Her father had been Imperial and Royal naval attaché in Constantinople near where Blanka had been born. Her grandfather had been a *Feldmarschalleutnant* in the Habsburg army and *Stadtkommandant* of Zagreb. Her mother, Colomba, had been a Turkish aristocrat and a great beauty – blessed, it was rumoured, with psychic powers. As a child Blanka had gone to school with her three sisters near the Grand Bazaar. 'Four Korwin girls and the *Aya*; we were marched each morning through the Bazaar hand in hand until we reached the German School.' Fluent in six languages including Albanian, Blanka contained within her the cultures of many different worlds. Her devout, unhesitating Catholicism was the religion of Sobieski and the Polish relief of the great Turkish Siege of Vienna in 1683 when an international coalition of Christian Europe saved Austria from the Ottomans. In her mysticism and observation of people and their behaviour there was a hint of the Near East. In matters of form and protocol, there was something almost Prussian in her discipline, yet her gentleness and her love of music and ability to improvise suggested a more Mediterranean inheritance too. She adored Rome and loved the Italians. Like so many Austrians of that generation, she was an embodiment of a culture which took such seemingly irreconcilable differences easily in its stride and whose sum was always greater than the constituent parts.

As spring advanced, the value of the heavy curtains and chocolate-and-cream-striped blinds became daily more apparent. I grew accustomed to sleeping less and waking up to see from my window Blanka, wrapped in a thick padded dressing gown, pacing the balcony to enjoy the early-morning breeze and the first glimpse of the rising sun. If I needed to get up early to catch a train to the University of Udine where I taught two days a week, Blanka would enter my room with a cup of strong Turkish coffee, theatrically announcing in warning tones that I must 'stay up!' as 'die Flotte' was weighing anchor. As the daughter of an Imperial Austrian naval officer, educated in Constantinople and then in the Convent of the Sacred Heart at Pressbaum near Vienna, she assumed that the surest way to get an Englishman out of bed must be to invoke the Royal Navy.

This admiration for all things English was born partly from a tempestuous love affair with the last British Ambassador to Nazi Germany, Sir Nevile Henderson. Henderson had fallen in love with Blanka in the 1930s when he had been minister in Belgrade. A few days before the war he had written to her from Berlin on embassy stationery dated August 1939, insisting that 'Les Allemands non voulaint la guerre.' The blue-embossed notepaper, together with postcards he sent her from Argentina, were kept in a bedside drawer. Henderson, despite his appeasement views, had a proud and unyielding character, fully convinced that no creature on earth was superior to an Englishman. He had regaled Blanka with many stories of English self-control. One which she enjoyed repeating concerned a consul called Smallbones. Smallbones had been in some forsaken Portuguese colonial African posting when, on a safari, he had discovered a high-ranking Portuguese official having an affair with his wife. Smallbones had stormed into the philanderer's tent and angrily demanded, 'Do you love her?' When the Portuguese replied with an air of cool insouciance, 'Hardly, old man. It was just a fling,' Smallbones had preserved his temper only by digging his fingernails tightly into the palms of his hands. 'So great is your England' was Blanka's verdict on this textbook example of the stiff upper lip. Although I did not know it at the time, Blanka's tale carried a kernel of wider significance. Many decades later, Robert Smallbones, late of Her Majesty's Consular Service, would be honoured for having saved hundreds of Jewish lives when as Consul in Frankfurt (under Henderson) he issued them with emigration papers to escape the Nazis. His handsome Scandinavian wife even took a riding crop to some Nazi thugs who tried to drag away a Jewish neighbour. Is *Selbstbeherrschung* (self-discipline) the foundation of all heroism? Clearly Blanka imagined that in this the British led the world.

At nearby Miramare Castle, a white limestone *castello* built by the Archduke Maximilian, who was later to become first and last

Emperor of Mexico, there is a painting of a Royal Navy launch manned by British sailors. They are saluting Franz Josef and the Empress Elisabeth stepping off the boat, but the artist, Cesare Dell'Acqua, has clearly been far more captivated by the long, thin, distinguished face of the English naval officer and his handsome crew than by the Habsburgs. For Blanka's generation, Britain indeed ruled the waves. Miramare was an hour's stroll along the coast from Blanka's apartment. The contrast between its white limestone walls and the blue sea and sky is another unforgettably vivid Triestine moment. The Archduke Maximilian, Franz Josef's brother, had come ashore near here after a Bora storm had capsized his yacht and he had immediately fallen in love with the place. The construction of the castle and its gardens occupied his mind right up to his violent death in Mexico in 1867. Inveigled by Napoleon III into accepting the 'throne' of Mexico, Maximilian had slowly recognized the folly of French machinations, but enlightenment arrived too late. A few days before the firing squad paraded to execute him, a scene immortalized in Manet's famous painting, the final details of this castle had filled his last waking moments: he had ordered Miramare's garden pavilions to be filled with nightingales. The castle's gardens include cypresses sent from Mexico as well as camellias, myrtle and laurel. Perhaps the thought of his enduring legacy at Miramare helped Maximilian face the firing squad with equanimity. The small black waistcoat he wore that day, which has survived, displays six bullet holes all close to the heart, a tribute to Mexican marksmanship and to their Emperor's unflinching character.

It is widely believed in Trieste, as a result of Maximilian's tragic end, that the castle bears a curse. On more than one occasion this has apparently condemned those who have slept within its walls to a violent death far from home. The Emperor Maximilian was only the first victim. The Archduke Franz Ferdinand with his wife and the Duke of Aosta were three of the more notable twentieth-century casualties. After the Second World War, two American generals, Bryant E. Moore and B. M. McFadyen, who were accommodated within its walls, met violent deaths on foreign assignments. A third general, the New Zealander Bernard Freyberg VC, avoided staying in the castle and pitched his tent in the grounds. He died peacefully at Windsor in 1963.

And yet to visit Miramar, as the Austrians call it, is not simply to evoke tragic events. Other, happier memories are held in its quiet pathways and woods, and on its unchanged balconies and terraces. The grotto in the gardens of the castle is a romantic spot where at least one Austrian naval officer plighted his troth to the girl he would one day marry. Countess Lanjus found romance in these pictur-esque paths in the brief weeks before her world ended. In her memoir, she recalled the happy days at Miramar in March 1914 with her future fiancé, Lieutenant Kastner, who had summoned up the courage to ask her to marry him in the grotto there. Describing tea the same afternoon with the German Kaiser Wilhelm, who was visiting, she remembered the bright sun shining on the white limestone of the castle, its stone balcony contrasting with the colourful uniforms of the Austrian and German imperial parties. 'Even though it was only late March, the sun bathed us in its warmth and we needed to erect umb-rellas to shelter us. Kaiser Wilhelm was so enchanted with the place that he was in the best possible humour, dispensing a beautiful watch to the Archduke's daughter and presents for her two brothers.' The German Kaiser's presence also reminded Countess Lanjus of the tensions of the world she inhabited: 'Although he was always kind to me, I could not stand him. His manner was so cold and arrogant and Prussian [comportamento prussiano].'

This Prussian stiffness must have sat awkwardly in such a pictur-esque place. Until recently the glass in the castle's upstairs windows was tinted rose to soften the bright light and romanticize the view, but the depredations of the harsh Bora wind over the last three dec-ades have smashed almost every one of these Bohemian glass windows and only a single pane of pink glass over the staircase reminds one of the attention to detail which obsessed the doomed Emperor Maximil-ian during his final moments.

Increasingly, my social life was becoming dominated by people old enough to be my grandparents. Between XXX Ottobre, the Bar Danubio, the Circolo del Bridge, the Teatro Verdi and the Caffè Tommaseo, there seemed little opportunity to meet anyone of my own age. There clearly were young people in the city, but their haunts

were far from the city centre and were best reached by Vespa, a mode
of transport I did not have.

Although by 1979 Trieste had ceased to be a significant port,
there were still a few ships passing through the harbour. One morning, a couple of months after I had arrived, walking along the Riva
on the way to Tommaseo's I saw a giant poster announcing a day-trip
from Trieste to Venice on the small 1950s Italian liner *Ausonia*. Tickets
were sold from an office which announced itself in giant capitals as
the Ufficio Triestino Azienda Turistico (UTAT). There, an elegant,
dark-haired woman with chestnut eyes sold me a ticket. After a few
minutes' conversation, she introduced herself as Graziella. She was
quietly confident and appeared to be almost my age.

Ruskin and many others after him have written of the unforgettable joy of approaching Venice in winter from the sea. After barely
two hours, the *Ausonia* entered the system of lagoons. In the over-
cast early-afternoon light, a hundred excursionists gathered on deck
for our first glimpse of La Serenissima. A silence reigned as we stood
stretching our eyes for a first view of land. Suddenly there was a faint
gasp. Through the grey-white horizon appeared first one, then two,
then a dozen thin vertical lines of pencil grey which, as the ship
steamed on, gradually took the form of campaniles. As we drew
closer, the campaniles became connected to the buildings below
them until, after ten more minutes, the entire architecture of the city
lay before us. Absorbed in this magical transition from Whistler to
Canaletto, I was awoken by a soft brown hand on my arm. 'What do
you say now?' Graziella asked slowly in English. As I later came to
discover, she was Venetian to her core. She may have worked and
lived in Trieste, but it was the spirit of the Doge's world and the rural
calm of the shimmering Venetian plain which invested her character.
The cosmopolitan ways of Trieste were remote from her conservative
Catholic upbringing in the villages to the east of Venice clustered
around the mouth of the Piave river, the *Fiume Sacro della Patria*
where in 1917 the Italian line broken by the Austrians at Caporetto
had almost miraculously held. After a few hours guiding me through
some of the more obscure *calli*, she left me near the Church of the
Miracoli to thread her way through the crowds back to her relations

on terra firma. I would return to Trieste that evening happy to have made a new friend.

In those days, ships from Trieste did not just sail to the West. I also found in an obscure corner of the Piazza Unità a poster announcing the weekly times of the one remaining passenger ship of the Lloyd Triestino line, the *Dionea*, the unarmed civilian equivalent of a small gunboat and, it turned out, serving a similar purpose. As part of the 1954 London agreements governing the ceding of Istria to Yugoslavia after the Second World War, Italy reserved the right to a near-daily maritime communication between Trieste and the Istrian peninsula whose coastal cities had for centuries boasted an Italian population. As the numbers using the route reduced, the vehicles of the line became increasingly modest until, by 1979, the *Dionea* was all that was left, her crew of fifteen generally outnumbering the passengers two to one. Every day at 8 a.m., the *Dionea* plied a picturesque route to Koper (Capo d'Istria) and the Venetian town of Pirano (Piran), continued to Rovigno (Rovinj) before ending at Pula (Pola), whose spectacular amphitheatre rivalled that of Verona. From Pula the Quarnero beckoned and the romantic resort of Opatija (Abbazia) with its villas in the Austrian Riviera style. Thanks to this little boat all these places could be visited without the inconvenience of long frontier delays.

This was certainly the quickest way to cross the difficult frontier between Trieste and Yugoslavia, which was in those days a barrier between two worlds – even though Yugoslavia was a more open Communist country than Czechoslovakia, Hungary or Romania. Nevertheless, as the scrupulous customs and police inspection always demonstrated, those who went behind the Iron Curtain were never sure that they would be able to continue their journey until they reached the other side. An atmosphere of unabated suspicion often permeated the frontier officials of both countries. Those who have read Stefan Zweig's *The World of Yesterday* will recall that a hundred years ago passports were unnecessary for travellers on mainland Europe, a generous arrangement the Schengen Agreement has striven to revive in our own times. In the 1970s, however, such freedom was a remote dream.

The formalities encountered at the port of Koper nonetheless were nothing in comparison to the indignities visited on passengers of trains attempting to cross the frontier. For two to three hours all trains crossing into Eastern Europe from Trieste were subject to systematic searches. However, this did not prevent Trieste Centrale, as the old Südbahn station was called, running ten international expresses a day to Paris, Milan, Vienna and Basel in one direction, Moscow, Budapest, Athens and Belgrade in another. Today, even though the frontiers are open, not a single international train any longer passes through Trieste. The city which played such a crucial role in linking the Alpine and Adriatic worlds finds itself more isolated from its hinterland in the twenty-first century than at any time in the last 150 years, at least by rail. Most of the blame for this must be ascribed to the government in Rome which is terrified that the city that cost Italy so much blood and treasure during the First World War will, simply by dint of its geography and self-interest, break away to resume its centuries-old links with 'Middle Europe'.

This severance of the city from the other great commercial centres and capitals of Central Europe is all the more curious when one considers the wealth once created by the three railway lines connecting Trieste with the heart of the continent. It was a wealth which supported (and still supports to this day) several of Trieste's most commercially successful families. If the brandy of the empire was largely distilled in the Stock factory beyond the station, most of Central Europe's coffee was imported along the railways from Trieste. Illy and Hausbrandt, household names eternally associated with the coffee bean, trace their origin to the oligarchy of Trieste. In the 1970s, Trieste could claim more millionaires per capita than any other city in Italy apart from Rome and Milan. Most of this was 'old money' and as a result the city enjoyed a relatively easy relationship with wealth, as it does to this day. But the ostentation of other cities is conspicuously absent here. The luxury brands which have erupted selling the same wares in every Italian (and, indeed, European) city have yet to discover Trieste, where older names, mostly unknown a few miles beyond its confines, still have precedence.

The casual visitor benefits from this in a variety of ways. First, because wealth is discreet, there is no aggressive suspicion and social tension, or hint of any blatant inequality distorting the social consensus. Second, the standard of cuisine in Trieste is higher even than in most other Italian cities, and can be compared particularly favourably with Venice. A discerning clientele is here accustomed to eating excellent food served with some of the finest though most inexpensive wines in Europe. Third, the *borghesia alta* is generally well educated: there is no shortage of bookshops. In Venice and many other Italian cities of comparable size, one looks in vain for a *libreria* of the character and quality of the Umberto Saba bookshop in Via San Nicolò or the Libreria Achille in Piazza Vecchia.

Predictably, as an 'old Austrian', Blanka knew many people living across the border. One sister, Greta, had been buried in Rijeka (Fiume), close to Opatija (Abbazia). Another, Christa Špun-Strižić, still lived in Zagreb, close to the former palace of their *Feldmarschalleutnant* grandfather. Blanka often visited Christa at short notice. Over breakfast of rolls and butter and Turkish coffee Blanka would suddenly playfully announce as if she was in her second rather than her ninth decade, '*Abfahrt* [Departure] ... Today I am off ... *ich verschwind mich gern ... Sie auch?* [I enjoy disappearing ... You too?].'

After several months, I was allowed to accompany Blanka to Zagreb to visit her sister. As we approached the imposing pre-Great War block of flats with its giant half-columns rising across three storeys, Blanka gave me some last pieces of advice, as if we were about to have an audience with a nineteenth-century sovereign. 'Kiss her hand. Do not say *Küss die Hand* and do not use the third person singular. I went to school with sixteen *Prinzessin* at Pressbaum and no one ever used this archaic formula.'

As we entered the imposing hall of Vlaška Ulica 5, we were met by an irresistible smell of grilled meat and onions. The small café near by sold some of the best *ćevapi* in the Balkans. The smell, so redolent of Sarajevo and the old Habsburg Military Frontier, brought back happy memories of the world beyond the demi-monde opulence of Zagreb.

The hall was unlit and it was only when we were a foot away from the ornate iron grille of the lift that I noticed a gaunt figure leaning motionless on two sticks. We were punctual – Blanka had reiterated as we had walked across Zagreb's main square that 'Bei uns sind die Leute erschossen wegen der Pünktlichkeit' (With us, people are shot on account of issues of punctuality). But, although we were absolutely on time, there was tension in the air. The two sisters greeted each other unemotionally and I was formally introduced. Christa abruptly cut short my opening courtesies and peremptorily ordered me to press the button for the lift. She had summed up my character in a split second, her sharp eye having digested stature, expression and clothes. 'Blanka! Man kann nicht herumlaufen mit Löcher im Pullover!' (One cannot run about with holes in one's pullover!), she muttered, ignoring me. The two sisters faced each other like scowling gladiators as I obediently closed the doors of the lift behind me.

As the lift rose it was clear that the dynamic between these two remarkable women had been set nearly eighty years earlier when Blanka, the youngest of the four sisters, had perhaps been appreciated by her parents more than by her eldest sibling. Stepping out of the lift as soon as I could, I saw the double doors to Christa's apartment opened by a female servant who noiselessly led us to the salon where tea had been laid for three.

Despite the social and political constraints of the Tito regime, Christa resided in considerable splendour. Her apartments on the Vlaška Ulica were imposing, with interconnecting doors and life-size portraits of Austrian ancestors including one of her grandfather, Feldmarschalleutnant Emmanuel, Ritter von Korwin, with a blue tunic and waxed moustaches. The family resemblance was unmistakable: Blanka shared the tightly drawn features and slightly whimsical expression of her grandfather.[*]

Christa managed to preserve these privileges through a combination of razor-sharp intelligence and fearless determination. With time, it became clear to me that this faded setting was not considered anything especially unusual in 1970s Zagreb, where a certain society had survived two world wars and the imposition of Communism with its aristocratic values still intact. Everything in Vlaška Ulica

---

[*] In the spring of 2017, on visiting the Vienna Military Museum (HGM) I was astonished to see a smaller copy of this picture forty years after I had first seen the original. At the time of writing it is exhibited in the first room to the right of the main entrance.

was spotless and expressive of a disciplined household, far removed from Blanka's more bohemian quarters in Trieste. But, as Blanka was fond of pointing out, her elder sister was 'eine grosse Nummer' (quite a number) and ran her rooms much as their father, the naval captain, might have run the officers' quarters of a Dreadnought.

In the salon an Edwardian silver teapot gleamed in the centre of a Biedermeier table. Around it, several cups, with a blue Meissen pattern which over the coming years I came to recognize throughout Central Europe, had been carefully arranged next to a larger plate with 'creckers', as Christa called them, covered in various pastes. As we took our allotted seats on the carefully arranged chairs, Blanka spotted a copy of *Paris Match* on a small table, picked it up almost absent-mindedly and settled down to turning its pages while the *Dienstbotin* began to pour tea.

With siblings one can rarely tell what is deliberate provocation and what is simply studied indifference. I had never seen Blanka so absorbed by any magazine before and I naively assumed that she was feeling at home in her sister's spacious, comfortable rooms. But of course she could find *Paris Match* in Trieste and she must have sensed what was coming. Christa, seated on the highest and most ornate of the chairs, looked across the table with an expression worthy of one who had been through two world wars, revolution, the assassination of at least one king and one archduke, massive social dislocation and long spells of persecution, but had rarely allowed any of these events to interfere with her daily routine of bridge, tea and the smoking of fifty cigarettes. 'Blanka!' she barked in her gravelly voice. The younger sister glanced up with a look of seraphic enquiry. Christa snapped, 'Man liesst nicht Zeitungen in Gesellschaft!' (One does not read newspapers in company). Then, casting a rather theatrical smile in my direction for a split second, she added almost seductively, 'Schaust Du den Richard an. *Er* liest keine Zeitungen' (Look at Richard. *He* is not reading any newspapers).

Christa clearly said nothing unknowingly. After so much formality, her fleeting bestowal of praise on someone she had met only a few moments earlier confused me. At the same time it drove a wedge between her two visitors, reinforcing one at the expense of the other and underlining her status as sovereign in her own drawing room.

Divide et Impera had been a Habsburg motto and Christa must have digested its lessons at a very early age. Without saying a word Blanka petulantly put the magazine down on the table, folded her arms and assumed an expression of studied indifference, but the attitude of juvenile truculence which I had not seen before in an eighty-year-old had not entirely disappeared.

Christa proceeded to interrogate me in a mixture of French, German and English. What did I want to do with my life? Why was I in Zagreb? What was my religion? Who were my people? When Blanka attempted to support my halting replies by saying, 'Perhaps he will become a diplomat,' Christa icily dismissed this idea with a withering glance: 'In England? Impossible; everyone knows there is no future in government circles in England for anyone who is Catholic. I thought you had studied history! These jobs are not available. *Ausgeschlossen!*' (Out of the question!)

Christa's only experience of diplomacy had been playing bridge with the consuls of Zagreb in the 1950s, although an uncle, Antun Mihalović, had been the last Ban (viceroy) of Croatia during Habsburg times and a photograph of him wearing the fur-lined coat and hat of office adorned a nearby table. Her opinions on this as on all matters brooked no opposition, and we settled back to listen to a prolonged exposition on the realities of European geopolitics. Blanka unconvincingly adopted an expression of submissive compliance.

As Christa lit her fourth cigarette, she continued to survey me with a cold analytical stare. The brief compliment for not reading magazines had not been followed by any more enduring evidence of goodwill. Yet, when all was said, these two sisters, so different in character and temperament, clearly both loved each other. When, a few years later, Christa fell asleep in bed while smoking her fortieth of the day and reading Agatha Christie, the ensuing conflagration proved fatal. Blanka was deeply affected by her passing.

Blanka had arranged for me to stay in Zagreb for a week in a small *pension* a few streets away. As usual in those days, I had brought my horn with me so as not to get out of practice. Each day I was able to use a room in the nearby music academy for a few hours. One morning, there was a knock at the door and an elderly professor asked if I could hear his star pupil, a fifteen-year-old whom he believed had a rare talent for the French horn. I happily agreed and was introduced to the young man, who did indeed display great skill on a dilapidated pre-war instrument far too primitive for his abilities but from which he nonetheless managed to coax a beautiful sound. Would I be able to give him some lessons on playing? I was happy to comply, little knowing then that within ten years this 'pupil', Radovan Vlatković, would become the principal horn of the Berlin Orchestra and a highly sought-after soloist. I would then be listening to his exquisite playing for guidance, rather than the other way round.

A few days later, I decided to make an excursion to visit distant relations of friends I had made a few months earlier in Trieste. One of these, Haleban, a man of advanced years, lived in a small town called Koprivnica (Koprinica) of which he was an historian. I did not know Haleban's telephone number or indeed his address. I had been told simply to take the train to Koprivnica and ask for him when I got there. A small train with old green carriages which allowed one to sit outside, dangling one's legs down to the tracks, moved off from Zagreb's main station at a steady 20 miles an hour in the direction of Hungary. A glorious winter sun offered surprising warmth. No cars appeared on the roads we passed and the fields were dotted with triangular hand-gathered haystacks.

Koprivnica had been established as one of a chain of fortified camps guarding the south-eastern flank of the Habsburg Empire against the Turks in the sixteenth and seventeenth centuries. Over many years, this 'Military Frontier' had absorbed peoples of different faiths and nationalities, welding them into 'a huge armed camp' in the phrase of the Napoleonic Marshal Marmont. *Ante Murale Europae, contra immanissimum nominis christiani hostem* ran the motto of Croatia after 1389 (The first defence of Christendom against her innumerable enemies). The beating back of the Muslim armies had been Koprivnica's incessant work for centuries. Here Ottomans who had converted to Christianity, Orthodox Serbs, Protestant Hungarians and gypsies as well as devout Croat Catholics had all organized themselves into a system of defence which was communal as well as military. In these settlements no individual held land; families alone were proprietors and the chief of each administered any revenue. When a family of the Frontier died out for any reason, the property returned to the Emperor, because it was only held in return for military service rendered. Sixty years after the end of the Habsburg Empire the legacy of these arrangements appeared to have survived the upheavals of the twentieth century. The paternal home was still the epicentre of all social activity and the head of the household was waited upon virtually hand and foot by the women of the family.

An hour after leaving Zagreb, the train pulled into Koprivnica and as instructed I asked the stationmaster for Haleban. He knew immediately who I meant and directed me towards a crumbling, red single-storey villa with a vine-clad terrace behind the station. The untarmacked streets were mostly composed of similar one-storey houses and at the end of each street fields stretched as far as the eye could see. Haleban came to the door and welcomed the stranger with unquestioning hospitality and the firm handshake of the Military Frontier. He spoke little modern German and at that stage I spoke little Croat, but I soon realized that my host understood and could speak the old German of the Frontier, Militärgrenze-Deutsch, an extraordinary amalgam of Slav and German phrases, the most repeated of which, uttered every two minutes, was *Ist gefällig*, a linguistic corruption of *Izvolite*, a Serbian phrase which could be translated as 'Please, after you', and the Austrian *gefällt's dir*, meaning 'Are you happy?' or 'Do you like it?'

Haleban's frame and hands were large and he moved slowly. He might have been any age between sixty and eighty, even older perhaps. His head was huge and bald, his face round and generous, Ottoman rather than Croatian. A headscarved woman, a relative rather than a servant I thought, appeared from a side room with Turkish coffee and a plate of bread, tomatoes and cheese, and our halting conversation began. She curtseyed for an instant before retreating to the kitchen. Judging by the Jugendstil detailing of the woodwork and the classical stucco detailing of the façade, the house dated from Austrian times, but there were no doors between the interior spaces, only large rugs hanging from the lintels. An old-fashioned bookcase held mostly Austrian novels, one of which was romantically entitled *Ulanenliebe* (Lancer Love). Its cover portrayed a thin, impossibly high-collared officer in boots and *czapka* (lancer helmet) fixing a monocle into his eye while a wasp-waisted Viennese lady in an equally high-collared, pneumatic blouse looked on admiringly.

Before our lunch was over, Haleban's face puckered into a smile and we were joined by three of his female relations who, taking chairs around our little table, sat watching the patriarch as he slowly drained his coffee cup. Suddenly, with a splendid *coup de théâtre*, he upended the cup over the saucer and gazed silently at the pattern made by the remains of the black liquid. The women bent forward to look. Haleban watched intently as the coffee formed its strange patterns on the saucer. I had never witnessed this particular example of fortune-telling and could not imagine how the abstract remains of our coffee might afford any indication of the future. But Haleban, drawing on the symmetry of certain shapes, soon proceeded to give a spirited prediction of his own good health and happiness, although many of his words were lost on me. Our female companions took it in turns to tip their own cups over and visit the mysteries of their own futures.

Before 1900, many of the inhabitants of the old Military Frontier had been illiterate, yet the Habsburg officers recruited there rose to high rank on account of their courage and quick thinking. Although often they could neither read nor write, they developed other skills. Instinct and intuition gave them much of the mental equipment required. Psychic prediction was another talent. In 1900, the ill-fated Archduke Franz Ferdinand had visited these parts and had been presented to an old soldier widely rumoured to have such powers. When the Archduke had shown the man his hand, the soldier had examined it and recoiled in horror, saying that it was a hand which would 'one day unloose a terrible war'.

This was the tradition of which Haleban was part, and he performed the rituals of this fading world of his predecessors with solemnity. He offered to accompany me back to the station and show me a nearby battlefield where 'thousands of Turks' had been killed during the long Turkish wars of the late sixteenth and seventeenth centuries. The ramparts he took me to were long overgrown and barely recognizable, but his face took on a grim expression as he described, as if it were yesterday, the fighting that had taken place here.

A few hours later, with a setting sun of spectacular richness accompanying the train, I was brought back to Zagreb. As I walked from the railway station back to Christa's apartment, the sophistication of an altogether more metropolitan world quickly reasserted itself. The following day Blanka, still in uneasy residence with her elder sister, took me to lunch with her friend Countess Kukuljevič who lived in the Upper Town near St Mark's Church. At that time, the Kukuljevičs were a shadow of their former glory as one of the families par excellence which had contributed to Croatia's intellectual and literary life in the nineteenth century. The Tito regime had however spared them much of the cruelty which had been visited on other aristocratic families in Central Europe after the Second World War. Like Christa, the Kukuljevičs lived in some comfort, although no doubt in the twenty-first century their surroundings would be considered austere. Large rooms with interlinking doors in the best Vienna style led to a salon with a fine cabinet of porcelain, the usual portraits of Habsburg military figures and Biedermeier furniture. We lunched well, and I barely noticed that the servants had withdrawn silently to another part of the palais. 'You see,' said Blanka, revisiting an old theme, 'you cannot get such *Personal* in Trieste these days.' As the light faded on the leafless trees of the Upper Town, we lay on various chaises longues and took a siesta for the customary forty-five minutes. By the time we awoke the room was dark and it was time to prepare for our return to Trieste.

A jovial lawyer, Gianpaolo Tamaro, often drove Blanka between Zagreb and Trieste in his Alfa Romeo. This time, he had agreed to take us both back to Italy that evening. A member of a famous Triestine legal and scholarly family, he was certainly *un uomo d'affari*, but he was also wise and kind, a great romantic who loved the unsophisticated simplicity of the Croatian countryside and its inhabitants.

As I came to know Blanka better, I discovered that Tamaro had played a significant role in persuading the Albanian authorities to allow her to leave that benighted country in the early 1950s. What possessed him to take up her case I never knew – he had come across it while researching his doctorate – but since Blanka's return to Trieste the two had remained firm friends, always joking and laughing when they were together. Not that Blanka by herself was ever gloomy or melancholy. She exuded a contagious sense of well-being and calm. Her detachment from worldly things was matched by an acute power of observation and humane curiosity which enabled her to converse with anyone of any rank with ease. On one of our trips to Zagreb I accompanied her first to the candle-strewn open chapel of the old town, the Kamenita Vrata, where she engaged cheerfully on a Marian theological point with some smiling old Croatian women before entering an ice-cream parlour run by Albanians, chiding the owner for his, in her view, eye-watering prices with a torrent of fluent Shqiptar (Albanian patois) to the astonishment of the teenage boys behind the counter.

That evening, the journey back to Trieste took us rather longer than expected. Near Samobor, a pretty village to the west of Zagreb to which Blanka's grandfather had retired, the car broke down with an engine problem. Having rectified that, a few miles further along Tamaro had to change a wheel next to the streams of lorries pounding along one of the principal arteries of east–west traffic in Southern Europe. Once the car was running properly again, Tamaro's style at the wheel was that of an Alfa Romeo test driver of the 1960s. No vehicle ahead of us was ever ignored but had to be overtaken at high speed. Politesse dictated that one should feign total sangfroid in the face of this display of high-speed machismo. Tamaro was without doubt a skilled driver but several near-misses with oncoming traffic made the journey a terrifying experience.

One morning in October, Blanka almost absent-mindedly announced over breakfast that we had been invited for drinks at the Castle of Duino that evening by Raimondo Torre e Tasso, a prince of the Thurn and Taxis family, and we would be heading off there by bus later that afternoon. Threading our way a few hours later up the long path from the village of Duino to the *castello*, we followed a red-liveried servant who led us into the castle's magnificent rooms, all decorated in a wonderful mixture of Italian and old Austrian styles. A group of septuagenarian men in double-breasted blue and grey suits looked up and the Prince bounded over to greet us with magnificent joviality.

'How is Prince Charles?' He looked at me seriously while I took in his splendid blue-and-white-striped shirt complete with princely coronet under which the initials TNT were (rather alarmingly) set out. Blanka whispered, 'Don't forget to call him Your Grace: *Durchlaucht!*' The Prince of Wales had certainly looked well in a photograph in the week-old copy of *The Times* I had just seen lying in Tommaseo's so I assured one prince of the well-being of another. As so often in Trieste, the conversation moved seamlessly on to 'England', a concept which for my host included Scotland and at times even Canada and South Africa. As always during the late 1970s, despite the difficulties of the moment, there was a mixture of admiration and envy of the way England functioned, the strength of its institutions, the continuity of its traditions and the confidence of its ruling class.

The salon we were in was painted yellow, making a pretty backdrop to the blue-upholstered Biedermeier furniture. Its windows overlooked some jagged rocks and, as a white-jacketed waiter served us canapés and prosecco, Blanka urged our host in almost theatrical excitement to 'Zeig uns die Felsen!' (Show us the rocks!). We moved to a balcony and surveyed the dramatic scene below us. The *Felsen* were the same magnificent limestone which had inspired Rilke to write his *Duino Elegies*. On a windswept morning in January 1912, the greatest expressionist poet of the German language had clambered on to the ramparts above the room in which we were standing and had contemplated the rocks 200 feet below in the brilliant sunshine and Bora wind. Rilke had been much exercised by a disappointing letter he had received from his publisher that morning. While he thought about a reply, with the wind howling around him and the sea reflecting the dazzling sunlight, a verse came to him as he watched the blue sea streaked with silver in the wind:

> *Wer, wenn ich schriee, hörte mich denn aus der Engel*
> *Ordnungen? und gesetzt selbst, es nähme*
> *einer mich plötzlich ans Herz: ich verginge von seinem*
> *stärkeren Dasein. Denn das Schöne ist nichts*
> *als des Schrecklichen Anfang, den wir noch grade ertragen,*
> *und wir bewundern es so, weil es gelassen verschmäht,*
> *uns zu zerstören. Ein jeder Engel ist schrecklich!*

(Who, when I cry out, hears me from the ranks of the angels?
And even if one of them pressed me suddenly against his heart
I should be consumed in that overwhelming existence.
For beauty is nothing but the beginning of terror
which we are still able to endure,
and we are so awed because it serenely disdains
to annihilate us. Every angel is terrifying!)

By the evening he had the first elegy on paper.

Stepping back from the sublime vista below I noticed how gentle and feminine the decoration of the room was; the pictures with views of Venice and portraits of the Habsburgs offset the cragginess outside the window. Everything seemed to confirm the supranational identity of an older order. Italian, Austrian, Bohemian and Hungarian art were all linked by the common thread of this venerable family. Our glasses chinked. There was the usual gossip about some errant mutual acquaintance. An hour later, with the sun setting over the autumnal horse chestnuts, Blanka and I took the bus back from Duino to the Via XXX Ottobre.

This cosmopolitan Trieste was a world away from its immediate neighbours. A few miles to the west begins the Venetian plain, which opens up beyond Monfalcone. There even in the 1970s the village parish priest still held in the palm of his hand the power of material advancement and spiritual oblivion. A few miles to the east, there was another completely different culture. In the beautiful foothills of the Julian Alps begins the unique world of the Slovenes and the charms of 'Inner Austria'.

The great Südbahn, the oldest of the Alpine railways, then still linked these worlds and its principal termini now punctuated marks in my approach to the Habsburg capital. Before finally reaching Vienna I was to work and live in Graz and Ljubljana, two cities of beauty, blessed with all the advantages of provincial Central European life: each had an opera house and theatre, fine-art galleries, good restaurants and superb local wine, and the opportunity to be in the deepest countryside in less than half an hour's walk from the city centre. Barely four hours of rail travel separates Trieste in the south,

Ljubljana and Graz in the north. Yet in those few hours the traveller encounters three different languages, half a dozen different dialects and all the nuances of national and confessional diversity which the old Habsburg lands offer.

In Ljubljana I was startled and amazed by the buildings of Josef Plečnik, an early twentieth-century architect who had studied in Vienna under Otto Wagner but had quickly developed his own personal style very different from the Viennese Jugendstil of his contemporaries. After a year in Trieste, I returned to London to study at the Courtauld Institute of Art where Anthony Blunt and Howard Burns encouraged my interest in Plečnik. The architect, then virtually unknown in the English-speaking world, would provide an admirable subject for a Master's thesis and a chance to build on the Triestine foundations of my time in Central Europe. There remained only the challenge of financing myself through the research in Slovenia. There were no language schools in Titoist Slovenia and a job in the university would have been impossible for a non-Slovene speaker, which at that stage I still was.

The then completely unspoilt Trnovo suburb of Ljubljana was immortalized by the nineteenth-century Slovene poet France Prešeren. Here he had first glimpsed the beautiful Julia, graceful, self-contained and shy, as she passed through the oak doors of the old church:

> *Kupído! ti in tvoja lepa starka,*
> *Ne bosta dalje me za nos vodila;*
> *Ne bom pel vaj'ne hvale brez plačila*
> *Do konca dni, ko siromak Petrarka*

> (Cupid! you fool me no more,
> I am not whom you are for;
> I will not sing your praise
> Like Petrarch till the end of days)

One morning, strolling through this still untracked and semi-rural suburb, I heard some words of English being spoken by two strikingly pretty young women. One was Slovene, the other was English. In those days, hearing English spoken in Central Europe was sufficiently unusual to occasion immediate mutual astonishment and we soon fell into conversation. They were both members of the National Slovene Theatre's corps de ballet. Somehow I must have mentioned to the Slovene woman with mesmerizing blue eyes that I was a horn player and indeed had my horn with me. In very little time, I had agreed to audition the following week at the Ljubljana Opera House.

The opera house was a masterpiece of Central European neorococo. Designed in the 1880s by two Czech architects, Hráský and Hruby, in the best Imperial Schlagobers (whipped cream) style, it made up in ornate decoration what it lacked in scale. As I approached the main entrance, horn case in hand, at the appointed hour, the door opened and a diminutive man in blue uniform bowed stiffly and escorted me up some side stairs into a practice room with a Bechstein grand in the corner. Once again bowing formally, he left me to unpack the horn and begin practising.

As I was warming up, a knock on the door announced a member of the house's staff who, giving me a knowing smile, placed a vast pile of music on the piano; this was my sight-reading and fortunately (a huge advantage) I had twenty minutes to look at it. I had barely scanned the last passage when with a great flourish the door was thrown open to admit the audition committee. This consisted of the principal trumpet, the deputy conductor, the principal trombonist, the Intendant's secretary and the same doorman who had met me so formally on arrival. The capable Marshal Tito had pioneered a form of Communism known as 'self-management' which meant that all important decisions were in practice taken by him and carefully selected lieutenants, while all decisions of lesser importance were made by a committee, thus emasculating any potential rivals. With the bureaucratic relentlessness of those times, this system had percolated down to the organization of every concern, be it political, economic or cultural, and now at the opera house it involved the doorman in the selection of the artists.

To my surprise and delight, after I had given a passable rendition of a Mozart horn concerto, the committee was unanimous in recommending me for the post of principal horn. Another porter, resplendent in blue uniform and cap – the old Habsburg traditions had not died completely – ushered me into a smoke-filled office where the Artistic Director of the opera house was vigorously extinguishing a cigarette into a flat copper ashtray. Maestro Cvetko was the archetypal provincial opera-house Intendant. Invariably dressed in brown suit, faded grey shirt and brown bow tie, he reserved the splashes of colour for his scarlet scarf and navy-blue beret. Large glasses magnified frog-like black eyes. On his desk were piles of paper, a pre-war typewriter and two unemptied ashtrays. He spoke the old Austrian German of the Slovene provinces with rolled consonants and guttural vowels and politely offered me an unfiltered Bosnian cigarette from a large silver box. He was a busy man who came straight to the point. Taking a file from beneath a pile of seemingly haphazardly arranged documents, he pushed a piece of paper before me, already filled out with immaculate copperplate handwriting, and asked me to sign at the bottom. 'You will start with *La Bohème* on 3 February. *Gut? Sehr Gut. Auf Wiedersehen. Hvala Lepa ... Nasvidenje.*' (Good? Very good. Goodbye. Thank you ... See you again).

I rushed to find the two members of the corps de ballet to thank them for their inspiration, only to find that both had resigned from Ljubljana the previous week and moved on to other theatres in Northern Europe in quest of the bright lights of the West. Alas, I would never set eyes on either of them again.

Like Trieste, Ljubljana was somewhat Austrian in atmosphere, but it had a youthful buzz which was very different from the old Adriatic port. The population of the city seemed much younger and more energetic. Most of those who became my friends were orchestral musicians more or less of my own age. The Slovenes were serious, with a penchant towards the sardonic in their use of humour. After the vivid personalities of the Italians in Trieste, they seemed at first almost introspective, with a great sense of precision and a pedantic concern for bureaucratic detail. Alpine environments breed self-reliant, physically and mentally tough people, but their horizons can be close at hand. After the sophistication of Trieste and even Zagreb, this was immediately apparent.

The regime at the opera house was benign. The 1970s Cambridge tradition of light preparation which had made us 'the best sight-readers in Europe' – two rehearsals for each concert, which meant up to fifty-two performances a term – on average nearly one a day – had not yet penetrated continental Europe. Operas were painstakingly rehearsed over several weeks before they were performed. As a result, an orchestra which was probably not as innately skilled as the one in which I had played at Cambridge – we had after all been conducted by Britten and Tippett and had accompanied Yehudi Menuhin in Elgar's Violin Concerto – nevertheless played with discipline and a fine sense of ensemble. We had sixteen rehearsals for *La Bohème* and months went by practising Prokofiev's *Romeo and Juliet*. Occasionally, the old Cambridge skills were required. In the great tradition of many Central European opera houses, the Ljubljana Opera House was also a repertory company: we did not always perform the same few operas for two months on end but instead might play through fifteen different operas a month. Some of the older productions could be revived at the drop of a hat. Quite often, even the musicians were taken by surprise.

One evening, after a few weeks of working at the theatre, I arrived ready to play the straightforward first horn part of *Rigoletto* only to be told that the Intendant had decided to cancel the Verdi an hour earlier and that I would now be playing the more challenging part in Borodin's *Knez (Prince) Igor*, a score I did not know and which was riddled with cuts and other uncertainties. My younger horn-playing colleague attempted to guide me through the cuts in the ten minutes before the curtain went up but there was still much to check when time ran out. We navigated the first hour successfully and my colleague and I were carefully counting our rests when there descended a solemn hush broken only by some nervous whispering. I looked up from counting my rests and saw Maestro Kobler, a giant of a man bursting out of his wing collar and white tie and with slicked-back Brylcreemed hair, urgently pointing his baton in my direction. I looked at the score in front of me and spotted a pencil line running down the page to a bar marked solo fortissimo. I blasted out the first two notes before being drowned out by a chorus of *ssshh* from the trombonists behind me. My colleague quickly pointed to another pencil line on the page which led to a single note to be played pianissimo and on which the tenor was waiting to begin his aria. Nobody in the audience appeared to notice my solecism and it led to no unfortunate consequences. Maestro Kobler had been broken in by earlier generations of Slovene musicians but, as an example of the perils of sight-reading revised opera scores, it remained vividly etched in the memory.

Nearly all the musicians were from the Communist bloc. A Swiss member of the *corpo balletto* and I were the only Western Europeans (*Gast-Arbeiter* we mischievously styled ourselves) employed in the house. Otherwise there were Russians, Romanians, Slovaks and Hungarians, paid what was in those days a readily convertible currency: the Yugoslav dinar. Indeed, we were reasonably well remunerated, certainly enough to enjoy the superb cuisine of the PEN International club restaurant, a few villas away from the opera house where unforgettable *Palatschinken* and tender fillet steaks could be had for a fraction of the price we would then have paid in Paris or London. After each performance, a group of us would make our way there to fall upon these delicacies with the ravenous hunger only post-performance musicians and athletes seem to share.

The opera-house schedule was undemanding and the orchestral musicians were considered to lead a fairly easy life compared to Ljubljana's two other orchestras, the Radio Symphony Orchestra and the Slovene Philharmonic, who regularly toured Yugoslavia. Our week began with a Sunday-evening performance, usually an Italian opera, *Rigoletto* or *La traviata* or *L'elisir d'amore*. As the week progressed there was at least one performance of Puccini, *La Bohème* or *Madame Butterfly,* or Borodin's *Knez Igor*, the last of which was a great favourite among the Communist *nomenklatura*. Interspersed between these were various Russian ballets and works by Rossini and Verdi. By Friday morning, everyone was looking forward to the weekend which, there being usually no performances on Friday or Saturday evenings, began immediately after a schools matinee performance. Marshal Tito's Yugoslavia may have closed down monasteries, arrested priests, banished convents and expelled most religious orders but it still took its Sundays very seriously. All shops were closed and Ljubljana was deserted at weekends until Sunday evening brought the stirrings of cultural and social life back to the city.

As soon as the Friday matinee was finished, a couple of colleagues and I would often hitch a lift down to the Quarnero coast. Like the

Red Sea, the Adriatic at its head forks into two branches, divided in this case by the triangular peninsula of Istria. The eastern arm, hemmed in by lofty mountains and broken up into long and intricate channels by rugged islands whose crests sometimes rival the height of those of the mainland, is known as the Quarnero. Opposite is the port of Rijeka, D'Annunzio's Fiume, which we would generally reach by 4.30 p.m., in time to catch one of the many early-evening ferries heading off towards Dalmatia.

In those days, drivers throughout Yugoslavia felt little hesitation in offering lifts to strangers and the journey south was easily accomplished, especially if one of the female members of the corps de ballet was of our party. Our most popular destination was Rab, known to the Italians as Arbe, an exquisite small island just two hours' sail from Rijeka. The island's lush vegetation of myrtle and pine could be smelt miles out to sea. Another horn player, Boyan, a native of Ilirska Bistrica, a village on the forbidding limestone karst, seemed to know where to stay, although he warned us not to get too close to the local young women, lest 'our intentions were misunderstood'. 'Island girls', he hinted darkly, 'need to be handled very carefully.' A natural reticence prevented my ever discovering the truth of Boyan's words, but Lillian, a dark-haired half-Italian, half-Swiss dancer from the corps de ballet, soon became the object of several of the island boys' attentions. Boyan kept a vigilant and protective eye on her, but our many hours on Rab were otherwise mostly passed in sunny ignorance of the dynamics of teenage life in communities where modern Communism had been reinforced by centuries of Roman Catholic conservatism. On Sundays, after an early lunch of local fish accompanied by an inexpensive bottle of Malvasia wine, we caught the ferry to Rijeka for what could be a tense race to hitch a lift back to the opera house to be in our black tie for the Sunday-evening performance. The leader of the orchestra, a charming elderly violinist who rejoiced in the name of Rotar, would throw us a cynical smile as his horn section settled in with just a few seconds to spare before the conductor strode on to the podium.

During the week, any spare time I enjoyed between rehearsals and performances was usually devoted to studying Plečnik in the Ljubljana architectural museum, which contained all his papers. His correspondence from Rome and Vienna was particularly interesting and revealing of his personality. Plečnik hated the noise and poor wine of Italy after his native Slovenia and had little patience with the sophisticated cosmopolitanism of Vienna. Like every Slovene, his food and wine mattered immensely to him and many of his letters from Vienna are punctuated by the phrase 'Jed je grozno' (The food is disgusting).

One of Plečnik's central beliefs was that the southern Slavs deserved their own style of architecture which could express their historical roots and their cultural aspirations. He rejected the imperial styles, both the classical 'Third Rococo' of the Habsburg cities and the Viennese Jugendstil, which he saw as a visual expression of German cultural domination. The Slavs, he believed, hailed from an older culture, that of the eastern Mediterranean, and therefore the Slovenes, the westernmost protagonists of the southern Slavic world, should have an architectural language which corresponded to that heritage. Just as Prague developed an indigenous Cubist architectural style after 1918, Slovenia also developed a few years later a new architectural vocabulary which indelibly shaped the appearance of its capital.

Studying in Rome before the First World War, Plečnik had become absorbed in the decorative details of vernacular Roman architecture. Near his rooms in the Palazzo Venezia, which was then the Imperial Austrian embassy, he saw capitals of columns placed haphazardly into the wall and he later sought to incorporate the design of these fragments into his works. In Ljubljana, he translated such forms into a series of structures which to this day give the old town its distinctive character, immediately distinguishing it from other former Habsburg cities. His Three Bridges, at the centre of the city, is an ingenious solution to the problem of preserving an existing nineteenth-century bridge of great merit. By adding two pedestrian bridges to the original he expanded its capacity. By adorning them with Ionic capital motifs he anchored the entire structure in a modern, novel reinterpretation of the ancient classical vocabulary which expressed a distinctive Slovene style. These bridges and the other elements of Plečnik's work in Ljubljana offer a striking contrast to the older Austrian fabric of the city which appears so similar to Graz and other

Central European towns. Harnessing Plečnik's genius to the planning of the city in the 1920s and 1930s, the Slovene authorities ensured that Ljubljana would become a place of pilgrimage for architectural students thereafter.

My studies were immensely assisted by one of Plečnik's pupils, Edo Ravnikar, a retired professor of architecture and one of the most prolific architects of late-1960s Ljubljana. Ravnikar was serious, intelligent and well informed about current events including even politics, a subject upon which most Slovenes were at the time generally reluctant to express a view. He was also a great gastronome. Each week, on the one afternoon I had off from the opera house, we would visit a private restaurant. The curious hybrid system of limited capitalism within the framework of state Communism which marked Yugoslavia in the early 1980s allowed private enterprise to flourish in limited areas. In Ljubljana, regulations only permitted private restaurants outside a 3-mile radius of the city centre. Inside that circle, all restaurants were, in theory, owned by the state, so this network of private places sprang up on the fringes of the city. Standards were high because owners took pride in their establishments, and wanted customers to leave feeling they had enjoyed the best cooking, wine and service in Slovenia.

Although Ravnikar had designed and built much of modern Ljubljana, he was not a wealthy man: the Titoist regime denied riches to all except a chosen few in the Communist Party leadership. Nonetheless the Professor had enough money to eat and drink well, and he made it his business to ensure that our informal 'seminars' on the architecture of Plečnik were conducted in a different private restaurant each week. In this way I was introduced to a wonderful range of Slovene wines, especially the prized Terran of Istria. One favourite haunt was a modest establishment in Trnovo, barely more than a Biedermeier bungalow, surrounded by vegetable gardens and run by a Bulgarian. The Bulgar was taciturn but renowned for the quality of his cellar. Perhaps as a counterpoint, he encouraged us to eat raw spring onions, unfailingly served as a *Vorspeise* which were also supposed to guard against diseases of the blood. Ravnikar looked on as I gingerly tried these delicacies for the first time. 'I suppose in London and Cambridge, this would not be usual,' he said with a note of pride, pushing another plate of onions, pungent, trimmed and washed, in my direction.

Ravnikar was in his early seventies. He always wore a jacket and long-collared shirt and peered thoughtfully at me through thick spectacles. He lived in the penthouse of one of the blocks of flats he had designed behind the main boulevard of the city, inevitably named Cesta Marshalova Titova. The flat, built of brick and wood, was generously planned though minimally furnished, and the space was filled with light. He was keen that I should understand as much as possible about Plečnik's mentality, his closeness to his brother, a Roman Catholic priest, his simple piety and his utter rejection of the modern Corbusian aesthetic. These would have been invaluable lessons for any student of architectural history, but for anyone developing a wider knowledge of the complex tapestry of South-eastern Europe they were a source of insight of enduring value.

Like the rest of Yugoslavia in 1981, Slovenia appeared to be in a state of political suspended animation. Marshal Tito, the pioneer of strategic non-alignment, delicately balancing favours from East and West, had begun his career as a Communist partisan fighting the Nazi Germans. He had died the previous May after a long illness. Newspaper editors throughout Europe had commissioned obituaries which had turned yellow with age as the dictator lingered on in a clinic a few hundred yards away from where I worked in the opera house. An elaborate plan had been devised to ensure that after his death the country's centrifugal forces (several different nationalities and religions) would not erupt, but no one believed that the system would survive long without him. The architectural historian Damjan Prelovšek warned me one afternoon as we were examining some of the remarkable Plečnik furniture in his villa. 'You will see. If you stay here for longer, you will really experience something.'

Such conversations hinted at Slovene separatist activities which the federal Yugoslav state was careful to monitor. That such an apparatus existed was evident. Once, when one of my colleagues from the orchestra joked that if Yugoslavia broke up Slovenia would be fine and could become an independent state, another colleague looked at us grimly. Bringing his wrists together as if they were handcuffed, he shook his head, unmistakably warning us to change the subject.

A second-hand bookshop in the old town of Ljubljana provided further education about my surroundings. Alongside novels by the Austrian Alexander Lernet-Holenia, I found a faded edition of that classic adventure *Eastern Approaches* by Fitzroy Maclean. Maclean had been parachuted into wartime Yugoslavia to act as Churchill's personal liaison officer to Marshal Tito, then just one of several partisan leaders. Maclean's support had been critical at several tricky moments during the war and when, after it, Tito broke with the Soviets, he turned to Maclean for help. In this way Maclean had played an important role in cementing Yugoslavia's fragile position between East and West.

From the first page, with its romantic departure from the Gare de l'Est in Paris in the compartment of a wagon-lit, *Eastern Approaches* is still a most absorbing book. That distinguished *Times* correspondent the late Peter Hopkirk wrote that for his generation Maclean's book was the natural sequel to Rudyard Kipling's *Kim* as an inspiration for fledgling foreign correspondents and players of the 'Great Game'. Certainly, at that moment few other books appeared as relevant to me as Maclean's. As the uncertainty over the future of Yugoslavia began to focus minds, I looked at his handsome face gazing at me from the frontispiece of my somewhat dog-eared volume and wondered what he would have made of current developments in Slovenia.

A couple of months later, after returning to England for a few weeks that winter, I was invited to give a lecture on Plečnik to final-year students of the University of Strathclyde's architectural class. The morning after the lecture, I visited Charles Rennie Mackintosh's famous Hill House in nearby Helensburgh. Unfortunately, it had rained heavily in the night and the house had flooded, so it was closed to the public. Disappointed, I retired to a simple café near by to read the day's *Times*. On the letters page was a short but stylish contribution from Fitzroy Maclean on the future of nuclear disarmament: 'Sir, I do not see how any rational observer of the international scene can fail to be amazed at the inept manner in which the superpowers are at present approaching the problem of nuclear disarmament. If ever there was an occasion for serious negotiation between experts behind closed doors, it must be this . . . surely the time has come for a little secret diplomacy.' I pondered this before returning to the railway station to catch the train back to Glasgow.

The station was deserted; its Edwardian waiting room seemed unchanged since the age of steam. I gazed out at the rather black clouds gathering over the hills to the north and prepared to cross over the track to catch the Glasgow train. The dramatic landscape stretched enticingly along the line to the Highlands, like a scene out of Alfred Hitchcock's classic film of Buchan's *The Thirty-Nine Steps*. As I took this in, a train heading north pulled up in front of me and, rather than wait for another train heading south to take me back to Glasgow, I was seized by a sudden compulsion to jump aboard and visit the next station along the line, wherever that might be. It was only two o'clock in the afternoon. I assumed I could always return on a later train. The carriage I entered, like the entire train, appeared to be virtually empty. The only other passenger was a grey-haired man in a black pinstriped suit with a green and heather-purple regimental tie who sat at one end reading *The Times*.

I looked for a conductor to enquire about our destination, but there appeared to be no conductor on board. Returning to the man still gazing at his paper, I asked him what must have seemed a witless question: did he know where the train was going? He looked up, rather surprised: 'To Arrochar and then on towards Mallaig' – two names which then meant nothing to me. He returned to his paper and I started back along the carriage. I noticed that his briefcase bore a label with an old-fashioned white *carte de visite*. The engraved writing gave addresses in Eaton Square and Argyll but above these in slightly larger letters stood the name of the briefcase's owner: Sir Fitzroy Maclean Bt.

As an example of what Jung and Koestler refer to as 'synchronicity', this encounter had a slight flavour of the paranormal about it. The odds against not only taking the same train but being even in the same carriage as someone whose letter I had read an hour earlier in a newspaper were of course immense. No doubt the rules of form or politesse insisted that I ignore this unlikely meeting on a train chugging through the empty landscape of southern Argyll, but so vividly had *Eastern Approaches* captured my imagination, that to be suddenly confronted with its author seemed unreal but also providential.

'Fitzroy . . . Maclean?' I asked in halting astonishment.

'Why yes . . .' His cobalt eyes held mine in an inquisitive and alert gaze.

We chatted about Slovenia for about fifteen minutes, and any barriers which might have been present evaporated. Maclean was curious, courteous and charming. Was I travelling far? Would I like to go for a walk? This appeared too generous an invitation to give up lightly. As the train pulled into a rainy Arrochar twenty minutes later, the door of a small car parked near by opened to reveal Fitzroy's wife, Veronica, dressed in royal-blue trousers with a flash of magenta about her heels. About half an hour later I was shown into a fine Georgian house where I was equipped from among various rainproof hats, coats, stick and boots all arranged along hooks in a brightly lit gun room. Thus attired in the impermeable regalia of the modern Highlander, I followed Fitzroy into a magnificent drenched landscape. The drizzle was interminable but the view starkly sublime, and my host was unperturbed: 'I always go for a walk in the rain when I get back from London. I find it clears the mind after the train.'

For two hours we walked and talked mostly about Yugoslavia and its prospects for the future after Tito. We also discussed Cambridge and Russia as well as the British constitution, the 'unnecessary' unmasking of Anthony Blunt and my plans for the future. Maclean's welcome was marked by genial informality which I later came to realize was one of the traits of the western highlands (in contrast to the altogether more formal manners of Edinburgh). He spoke candidly of politics and history and seemed happy to have the company of someone familiar with the latest conditions in Slovenia. Beneath his sincere joviality, I sensed his brain was always working; his questions were to the point and well informed.

After a glass of the Famous Grouse at Strachur, he escorted me to a nearby inn called the Creggans, whose darkened, wood-panelled interior was filled with smoke. Outside the rain beat down on the windows. We entered this tobacco-rich landscape like two figures from a Richard Hannay adventure. 'My friend here needs to get back to Glasgow,' the laird said with a certain matter-of-factness. 'Is anyone headed in that direction?' A low murmur filled the room for a few seconds before a small weather-beaten man piped up with the offer of a lift. This man took me to Dunoon, giving me an informed *tour d'horizon* of his views on the poor fighting quality of US soldiers as we passed an American base. Two hours later, I returned to Glasgow. 'So the Mackintosh house was flooded and closed,' commiserated my host from the architectural faculty that evening. 'What bad luck. You must have had such a boring day.'

The following week, back in Slovenia, the memory of this encounter with the architect of Yugoslavia's relationship with Churchill was a constant source of reflection. When I travelled by train to Trieste, I could now gaze out at the ruined stones of the bridge at Borovnica, once the most imposing viaduct of the Südbahn, and recall that it had been blown up in 1944 by the man I had been walking with in Argyll just a week before. It stood (as parts of it still do) as a memorial to the bitter fighting Yugoslavia witnessed during the Second World War. Such a beautiful bridge, I had remarked to Maclean during our walk. His reply had been dispassionate: 'Yes, but I'm afraid it had to go.'

As the months wore on, the fragility of the Yugoslav political situation became more and more apparent and even the usually mild Professor Ravnikar noted grimly that he did not expect matters to continue as before for very much longer. Some months earlier, in March–April 1981, an uprising in the Albanian-populated Kosovo region in the south of the country increased nervousness, although life at the opera house continued its routine as before, punctuated by tours of Carinthia and Croatia. At a performance of *Madame Butterfly* in Rijeka, it was easy to imagine I was back in the days of a multinational and multilingual empire. Lieutenant Pinkerton, played by a singer from an old family in Istria, sang in sonorous Italian, while our demure Madame Butterfly responded to his advances in slightly harsh Slovene. The chorus, 'lent' to us by the local opera house in Rijeka, watched on before entering in a deafening Croatian.

At the end of the 1982 season the opera house offered to renew my contract for another three years but I did not wish to linger. I had finished my thesis on Plečnik which would no doubt gather dust for decades to come on the shelves of the Courtauld Institute. Ljubljana was still quite rigidly Communist and over-comfortably provincial. Having spent the best part of three and a half years along the southern Südbahn axis, my next port of call was, almost inevitably, the northern terminus of the railway – Vienna. The challenge would be to find the appropriate entrée. While Christa Špun-Strižić had warned me rightly or wrongly in Zagreb that entry into the Foreign Office might be difficult, Fitzroy Maclean had spoken warmly of *The Times*, whose editor was another impressive Scot, Charles Douglas-Home.

The demands of the Cold War dominated newspaper reporting from the heart of Europe in those days. Apart from Poland where the aftermath of martial law merited a permanent *Times* office, the rest of the Soviet European empire was largely uncovered. The aspiring correspondent could attempt coverage of Czechoslovakia, Hungary and Romania, but there were formidable restrictions on doing so. Western correspondents were not allowed to reside in those countries because the authorities feared they would spread subversion and propaganda. The would-be correspondent's residence in Central Europe was therefore possible only in Vienna, a place which in those days was neither a Western European nor an Eastern European city but which offered a geographical and infrastructural base from which to 'cover' Central Europe comfortably. 'Neutral' Vienna had its own peculiar atmosphere and mentality. It was sufficiently far to the east to keep a watchful eye on Warsaw Pact countries while enjoying many of the freedoms of Western Europe. At an appointed hour one evening, buoyed with a sense of opportunity, and no doubt exuding the brazen confidence of youth, I breezed into Gray's Inn Road, then the headquarters of *The Times*, and confidently asked to see the Foreign News Editor.

With the naivety of inexperience, I thought I would encounter a certain bonhomie, even enthusiasm, in response to my efforts, but in this, as in so many other things to do with journalism, I was mistaken. The Foreign News Editor of *The Times* was cautious. Bearded, formal and with a pen dangling on a band around his neck, he appraised me through sceptical, humourless eyes. He appeared far removed from the trivia and banter which I, after digesting Evelyn Waugh's *Scoop*, had imagined were the oxygen of any Foreign Desk's activities. I swiftly recalibrated my gushing phrases and assumed a no doubt wholly unconvincing air of constipated sobriety.

'Of course, you could not have chosen a more difficult place to report from than Vienna' was how the newspaper man glacially opened the conversation. He continued equally unpromisingly: 'Nothing happens there these days ... bit of a backwater. And of course further to the east we are, as you know, well covered.' His dispassionate voice only underlined the general insignificance of Austria, Central Europe and anyone foolish enough to wish to work as a correspondent there. The implied message, unconcealed even to the rawest of potential recruits, was quite simple: 'Why bother?'

I queasily asked for a letter of introduction, something I imagined from reading *Scoop* was an automatic requirement, easily asked for and easily given. The Foreign News Editor's eyes narrowed suspiciously as if I was requesting something he had never heard of. In a neutral tone of voice suggesting that such favours were not granted lightly, he hinted that such a letter might eventually be forthcoming, but he did give me the telephone number (to be used sparingly) of the Foreign Desk and the telex address to which I could send 'any copy'. Nothing was said about payment. He wished me 'Good luck' but gave a convincing impression of believing that any further contact was unlikely.

Undeterred, I made preparations to move to Vienna later that summer. A passage from a hastily acquired copy of *Teach Yourself Journalism* by E. Frank Candlin seemed to place my low-octane encounter with the Foreign News Editor into context: 'Fleet Street fully justifies its reputation for hustle, for the demands it makes on its denizens and for the cut-throat competition which exists therein. It is no place for weaklings or for the idle and easy-going. Those who lack dynamic drive, personal initiative and a supreme confidence in their own abilities will do well to save their train-fare.'

Before setting off for Vienna, it was necessary to make one more important visit as part of the preparations for taking up life in the Austrian capital. A few months earlier, I had found a copy of Osbert Lancaster's *With an Eye to the Future*, published in 1967 but written in the Macaulayesque rhythms of an earlier age, splendidly acidic in its observations of the Austrians and their ability to mask darker motives behind a disarming front of charm. Lancaster had got the measure of the Austrians in the 1930s just as he had, also correctly, taken the temperature of what he described as the 'mentally underprivileged members of the Bullingdon' at Oxford. His description of life in Salzburg, Budapest and Vienna was vivid and illuminating. Such expertise would be invaluable, and somewhere in London, I knew, he was waiting to be found.

After graduating, my first paid work in London had been with the *Architectural Review*, then situated in a fine eighteenth-century house in Queen Anne's Gate. In its basement there was a private hostelry called the Bride of Denmark, resplendent with gin-palace mirrors and a glass cabinet containing a stuffed lion, items which had been painstakingly assembled from the rubble of demolished Victorian pubs by John Betjeman and Osbert Lancaster, both of whom had worked at the *Architectural Review*. The *Review* was collegiate, intellectual and adventurous. Its editors included many eccentrics, among them the eminent Georgian specialist Dan Cruickshank. Some wore waistcoats and shirts with detachable collars and, in the case of the Paris correspondent, a silk cravat of almost Beau Brummell-like extravagance. The Bride provided a focus for 'editorial drinks', an almost obligatory requirement in those days of all creative publishing in the capital.

It was to this freemasonry of architectural historians that I turned in my search. Cruickshank quickly supplied an address for the retired Lancaster and I was soon invited to tea in an apartment block overlooking the Chelsea Physic Garden. There Osbert's wife, Anne Scott-James, warned me that although Osbert was only seventy-four, his faculties had already begun to fade, though he might well have 'some better memories of earlier events'. Long years of life in the upper reaches of clubland had exacted their toll.

I was shown into a pretty drawing room furnished with Gillray pen-and-ink sketches, including a memorable one for his cartoon captioned 'Brigade Major – Weymouth 1797'. On a chair by the window, sitting immobile and silent like a faintly glowering Buddha, Osbert Lancaster leant forward with an inscrutable expression. He spoke slowly and unemotionally, but in this deadpan style he delivered one amusing insight after another. He recalled the German pre-war predilection for hierarchy. On crossing into Bavaria one summer in the 1930s, he had surrendered his passport for inspection, only to prompt a great deal of heel-clicking and saluting. The German customs officials had misunderstood Osbert for *Oberst* (Colonel) and had immediately elevated the twenty-one-year-old Englishman to field-officer status.

Lancaster had great affection for the baroque and he urged me to spend as much time in Salzburg as possible, noting that the Café Bazar was still one of 'the most civilized places on earth'. The Vienna Ringstrasse and the glories of Budapest, however, left him rather cold: 'very impressive but really all filthy stuff'. He glided effortlessly from the architectural to the military. He recalled the thrill of seeing a Corpus Christi procession led by the Hungarian Regent, Admiral Horthy. The Regent had been accompanied by all the great magnates, dressed in hussar uniforms and dragoon helmets as if they 'had been in an Erich von Stroheim film'. The whiff of formaldehyde had been quite overpowering.

Our conversation meandered over these Central European topics for about an hour before I sensed my interlocutor was tiring and I reluctantly moved to leave. Suddenly Lancaster seemed to spring to life with a flicker of a smile. The Austrian girls, he recalled, were one of the lost glories of the Habsburg Empire and, for some reason, were all called 'Mitzi'. Dispatched by this practical if curious parting shot, I set off across London to pack.

A few days later, the Foreign News Editor's letter of introduction duly appeared and I prepared to spend the rest of the summer in Graz, where I hoped to improve my decent but still imperfect German. Two summers earlier I had lived in the villa of the redoubtable Frau Höhnel, the daughter of a *fin de siècle* architect who had designed many of the city's pretty villas in a mixture of Jugendstil and neo-Gothic. I now returned here for the summer. Frau Höhnel still exuded propriety and discipline. Her hair was neatly tied and her collar starched. This neatness invested her home. The Villa Höhnel stood in the gas-lit Schubertstrasse on historical ground between the Graz Stadtpark and the Hilmteich Lake. As Gottfried Banfield had intoned with childlike glee when we had first met in Trieste a few years earlier: 'Graz liegt am Hilmteich. Rings herum liegt Oester-reich' (Graz lies on Hilmteich. All around is Austria). Here was the heart of Inner Austria.

The villa had a fine 'English garden' punctuated by tall trees which meant that in every direction the views from the first floor were of lush green foliage. Although it was barely ten minutes' walk from the main city square, not another building could be seen from the upper floors of this enchanting house. Inside nearly all the furniture and paintings appeared to date from before 1914. In the middle of the garden stood a small pavilion with frescoes, erected in the late eighteenth century to commemorate Mozart. It predated the villa and had been commissioned by well-wishers of Mozart shortly after his death in 1791. A Biedermeier inscription noted that it was the first (and therefore oldest) monument to be erected to the great composer's memory. In this respect, the 'brethren' of Graz had been ahead of both Vienna and Salzburg.

Life in the Schubertstrasse was very relaxed. There were walks and card games during the day. The sun shone brightly almost every day until a thunderstorm rumbled in around 6 p.m., drenching the tree-lined streets and gardens, and lasting about an hour before the setting rays of the re-emerging sun softly illuminated the early evening. As dusk fell, the moist air was so rich with the fragrance of the gardens that the effect was intoxicating. There were far fewer cars than in Western cities and in the perfumed air it was hard not to feel the Biedermeier beauty of the place, evocative of a Carl Spitzweg painting. Near by, a path led up to the Rosenberg Hill and beyond to the high plateau or Platte. As the billowing white puffs of cloud raced across the sky, the tall trees swayed in majestic accompaniment, their leaves shimmering in the wind. In the distance, a splash of imperial yellow on the horizon, stood the beautiful rococo pilgrimage church of Maria Trost, one of Styria's many Marian shrines. The celebrated Austrian writer Anton Wildgans had captured this atmosphere in a letter to his wife written in October 1924:

> Today, I walked from the Rosenberg over the 'Platte' to Maria Trost. It was a glorious autumn day; cool and at the same time warm because of the sun. This region is unique in its beauty. I can only compare it to

the area around Naples. Spanish chestnuts grow all around in the woods and gardens and the lush meadows are filled with every conceivable wild flower.

Frau Höhnel, then in her eighties, had studied in Birmingham before the war, and she continued to centre the afternoons around a formal English tea. This was held either in her dark-panelled salon or, when the weather allowed, on the terrace overlooking the Mozart pavilion. Her affection for England was undiminished by her age or the vicissitudes of the twentieth century. She liked to dwell on 'English values' which she believed were so important for the world and represented an alternative to unbridled materialism. It was indicative of her generation's outlook on life that when I offered to pay rent for a few extra weeks, she replied, 'Don't worry. We are not so mercenary here. Stay as long as you want.'

The Urania adult education institute in Graz complemented these early stages of my Austrian training. A remarkable legacy of enlightened imperial times, it occupied a fine palais behind the Herrengasse opposite the Gamlitzkeller. I had immediately felt welcome when, upon entering the Director's office, I spotted a large oil portrait of Disraeli hanging on the wall behind his desk. This seemed a curious adornment to a baroque palace in Styria. The Director, a bow-tied septuagenarian called Dr Schall, taking me kindly to one side and offering me a glass of schnapps, explained, 'A hundred years ago, Disraeli supported the Austrian occupation of Bosnia-Herzegovina. I felt we should commemorate this somehow.' I would soon learn that this exchange was typical of old Austrian ways. Under a façade of almost haphazard events, the foreign visitor was flattered, informed and even comforted.

Visits from friends in England were rare, but one morning in the Schubertstrasse I was delighted to receive a telegram from London giving me the details of the imminent arrival by train of a close friend who was en route for Dubrovnik, hoping to spend the summer painting watercolours of the Dalmatian coast. She was an adventurous and practical young lady, such as London seemed to produce in great numbers during the 1980s. As I was showing my guest the delights of the Graz Stadtpark rose-garden, I bumped into an old friend from the local *Kleine Zeitung* for which I had penned some articles and whose staff were unfailingly eccentric and kind.

'What are you doing tomorrow?' he asked me genially. 'The Empress has just arrived in Styria and has invited me to tea at Schloss Waldstein. Would you like to join me? I am sure she would like to meet you.'

The Empress was none other than Zita, last Empress of Austria, last Queen of Hungary, Queen of Bohemia, etc. etc. I had read in the papers a few days earlier that she had returned to Austria for the first time since she and her husband, the Emperor Charles, had left Vienna in 1919. She was now in her ninetieth year. Naturally, I needed no encouragement to accept this spontaneous invitation to visit one of the outstanding personalities of the last days of the Habsburg Empire. 'I'll pick you up from the Schubertstrasse tomorrow at two.' With that he bade us farewell: '*Servus. Christi.*'

The immediate dilemma, as my English friend with her discerning eye pointed out, was what on earth should I wear? The summer clothes of a fledgling young correspondent of limited means were simple indeed. I had a pair of cricket flannels, a few second-hand shirts with detachable semi-stiff collars and a burgundy silk waistcoat. For an audience with the last Empress of Austria, these did not seem sartorially sufficient.

Gottfried Pils, a neighbour in the Schubertstrasse whom I had met a few weeks earlier, was an artist with a profound interest in the Habsburg army. He quickly came to my rescue. Ushering us into his study, he opened a cupboard with a flourish and pointed to a gleaming blue dragoon officer's uniform dating from 1914, complete with crested classical helmet, sabre with black and gold porte-épée sword-knot and cross-belt with silver cartridge case. Here was a chance to bring Osbert Lancaster's world into reality. In a few minutes I had myself been transformed into one of the heroes of an Erich von Stroheim film. Herr Pils eyed my appearance critically with the eye of the specialist. There was a reluctant consensus that the helmet did not fit and, in a flash, another cupboard was opened to reveal the full-dress uniform of an adjutant of Uhlans. Once again I was unbuckled and reattired amid a baroque running commentary of theatrical expletives. 'Tighter! *Jesus Maria!* The sword belt must be tighter . . . What about the Uhlanka? *Du lieber Gott.* Where is the Uhlanka? *Stiefeln? Um Gottes willen.*'

Arresting though the finished product was after sabre and tschapka had been carefully fitted, it occurred to me that to adopt the parade uniform of an officer of an army, however distinguished, which had taken up arms against my own was perhaps not the best choice for an aspiring foreign correspondent of *The Times*. Reluctantly, I surrendered my spurs, sabre and Uhlanka and returned to more conventional attire. With some help from my watercolourist friend's sewing skills, I somehow managed to appear reasonably respectable in that charity-shop stalwart of certain Cambridge graduates in those days, the faintly pinkish Egyptian cotton jacket. My Austrian friends pointed out that in any event 'as you are English, no one will mind.'

The following day we drew up outside the Castle of Waldstein where the Empress's youngest child, the Archduchess Elisabeth, lived with her husband Prince Henry of Liechtenstein. Their son, Vincenz, charming and smiling, appeared in a linen Styrian summer hunting jacket carrying a decanter of ice-cold Welschriesling, that most refreshing of Styrian wines, still utterly unknown outside Austria. He cast an amused eye over me and sighed, 'What a pity,' when I politely refused his offer of a glass. It was after all only three in the afternoon.

He led me along a corridor bedecked with antlers to a room with a fine vaulted ceiling, where his parents awaited me. There the Archduchess Elisabeth was soon telling anecdotes about her mother, before suddenly standing up and gently escorting me towards a lady leaning on two sticks who had emerged on to a nearby corridor overlooking the courtyard. She was dressed in a black cardigan and black fur-lined slippers. The Empress Zita had worn black since her husband's death in exile on the island of Madeira in 1922. Since the 1950s, she had lived not far from the Austrian frontier in a convent building put at her disposal by the Swiss Bishop of Chur.

While in Trieste I had heard much of Zita. As a young Empress she had had a blazing row with Banfield. Both in their twenties, they had angrily clashed in 1917 on the bombing of Italian cities. When he was presented to the Empress, Zita had demanded to know why he 'had deliberately disobeyed' her orders and 'bombed Italian cities'. Banfield had replied evenly, 'Your Majesty should save her feelings for our cities which the Italians are bombing daily.' This stand-off between the two young headstrong personalities had been described by eyewitnesses as electric.

There was obviously more to discuss than this fractious episode and we turned to the question of the difficulties her husband had had with Berlin in 1917 and the Prussian generals. The Empress was keen to emphasize that her husband had repeatedly tried to persuade his German allies not to send Lenin back to Russia in the famous *plombierten Zug* (sealed train). 'He knew that Lenin was a virus, *Gift* [poison].' The word was articulated with such force it appeared almost to ricochet off the walls of the room.

The Empress had also helped organize the ill-fated Austrian peace-feelers of spring 1917 through her brother Prince Sixtus, an officer serving in the Belgian army. Her consistently anti-German position during the war had led the Germans not only to spy on her that year but also to conduct a well-orchestrated press campaign against her, stressing her Bourbon-Parma lineage and Italian sympathies. (She was the seventeenth child of the Duke of Parma, deposed in 1859.)

With characteristic cravenness, the post-war republican Austrian authorities had also been far from generous to her. When her daughter Adelheid died in Austria in the 1970s, the Empress had wanted to return for the funeral. Most of the younger members of the Habsburg family had eventually been permitted to visit Austria, but the officials of the Second Austrian Republic pedantically clung to the anti-Habsburg laws of the 1920s, which insisted that such 'privileges' were not granted to any Habsburg born before 1919. Zita thus had had to wait for her ninetieth birthday before returning to Austria when, thanks to the direct intervention of Pope John Paul II with the Austrian Chancellor Bruno Kreisky, the law banning her from Austria had finally been overturned.

After twenty minutes, we were joined by other members of the family and my friend from the *Kleine Zeitung*. The Empress looked for a moment disconcerted but then smiled as she realized that one of her five-year-old great-granddaughters, also called Adelheid, had hidden her walking sticks. In an answer to a question, she stressed that neither she nor her husband had ever abdicated. The conversation moved swiftly to lighter topics and any initial stiffness was quickly set aside.

Her smile and laughter were infectious, and she seemed to radiate an inner harmony born of an indifference to material things. I was aware of being in the presence of a deeply spiritual person, one for whom the perils of the world no longer held any threats. 'Man ist was man ist' (One is what one is), she told us with a smile.

I had always imagined the republican Austria of the 1980s to have left behind the courtesies and formal modes of speech associated with royalty. Socialism in Austria, even more than in Italy, seemed to strike a robust pose when confronted with the legacy of monarchy. The Austro-Marxism prevalent in the Second Republic could be notably *adelfeindlich* (nobility-hostile). It was therefore a surprise to hear my colleague from the *Kleine Zeitung*, whom I had always imagined as a 'progressive' socialist, lapse seamlessly into the formal language of the Dual Monarchy. *Kaiserliche Hoheit* (Imperial Highness), *Kaiserliche und Königliche Majestät* (Imperial and Royal Majesty) – these phrases tripped off his tongue as if he had been moving in court circles all his life rather than in the editorial offices of a newspaper of largely unreconstructed republicanism. But then, I remembered, this was Styria.

The Empress remained discreet, and those who attempted to ask questions designed to coax out her opinions on current events and personalities were met with a smiling 'Keine Ahnung' (No idea). On some historical subjects, however, she offered firm views which challenged the conventional narrative of events. One of these concerned the tragedy of Mayerling, the hunting lodge where in 1889 Crown Prince Rudolf was found dead with his mistress Marie Vetsera. These tragic events, immortalized in films, books and even ballets, have long been considered a suicide tryst. According to the Empress, the reality was more complex and it involved power politics and *raison d'état*, as was often the case with Habsburg tragedies in the late nineteenth century. Rudolf, she said, had become embroiled in a plot to depose his father, Franz Josef, and realign the monarchy away from Germany and towards France. Key to these designs was the support and participation of the Crown Prince, who held enlightened views, was undeniably Francophile and had struck up a close friendship with several men who would later reach considerable prominence in European affairs. One of these was Georges Clemenceau, a bitter opponent of the Habsburg monarchy and France's intractable war-time leader. Clemenceau was a frequent visitor to Vienna, where his brother had married the daughter of Moritz Szeps, the powerful editor of the leading Viennese newspaper *Neues Wiener Tagblatt*. Rudolf, who had a close relationship with Szeps, began to see a great deal of Clemenceau. At some point in their discussions the need to support the modernization of the empire and detach it from a potentially subservient relationship with Berlin crystallized into moves to bring about dramatic political change. Rudolf eventually realized he was becoming embroiled in a dangerous plot against his own father which could destabilize the monarchy, so he desperately tried to withdraw. But the men he was dealing with had not come thus far to be so easily dissuaded. They blackmailed the Crown Prince, threatening him with exposure as a potential regicide. When Rudolf still refused to fall in with their plans, and indeed counter-threatened to reveal their machinations to the Emperor, they decided to murder him. The Empress's revelations were mostly politely ignored and even her son, the Archduke Otto, felt compelled to treat his mother's words with caution.* The definitive account of what took place in the hunting lodge of Mayerling still remains to be written, although many of Austria's leading historians have decided that Rudolf's death was not suicide.

Our conversation moved to a close. At 4.15 promptly, tea was served and half an hour later we said farewell to the last woman to have worn the crown of the Queen of Hungary. 'Give my best wishes to England,' she said, and then surprisingly, 'and especially to the Isle of Wight where I learnt English so many years ago at Ryde Convent.'

A week later, I took the train to Vienna. The comfortable and spotless cream and blue carriages drew up at Graz railway station ready to ascend the Semmering Pass to the Austrian capital. The stationmaster wore a velvet-collared cape and smart red and gold cap. A few Styrian friends from the Urania had come to bid me farewell. As the carriage moved off, I saw Dr Schall and Frau Höhnel wishing me luck as if I was a great-nephew heading off on a journey

---

* These details would become more widely known a few months later when Zita confided her version of the story to Erich Feigl, a Viennese writer working on a biography of the Emperor Charles.

around the world. Although Graz was scarcely a hundred miles from Vienna, my Styrian friends knew no one whom I might look up in the Austrian capital. The federal structure of Austria engendered enormous cultural, linguistic and psychological differences between Vienna and the provinces. In addition, as in England, cadence, accent and intonation still revealed sharp class differences.

Happily, at a party in London, I had encountered the vivacious Babsi von Ow, then a young Reuters trainee who in the teeth of parental opposition had fought her way into Oxford to emerge as one of the brightest of her generation. Fixing me with her dark eyes and all the cynicism one might expect from an embittered octogenarian, she had given me a merciless verdict on modern Vienna. 'The contrast between the eternally glorious past and the permanently banal present impinges at all times.' Generously she gave me the names of two distant cousins, Victor Attems and Karl-Eugen Czernin. She also wrote down the address of a small *pension* called Alt-Wien in the Spiegelgasse where, she said, 'You will find your feet.'

The Charm of Old Austria

Vienna–Salzburg–Pannonhalma–Budapest

As the train chugged slowly up to the Semmering, the landscape became rockier and more Alpine. On a distant outcrop of rock I made out a chamois gazing across the cloud-filled valley below. As we ascended ever higher, we broke through another layer of cloud to a sunnier world where castles apparently floated on air, perched on precipices of grey limestone whose lower reaches were enveloped in fog. A shaft of sunlight cut through the murk before the train, gathering speed, penetrated the swirling wreaths.

Large Edwardian hotels in the Alpine style peeked out between the trees, their balconies deserted and their windows shuttered. At the Semmering station, the train halted for five minutes. Pushing down the window I breathed in the Alpine air and savoured the monument erected to the memory of Ritter von Ghega, the gifted engineer who had constructed the Südbahn. Ghega was a familiar name and figure in those days, thanks to the beautifully designed chocolate and cream 20-Schilling note from whose reverse his whiskered features stared out.

Born in Venice, Ghega was, as his name implied, of Albanian origin, yet another example of the pan-European traditions of the Habsburg lands. Between 1848 and 1854, he worked tirelessly on the route of the railway which would link the Adriatic with the imperial capital. In the face of many doubters who simply did not believe it possible to construct a railway over the Semmering, he succeeded in building an elaborate series of hairpin bends which enabled locomotives to manage the gradients without the addition of extra gears. Thanks to the personal intervention of the Styrian Archduke Johann, the route to the Adriatic went through Graz, thus linking Styria with the Mediterranean world as well as the Danube.

The traveller can appreciate Ghega's talents to this day: the beauty of the viaducts and tunnels he constructed to help the railway navigate the ascent from Gloggnitz to the Semmering is breathtaking. These viaducts, with their ever-changing vistas, are one of the wonders of railway history. While the journey time between Graz and Vienna is undoubtedly not a quick one, no one of sensibility who has encountered the Südbahn would wish to replace them.*

Beyond Payerbach, the railway cuts down into the pine-forested plain to the south of Vienna whose distant spires are glimpsed for a few moments on a clear day just before the train begins its descent. This plain is a dry and monotonous space in the late summer heat. Pines of the Italian rather than the Alpine variety are planted in regimented rows on a sandy soil. From there to Vienna, the train meanders through the suburbs before arriving at the Südbahn station, virtually opposite the Belvedere Palace.

Like so many in Austria, this once great station was bombed during the war and rebuilt in the 1950s in an austere, unadorned style. Its six platforms correspond to Vienna's principal routes to the southern lands of its former empire, but in the 1980s the station was usually empty for the simple reason that 30 miles in most directions stood the Iron Curtain.

The train decanted its few passengers and I made my way through an empty ticket hall on to the road where the copper-green roof of the Belvedere Palace beckoned me towards its gardens and the path down to the Schwarzenbergplatz and the centre of Vienna. In the dusk, the streetlights were illuminated but there was little traffic. In contrast to Trieste and Zagreb, the trams moved at a glacial pace. From the Schwarzenbergplatz, my old Baedeker guide pointed me in the direction of the towering Cathedral of St Stephen, from where I would find the small Spiegelgasse and, halfway up on the right, the Pension Alt-Wien.

There were far fewer cars in the centre of Vienna than I had become accustomed to in Trieste and even in 'Communist' Ljubljana.

---

* Unfortunately, as I write, the Austrian railways' obsession with saving thirty minutes' journey time has resulted in the beginnings of a vast tunnel under the Semmering. It is not yet clear if this will spell the end of regular travel along the oldest and most spectacular transalpine railway.

A silence hung over everything around the cathedral. At about 8 p.m., I entered the *pension* through a small wooden door cut into a much larger neo-baroque gateway: the main entrance to this *dritte rococo* palais. After climbing a few steps I found myself in a marbled hall from which a grand staircase ascended to a landing. Here a small door opened on to a room which seemed to function as a porter's lodge.

As I approached the steps, I saw a compact leather suitcase, distressed by age but with a gleaming patina, marooned in the middle of the hall. A female voice echoed from the porter's lodge, and I immediately offered to carry the suitcase up the stairs. But the voice coolly replied that it would not be necessary: *die Fürstin* (Princess) would be along presently. A short, thin but erect lady with white hair and a tweed skirt emerged and walked past me, throwing that 'easy smile' which had so captivated Edward Crankshaw writing about the Viennese before the war. Such charming politesse, as Crankshaw had noted, did not denote the falling away of archaic social barricades. Rather it 'created a barrier which was as impenetrable as any Prussian fortress'. Behind her in the small 'lodge', a lady of similar vintage was neatly and painstakingly folding into four a large piece of cream-coloured paper on which *die Fürstin*'s expenses were noted in an immaculate copperplate hand.

The Pension Alt-Wien was indeed a *Fürstenpension*, a term which today might suggest material wealth but had a very different meaning then. Today, when dukes have the windows of their houses coated in gold leaf, and Alpine princes insist on painting their escutcheons on the lanterns hanging on the façades of their palaces, it is hard to imagine that so recently the material wealth of this class had been almost obliterated by war and its aftermath. Thirty-five years ago the term *Fürstenpension* evoked an aristocratic poverty bordering on destitution, the result of twenty-five years of Austro-Marxism following hard on the heels of a decade of Soviet occupation.

'Grüss Gott,' said the lady drily, still slowly folding the copy of the bill of the departing guest with the help of a bladed letter-opener. 'Grüss Gott,' I replied, adding that I wondered if they might have a room for a week and that I had just been staying in Graz with Frau Höhnel. It was an early indication of the Viennese insularity I was to come to know so well that these references to places and people beyond the boundaries of Vienna evinced complete indifference.

The lady finished her folding and leant towards me with an unemotional expression offering a key. 'Zimmer 36. Dritten Stock. Etagenbad' (Room 36. Third floor. Bath on the corridor). Without waiting she returned to her paperwork. After the expansiveness of Styrian hospitality, this seemed a poor introduction to the legendary city of *Milde und Munifizenz*.

There was no lift so I walked the three storeys up to Room 36. Entering it, nothing appeared to have changed since the 1920s. It was furnished with a single Biedermeier bed with four enormous pillows, crisp and white. A large jug of iced water stood on a marble-topped table. A folding card-table with a green baize surface and a chaise longue occupied the rest of the room. The view from the window was across the back of the Spiegelgasse towards the huge copper dome of the entrance to the Hofburg. I was in the heart of a once great imperial capital, but I heard nothing. Even after opening the double windows, I could barely detect a sound. The air wafted in, a cool breeze, a faint scent of stone and ice. Was I alone in this *pension*, in this street, in Vienna?

The following day being Sunday, I was woken by church bells. Outside the temperature was autumnal, the light strangely diffused by dust. Walking up to the end of the Spiegelgasse I soon found myself opposite the Augustinian Church. A door opened into an empty interior. As my eyes became accustomed to the darkness, I found myself opposite the white marble pyramid which is Antonio Canova's funerary masterpiece, the magnificent memorial to Archduchess Marie-Christine and one of the wonders of the neo-classical age. The ephemeral quality of the winged Victory, the intense grief of the lion, the sombre cortège of the Virtues: I was mesmerized by the sheer scale and power of the composition. This quiet reflection of the early morning was rudely interrupted by a roll of timpani. The electric lights were switched on to reveal an orchestra about to begin rehearsing Mozart's Coronation Mass. A man in a dark grey and green suit approached me with a look of chagrin and spoke at me in voluble dialect. I could not understand most of what he said but I gleaned that I was not where I was supposed to be. The church was closed until half an hour before the 10.00 mass, and I had to leave.

Outside, the giant caryatids of the Palais Pallavicini, participants in a memorable scene in *The Third Man*, were soon disgorging on to the square a group of impeccably dressed young men and women. The men wore brown houndstooth tweed while the women sported pearls and Hermès scarves. As they walked towards the main entrance of the Augustinian Church, they were joined by other young couples, similarly attired. The men seemed to enjoy waving at each other with foppish grins as if it were part of a well-tried ritual. One, spotting my tweed coat, even waved at me until, struck by my failure to respond, he realized it was a case of mistaken identity. I later came to know many of these people well, but at this stage I had only a dim awareness that I had somehow stumbled across one of the weekly gatherings of what passed during Cold War Vienna for *jeunesse dorée*. These were neither the focused young, financial men and watercolourist women I had left behind me in London nor the relaxed, hospitable but intellectually questioning friends I had made in Graz and Trieste. Here was a new caste with an unfamiliar sensibility, one that in time I would grow to appreciate but which in its early manifestations confirmed all Blanka's strictures on the effervescent superficiality of the Viennese. 'Nur nicht die Sache Ernst nehmen' (Never take matters seriously) had been one of her mantras for warding off the disappointments of unrequited romance and other forms of melancholy. As I surveyed this giggling crowd before me, catching fragments of meaningless courtesies, it was hard not to conclude that this was an unhappy example of taking such advice to extremes.

I was tempted to wait the fifteen minutes until the Augustinian Church opened and then follow them in, but I suddenly felt weary of the formality such an experience appeared to demand. Instead, I determined to seek an assignation at the Neue Galerie with the one woman I knew was always waiting for me in Vienna. Her brown eyes, slightly reddish hair, tightly drawn rosy cheeks and noble brow spoke of intelligence, vulnerability and carefully concealed passion.

Sonja Knips had been painted by Klimt in 1898. The painting has never enjoyed the blockbuster appeal of the portraits of his 'golden' period, notably the coolly sensual Emilie Louise Flöge (1902) or the celebrated Adele Bloch-Bauer (1907), and yet it has something absent in the others. In the early 1980s, the portrait was ingeniously hung in an upper room of the Belvedere Palace. You ascended a rather simple and undecorated flight of stairs, turned a corner and there, without warning, were brought up short by the sight of this ravishing woman in pink. Her gaze seemed to be fixed upon you, the new arrival in her salon. The nervous suppressed excitement she is obviously feeling, and which Klimt captures so skilfully, seemed to race across the room and for a brief moment you might even imagine yourself the cause of her mood.*

Her passion is subjected to a studious control. There is formality, especially the firm line of her jaw and high ruff of her dress, and yet accessibility is also suggested. Her intelligent face seems to long for mental stimulation. In her right hand she holds a small red notebook and the pose and the dress capture the contradictions of her life. She is the daughter of an aristocratic but impoverished imperial officer and she rejoices in a name redolent of the great victories of the War of the Spanish Succession. But Baroness Sonja Potier des Echelles was born in Lemberg in Galicia where the intellectual poverty of garrison life, evoked with much feeling by Joseph Roth in his novel *Radetzky Marsch*, deprived her of the stimuli of a more metropolitan existence.

These riches she subsequently acquired by dint of marriage to a wealthy industrialist, Anton Knips, a move that cannot have been straightforward for the daughter of a military caste notoriously dismissive of trade and commerce. Yet this union offered an escape. Klimt's genius captures all this, as well as the paradox of her fragile femininity side by side with her clear strength of character. In doing so he immortalized a type that I was to come across often during the next five years in Vienna: beautiful, often aristocratic, intellectually curious, passionate and neurotic but at the same time stiffly conservative in externals. This was a heady mixture. After ten minutes or so I left her reluctantly and moved on to look at other paintings which also, over time, became wonderfully familiar: a beautifully proportioned Anton Faistauer nude, Anton Romako's Admiral Tegetthoff

* Today (2019) inexplicably Sonja Knips alas hangs in a dark corner of a gloomy room, remote from any possible *Begegnung* (encounter) with her admirers, old and new.

on the bridge of his flagship at the height of the battle of Lissa, and of course Frau Adele Bloch-Bauer, now in New York.

That evening I sat at the English *Stammtisch* in the Café Hawelka whose proprietor, the redoubtable Frau Hawelka, I now met for the first time. She was lively, short and grey-haired with a piercing gaze. She seemed to take one look at my tweed coat and pushed me towards two unknown but similarly attired young men who were playing cards. Gradually I came to know this group of young English exiles, who regularly descended on the café on Sunday evenings and enjoyed their own reserved table. Frau Hawelka and her immaculately bow-tied but more somnolent husband Leopold had preserved the café as a link with the bohemian 1920s. Soft, faded lighting and still more faded red velvet armchairs and marble tables made an elaborate choreography across a single room whose dark panelling and Jugend-stil motifs interrupted the space at asymmetrical moments. It was intimate yet anonymous, formal yet undeniably demi-monde.

Frau Hawelka was ably assisted by a brace of dinner-jacketed wait-ers of what would now be called the 'traditional Viennese school', men of the working-class suburbs with slicked-back black hair who spoke with the working-class district Meidling 'L' which gave their language a honky-tonk intonation. Their effortless obsequiousness tinged with hauteur constantly hovered on the cusp of insolence.

I came to realize that these weapons of words and manners, honed over centuries of imperial unpredictability and court caprice, were an essential part of Viennese café life. Irritating though they were at first, they expressed a level of almost baroque sophistication, allow-ing insults to be transmitted without any erosion of temper. A kind of theatrical banter was permanently on offer. Only when my knowl-edge of Viennese patois and nuance had been sufficiently developed could I meet this barrage head-on and join this unending *tableau vivant* during which insults could be hurled without the slightest risk of any descent to violence.

The *Stammtisch* cemented lifelong friendships and – by no means a given at that time in Vienna – had the added benefit of including women among its clientele. One of them promptly invited me to the Wednesday Club, a luncheon society organized by Renée Nebehay, the English wife of an art collector and gallery owner, Christian

Nebehay. I had walked past his impressive gallery in the Annagasse earlier that day and gazed at the fine lithographs in the window.

Like the Hawelka *Stammtisch*, the Wednesday Club offered an unceasing carousel of young English people, although in this case mostly women. They were passing through Vienna, either as part of their university degree courses or as a result of some mysterious unrequited romance in England of which their parents had sufficiently disapproved to exile their daughters to Vienna for six months. One of these, the former head-girl of an illustrious school near Windsor, had only just been rescued from the clutches of a 'highly unsuitable cornet' in the Dragoon Guards by her mother who had speedily packed her off on the Ostend–Vienna express a few days before our meeting. Another was the studious daughter of a well-known aristocratic Northumbrian family, with a keen intellectual appetite and a fine retroussé nose. She was promptly given by the more philistine men present the nickname 'Ethel'.

The Wednesday Club offered delicious Austrian food and wine, and our hosts clearly enjoyed the interaction it allowed them with a younger generation. We gathered at 12.30 sharp in the Nebehay salon, above the gallery, for a glass of Veltliner before we were summoned up a further floor to a dining room furnished in the ubiquitous Biedermeier style. At the end of the meal, after coffee and chocolates, the conversation turned to art and we were all asked to name our favourite painting in Vienna. I mentioned to Christian, a stalwart of the *Wiener Bürgertum*, invariably immaculately attired in bow tie and dark pinstripe suit, that I had been much taken by Klimt's portrait of Sonja Knips and felt almost a chemistry with its striking subject.

'Have you looked carefully at the painting?' he drawled, with an expression of benign amusement on his lips. Wondering what might be coming next, I replied that I had.

'Did you notice that she was holding something in her hand?' He walked over to a glass cabinet and bade me follow. Taking a key from his waistcoat pocket, he solemnly opened the door to the cabinet, took a small red suede notebook from a shelf and handed it to me. I felt its soft cover and realized that it was identical to the one Sonja was holding in the painting.

'It is her notebook; the very one she is holding in the painting. Now you have established another bond with her. You see how small our world is.'

As an early lesson in Viennese 'magic', this struck me then (and still does today more than thirty-five years later) as another remarkable coincidence. I held the booklet reverently for a few more seconds enjoying the softness of the suede against my thumb and finger and then handed it back to Christian who carefully returned it to the glass cabinet, relishing the sense of wonder it had generated in me. Vienna had demonstrated early its capacity to surprise and stimulate.

Thanks to these welcoming events, the period of settling into Vienna proved short and free from the bureaucratic and other obstacles which Italy and Poland would inflict on me a few years later. Nevertheless, certain formalities had to be endured, including registering for a special visa which the Austrians called a *Sichtvermerk*. This enabled me to reside in Vienna, and to make use of the Press Club situated in an imposing palais on the Bankgasse near the Hungarian embassy.

My predecessor on *The Times*, David Blow, was leaving Vienna to take up a post with the BBC in Berlin, and was full of useful tips. Over lunch in the Café Landtmann, this tall, well-spoken former pupil of the great Stoic historian William McElwee explained some of the advantages of my new 'position'. It became apparent that the prestige of certain English newspapers still rode high in Vienna. As long as I wrote one opera review at some stage during my stay in Vienna, I would be able to avail myself on most days of two free stalls tickets for any performance at the Vienna Staatsoper. Then there was free first-class travel on any of the country's railways and, of course, the usual discounts for entry to museums and exhibitions. In fact the perks were sufficient to ensure one would never starve or be bored or even be forced to stay in Vienna longer than one wished. After the previous two years of mildly impoverished life as a musician, this all sounded like a windfall.

Today, aspiring foreign correspondents are probably expected to have 'proper journalistic experience' before they contemplate the inky profession and have to learn a great deal which is no doubt professionally relevant and useful. But in those days neither I nor my predecessor, who had been a notable historian of ancient Persia, had any journalistic background. Neither of us had ever written for student magazines or posed as literary hacks in our university days. Other colleagues also failed to conform to type. One had been a clergyman, while another, like me, had worked in an opera house, though in his case as a tenor in a Hungarian chorus.

Such diverse qualifications appeared to be generally accepted as standard for being a foreign correspondent. 'How very *Times*, a bit of academia and a bit of music,' observed the aged Director of the British Council into whom I bumped one afternoon in the Bankgasse. 'Oh to be in your twenties and *Times* correspondent in Vienna,' he enthused wistfully.

Certainly the theatrical calibre of my colleagues in the Foreign Press Club was very high. An émigré Hungarian who worked for a provincial American newspaper and dictated his copy in a fortissimo voice came to my assistance when I was puzzled by the meaning of a German word that was appearing a lot in the Austrian papers: *Verleumdung*. I had never encountered the term before in Graz or Trieste, but every Austrian politician appeared to be using it freely in response to journalists' questions. When I asked my Hungarian colleague its meaning, he immediately stopped what he was doing, stood up, fixed his eye on the middle distance and struck a solemn operatic pose. After a five-second silence, he took a deep breath and raising his arms slowly skywards began singing 'La calunnia' from Rossini's *Barber of Seville*.*

In those days, the use of the telex machine for filing reports from abroad was widespread. In the absence of my own individual office, I had to cross the First District to the k.k. Telegraphenamt, a quintessentially Ringstrasse palais, where three telex machines were available for general use. The machines resembled typewriters but required different shift keys to be pressed every time you switched from numbers to letters and vice versa. As a result, the unpractised could end up with a typescript full of extraneous characters which then had to be laboriously removed from the ticker-tape. Two splendid

* *Verleumdung* = *calunnia* = calumny.

ladies in white coats, whose scientific attire suggested they might have been working in a chemist's, had mastered how to read ticker-tape and helped me as I struggled to remove a letter or numeral which had entered the text by mistake. At first, a short dispatch of 500 words could take me more than an hour to type and send, but gradually my proficiency increased and the twenty-minute walk across town to the Telegraphenamt was a prelude to a pleasant after-noon, after which either a *Heurige* (vineyard tavern) or Hawelka beckoned. Rarely did anyone else appear to use the telexes, so I usu-ally had the building to myself.

I had to be careful not to arrive after 4.30. Although de jure the offices closed promptly at 5.00 p.m., or on Fridays at 3.00 p.m., signs of the imminent departure of the telex staff began to manifest them-selves much earlier, especially in the run-up to the frequent Catholic holidays which punctuated the month of May. On Sundays a cheer-ful retired postman opened up the Amt for six hours. His smiles were sincere: trade union leverage ensured he was paid an especially gen-erous rate for working that day.

For most people not employed in the newspaper world or other 'essential services', the Vienna weekend, like that in Ljubljana, began shortly after lunch on Friday and built up a momentum of somno-lence which, by midday on Saturday, had reached its first major climax with the closure of all shops – food and drink suppliers included. From then until Monday morning, if you required as much as a bread roll, you needed to make the long trip to one of the out-lying railway termini where the *Reiseproviant* (travel provisioner) would supply a *Kipfel* or *Semmel* at inflated prices. Elsewhere in Vienna, this retail regime created parts of the city from where by Saturday afternoon virtually every sign of human life had vanished.

At first these weekends, foggy in the winter, stuffy and humid during the summer, were a trial. The melancholy still summer week-end days were probably the worst. At the beginning of *The Man without Qualities*, Robert Musil describes Vienna's lethargy at the height of a dusty dry summer's afternoon. 'It is an August day in 1913 ... Tension and relaxation, activity and love are meticulously kept separate in time and are weighed out according to formulae arrived at in extensive laboratory work. If during any of these activities one runs up against a difficulty, one simply drops the whole thing.'

In 1983, Vienna still had a *kakanian** feel to it. By Saturday afternoon, the mostly empty streets of the inner city took on the aspect of a sepia postcard. Fortunately, an interest in history and architecture invested even the briefest of walks in the *Vorstadt* (suburb) with considerable interest. An acquaintance encountered at a party soon after my arrival in Vienna offered a flat in her family palais in the Josefstadt opposite the Piaristenkirche. It was small but high up with light, airy ceilings. One neighbour was a vivacious young *comtesse*, the other, Sophie Nostitz, was the octogenarian daughter of the assassinated heir to the Austrian throne, Archduke Franz Ferdinand, and his wife, the Duchess of Hohenberg. Coming out of the nearby Piaristenkirche after mass one Sunday, Sophie Nostitz and I exchanged some words. Perhaps because of the tragic fate of her parents, she well understood the concept of *Ehrenfurcht* (fear of the Lord).

Living in the Josefstadt, I gradually came to know the many side streets which at times appeared to be a veritable roll-call of the once great *Wiener Bürgertum*. The names commemorated on the walls resonated with history. Opposite my flat stood the grand baroque Piaristenkirche and college where Bruckner had played the organ and where a generation later George Weidenfeld had gone to school. A few houses further along, a plaque noted the apartment where the founder of modern cinema, Fritz Lang, had been born. In the nearby Gardegasse, Alcide De Gasperi, the founder of Italy's Christian Democratic Party, had lived and studied. Another plaque heralded the birthplace of the composer Joseph Lanner, the inventor of the waltz, while on the Auerspergstrasse, a severe neo-classical house with lovely Biedermeier detailing, subtly indicated by a small stucco musical lyre on its façade that Beethoven had lived here. To be a

* *Kakanian:* Musil's reduction of the ubiquitous *k.(u.)k. – kaiserlich und königlich* (lit. Imperial and Royal).

Josefstädtler was to have become a member of a distinguished cultural club.

Between the Josefstadt and Gumpendorf in the west one could thread one's way through three remarkable Biedermeier *freiwillige Durchgänge* (pedestrian thoroughfares). The first of these however had a rather sinister atmosphere. It was high and narrow and it was hard not to think of it unchanged since the dreadful days of the Anschluss. The nearby Neudeggergasse confirmed the recollection of days when Vienna was not all sweetness and light.

A simple plaque noted the site of one of the district's synagogues, razed to the ground during the horrendous Reichskristallnacht of 9 November 1938. With that exquisite Viennese irony I would come to know so well, the building next door revealed a single column, symbol of the Enlightenment, and the inscription 'Zum Römischen Kaiser' accompanied by the monogram of the Emperor Joseph II, the Habsburg who had 'set the Jews free' with his Patent of Toleration in 1781.

A few streets away another passage brought one to Ulrichsplatz and, high upon a wall, the delightful bronze statue of a seventeenth-century cavalryman riding down an Ottoman janissary. A faded inscription here reminded the passer-by that on this very spot Kara Mustapha, the Turkish commander overseeing the Siege of Vienna in 1683, had pitched his tent. The nearby Spatzennest Gasthaus carried a vast mural depicting the siege. From here the Stiftgasse eventually brought one to the last of the passages, the Ferdinand Raimund Hof, named after the Biedermeier writer, and then to the Gumpendorferstrasse with its memorial to Franz Werfel and that most atmospheric of cafés, the softly lit Sperl. Walking these streets in the evening twilight, it was rare that I encountered anyone.

Gradually, I made friends with Austrians who shared the secrets of escaping the enervating weekends. The main avenue of refuge was to visit a relation's country house for tea on Sunday or even stay at one of the many beautiful castles which were still in aristocratic hands, much to the chagrin of the nouveaux riches who, despite their millions, struggled in vain to find a decent schloss where they might act out the life of a *Land-Graf*.

Despite two world wars, the end of empire and occupation by the

Nazis and until 1955 by the Red Army, most of the old families had clung on to their properties and libraries. Nevertheless, many castles betrayed signs of foreign military occupation. At Steyersberg, the paintings were marked by bayonet cuts inflicted by Soviet troops. At Ernstbrunn, Prince Reuss showed me the large salon which had been vandalized by the Russians. The priceless Reuss collection of manuscripts had been carted off to the Hermitage. In its place the Soviets had left stencilled illustrations of their tanks on the walls. No doubt they could have been removed easily, and the room restored, but it suited the Reusses to preserve this memento of recent times as a warning against complacency. 'If you have been occupied by the Red Army once, you cannot pretend it might not happen again,' the old Prince explained.

Tea at the Reusses' was always a convivial affair, with a stimulating mix of people and generations. Most of the older generation spoke of the Habsburg monarchy as if it had ended a few weeks earlier. In many cases their fathers had played key roles in the July 1914 crisis running up to the First World War. I was introduced to the children and grandchildren of the diplomats – Hoyos, Szapáry and Musulin – who had held the fate of Europe in their hands. For many of them, the contrast between the lives of their parents before 1914 and their families' uncertain paths after 1918 had nourished a philosophical outlook on the world. The glittering careers which they might have expected by reason of their birth had been denied to them, although through charm and intellect many had found ways of compensating. This ceaseless round of parties was an inescapable feature of Viennese life. Strange though it must sound today, a young Englishman with an interesting job was something of a rarity in Vienna then. Such was the mystique of *The Times* in those days all doors appeared to be opened to me, even though I knew that my opinions, if not completely worthless, were only as good as the next man's.

During the Cold War, it was an ill-advised *Times* foreign correspondent who did not make some effort to interact with the representatives of what was then usually considered the most important of British institutions in any Central and Eastern European capital, the British embassy. Frank Giles, later editor of the *Sunday Times*, had been advised by the legendary Bill Deakin,* 'In any city the most important Englishman is the British Ambassador but never forget: the second most important Englishman is always the *Times* man.' (Deakin had added comfortingly that if the correspondent was killed on active service for the paper, a good obituary was guaranteed.)

Within a few days of my first articles being published, a letter on headed paper came from the embassy inviting me to lunch with the press attaché. A bright (they were always bright) young man (they were always men) appeared at the appointed time in one of the more discreet of the restaurants of the Third District. In contrast to the suave manner of the consuls I had met in Trieste, this young diplomatist was keen to demonstrate solid proletarian credentials. My colleagues had warned me that 'Of course everyone in the embassy is a spy,' but even I, a tyro in such matters, found this earnest, gumchewing young man an unlikely candidate for the second oldest profession. His relentless talk of football and reggae was not likely to prise open any indiscretions or encourage confidence, at least mine. No doubt the antipathy was mutual.

This hapless young diplomat was probably the only Second Secretary in the embassy who in those days was not a spy, except, I suppose, that he might have been taking my measure ahead of my meeting with his boss, the Ambassador, at the annual Queen's Birthday party, to be held a few weeks later. This event, until its abolition on grounds of cost some years later, was the highlight of the embassy social calendar. It brought together many members of the rather eccentric but small English community as well as the diplomats from the three British missions in Vienna. Thanks to the superb architectural setting of the Residence on the Metternichgasse, the event if unstimulating in conversation was always a feast for the eyes.

Towering above all others present was the formidable British Ambassador, Sir Michael Alexander. Tall and spare, he commanded through force of intellect rather than patrician inclination. Alexander's father had been one of the top three codebreakers at Bletchley

* Bill Deakin (1913–2005), research assistant to Winston Churchill before the Second World War and first Warden of St Antony's College, Oxford. Fitzroy Maclean's predecessor as Churchill's liaison officer with Marshal Tito's partisans and during the 1950s a regular contributing Eastern European affairs expert to *The Times*.

Park during the war; his son had inherited his brain and many of his acute powers of observation. It was said that old Alexander had a sharp manner with subordinates, a characteristic his son had also clearly acquired. He had worked in Mrs Thatcher's office after she became Prime Minister and had established a rapport with her which made him one of the very few diplomats she ever trusted. This direct line to 'Margaret' gave him a shield which no doubt came in useful in his frequent struggles with the more conservative elements of his department, ever suspicious of the brilliant maverick. Alexander organized Mrs Thatcher's summer holidays in Salzburg, and his residence became a regular stop for visiting British royalty and other well-known figures. With a certain sense of *mérite oblige*, Sir Michael also arranged glittering lunches at which some of the more dashing elements of Vienna society were brought out to entertain these distinguished visitors.

Occasionally one of the VIPs fell by the wayside and had to be replaced with less glamorous fare. One fine spring morning the Ambassador's secretary rang to say that a guest for lunch the following day had dropped out and would I care, 'despite the frightfully short notice', to take Elton John's place? I readily agreed and found myself next to Princess Margaret and the beautiful Countess Gaby Seefried. It was the day of the American attack on Libya when several US aircraft had taken off from their bases in the UK and bombed Tripoli in a deliberate attempt to kill the Libyan leader Gaddafi. My regal neighbour threw me an enquiring glance with her marine-blue eyes and said it must have been 'very difficult' for Mrs Thatcher to allow the American jets to use British bases for such a mission. 'Did they hit anything?' she asked. 'Only the French embassy,' I replied. 'Serves them right for denying us the use of their airspace,' chipped in one of the diplomats around the table to nods and murmurs of general agreement.

Gaby Seefried, a vision of impeccably dressed middle age with bright red lips, had been one of the favourite secretaries of Hitler's spy chief Admiral Canaris during the war. Like most of the staff working for Canaris she had shared the Admiral's opposition to Hitler. Canaris had asked her to hide a huge chest of funds to help the German resistance in the event of the July 1944 assassination attempt on Hitler being successful. Unfortunately, the attempt failed, the Abwehr was dissolved and Canaris was executed, along with many other conspirators, in the last days of the war. Countess Seefried survived and married the Emperor Franz Josef's favourite great-grandchild. She had an utterly captivating elegance. After lunch, she sat calmly smoking a cigarette, her legs crossed as she leant back into one of the small sofas which then adorned the Ambassador's draw-ing room. Prince Rupert Loewenstein, the financial manager of the Rolling Stones, acted as a masculine counterweight to these Austrian graces. A man of paradoxes, this scion of an ancient German family was, despite the raucous, rebellious temperament of his world-famous clients, a devout Roman Catholic.

Being the youngest there by several decades, I was questioned closely on the distractions of Viennese life. 'Was there enough to do? Was it sufficiently stimulating?' I caught my host's eye for a fleeting second and noticed a faint smile cross his usually gaunt face. In the course of the next ten years I would come to know a number of Brit-ish ambassadors; though they had many capacities very few came anywhere near the intellectual calibre of Michael Alexander. His duties in Vienna seemed too modest for his abilities, so it was pleas-ing to see him finally given the top job at NATO, where he was reunited with a politician he, and so many diplomatists, much admired, Peter Carrington.

The rest of Alexander's staff in Vienna were mostly amiable men (the only women in the embassy in those days were cypherenes).* Dressed in blazers and club ties, and with voices honed in the major public schools and 'crack' regiments, they seemed languidly at ease in the grand Third Rococo reception rooms of the embassy or the well-stocked and extensive garden in the Metternichgasse – on top of which regrettably a new chancery building was erected in 1987, much to Alexander's dismay.

June brought many invitations from embassies and government departments. It also began the summer ball season, the highlights of which were the Rosenkavalier Ball in the Schwarzenberg Palais and the Johannsclub Ball at Eckartsau on the edge of the great

---

* Cypherenes: Cold War patois for female cipher clerks.

Pannonian plain. There are few places more romantic than Schloss Eckartsau, hidden in its park on the Marchfeld, the great plain to the east of the Austrian capital. Unlike many of the balls I later attended in Vienna during the winter, this party was both intimate and spacious with a dance floor that was never a crush. Is there a more intoxicating experience for a young man than dancing a Viennese waltz with an Austrian or Bavarian woman who knows how to guide, flirt and bewitch her partner, while all the time giving the impression that he is really in charge?

The glorious heat of midsummer on the Marchfeld meant that one could recover from these exertions as midnight approached by stepping outside and taking a path to the bridge over a moonlit stream to gaze at shooting stars before returning slowly to the music of Strauss and Komzák. By four in the morning, the castle was virtually empty, but with a few friends one could see the unforgettable gold disc rising over the flat fields where Napoleon had fought some of the greatest battles of his career.

The blaze of crimson, which marked the slowly ascending midsummer sun, bathed the plain in a dazzling radiance while the only sound to be heard was the song of a thousand birds. Despite the overwhelming beauty of the place, one could not help being reminded of the melancholy of the departing Habsburgs who had spent their last days on Austrian soil here at Eckartsau in 1919. Until she returned to Styria in 1982, the Empress Zita had spent her last night in Austria here, guarded by some loyal retainers and a single British officer, Colonel Strutt, whom George V had sent to keep a protective eye on the imperial couple. Although it is now a museum, in those days Eckartsau was rarely open to visitors. Superficially, it was virtually unchanged from the days when Kaiser Karl and Kaiserin Zita had wandered through the park.

The Rosenkavalier Ball back in Vienna was a more worldly affair. Organized by an American debutantes' society, it aimed to match wealthy young American girls with the impoverished scions of the *Erste Gesellschaft*. The more poverty-stricken of my acquaintances from the aristocracy had prepared for this upper-crust *Volksfest* many days ahead. It promised a week of lavish entertainment and frequent excursions to Schloss Fuschl, near Salzburg, all culminating in the ball, where the precocious demands of the American debutantes were expected to stimulate high performance from their coroneted partners.

The Schwarzenberg Palais was a less romantic venue than Eckartsau, but it was considered far more glamorous. Its ballroom was one of the miniature masterpieces of Viennese baroque, although it was a small space in which to dance. The magnificent garden of the Palais was also less spacious than the park at Eckartsau, but it provided ample cover for decadent scenes. The Austrian patron of the Rosenkavalier Ball was a cousin of Raimondo Torre e Tasso's in Duino, the octogenarian Prince Willy Thurn und Taxis, who presided over the details with the eagle eye of a former head of protocol to the Imperial House. Short, erect and with a shock of black hair which belied his years, TNT, as he was called, was a figure from an earlier age. Like every Austrian *grand seigneur*, he had a more modest side. As the various couples he had brought together slunk off into the undergrowth of the palace gardens, he sat alone in his tail coat at an outside table, napkin tucked into his wing collar, enjoying his Schnitzel and *Erdäpfel Salat* with only a two-litre bottle of Blaufränkisch for company.

The Schwarzenberg Palais was usually a far less exuberant place. One part had been converted into a luxury hotel but the family still held on to much of the rest. Living in one of the outbuildings behind the main palais was a lady my friends called 'Tante Lorie'. The aunt of the incumbent Prince (Kary) Schwarzenberg, a rather raffish figure on the Vienna night scene and later Foreign Minister of the Czech Republic, Tante Lorie was intelligent, serious, austere and hugely hospitable. She was a lady for whom any possibility of bling would have been repellent. Indeed so modest was she in her appearance that a few weeks earlier, when she entered a smart shop on the Kärntnerstrasse to buy some lipstick, the officious counter staff had quickly moved to escort her out, thinking by the holes in her coat that she was a tramp. Tante Lorie held her tongue until, passing out of the shop, she thanked the lady, saying in her nasal but impeccable *Schönbrunnerisch* dialect, 'Well, if you have not anything decent for a Princess Schwarzenberg, then I must find another shop.' The crestfallen attendants realized their mistake, but by then it was too late; Tante Lorie was gliding down the street.

Tante Lorie's only luxury appeared to be her books. She was well informed about architecture and music, and she had a sharp, incisive mind which no doubt in England would have led her down an academic path. In her disdain for worldly material comforts, she reminded me of the older dons at Newnham College, Cambridge. Her austerity was all the more marked by the fact that she had only to walk five minutes across the lawns of the Schwarzenberg garden to be in the grandest of all Vienna's hotels.

The Rosenkavalier Ball and its imitators, such as the prestigious Theresianisten-Picknick held opposite the Schwarzenberg Palais in the Haus der Industrie, were private affairs where connections were helpful. The Theresianum, despite decades of socialism, was still Central Europe's oldest *école d'élite*, and it resurrected all the weapons of the old ruling class to deter gatecrashers to the Picknick. In theory entry was possible only on presentation of identity papers checked against a formal list of graduates of the college, scrupulously administered by an octogenarian princess, but in Vienna everything had inbuilt flexibilities. Austrian passports and identity cards were somehow procured to ensure that a sizeable Anglo-Saxon contingent was present at the ball, none of whom had ever previously been inside the Theresianum.

On the whole, the so-called public balls were less rigidly policed. The exception to this was the highlight of the official social calendar, the Opera Ball, which was a vast jamboree taking over the State Opera House. All the stalls seats were unscrewed and removed to create the most lavish ballroom in Europe. Thousands of flowers were brought in to decorate the auditorium and a small casino was erected in the foyer of the grand circle.

Two tickets were the prerogative of every foreign correspondent *en poste* (we were barely a dozen), and as the day neared I anxiously considered whom I should take with me. This challenge revolved around my head as I attempted to organize the other essentials of the Viennese ball season: impeccable tails and a stick-up collar, the so-called *Frackzwang*. On these occasions fate often intervenes, and so it was that walking across the Tegetthoffplatz to buy a stiff collar from Herr Ružička at the Zum Jockey Club outfitters, I bumped into the most radiant of the English contingent in Vienna and summoned up the courage to ask whether she would be free the following evening. I could have asked for no more engaging companion. We meandered arm in arm across the various rooms of the opera house gazing at each other rather more than at the elegant representatives of the Second Austrian Republic.

One dancer, however, immediately drew our attention, a blonde woman whose hair was in elaborate Alpine plaits. She was not dressed in a ballgown but daringly in a man's white tie. As she waltzed across the dancing floor, she cut a figure of elegance and grace. Alex, as she was called with deliberate ambiguity, was one of the more unconventional of the younger Viennese, not least in her easy contempt for the traditional mores of the day which, in Vienna, dictated that women should always look feminine and wear dirndls or dresses.

Alex had clearly learnt Blanka's important injunction that 'Mit einem rühigen Gesicht beherrscht man die Welt' (With a calm face one can dominate the world). One of the more harassed representatives of the press present that night was visibly rather more stressed. Helga was a tall blonde photographer whom I had met at a press conference in the Café Landtmann a few weeks earlier. She was, she explained, *in Dienst* (in service), working as a photographer for the Vienna popular daily *Kronen Zeitung*. Dressed in a brown, almost Communist-drab dress, she was ill at ease, and she soon disappeared through the crowds. It was notable how very few of the old aristocracy were to be seen that evening. There may have been visiting royalty, and some of the German guests flashily wore the ribbons of long-extinct orders of chivalry, but of the old Austrian *Erste Gesellschaft* there was no sign. The event was much too middle class, arriviste and *bürgerlich* for their tastes, and in the class-conscious society of 1980s Vienna these things still mattered.

One serious figure of the older generation who was an exception to this rather limiting caste loyalty was the father of a close friend. Max Thurn was a direct descendant of Count Mathias Thurn who had defenestrated two imperial councillors from Prague Castle in 1618, thus precipitating the Thirty Years War which had laid waste to most of Germany. Twelve generations later, despite an infusion of Scottish blood via a Highland grandmother, Max still resembled his famous ancestor. He was immensely tall, well over 6 foot 6 inches, with a head resembling a block of carefully carved late-medieval granite. The gravity of his demeanour belied a brilliant sense of humour. To this quality was added a streak of independent thinking which illuminated any discussion in a lively and sometimes acerbic way. After the usual Austrian monastic boarding school run along near-feudal lines, his Scottish grandmother had packed him off to Queen's College, Oxford where exposure to liberal values had left enduring legacies. When the Nazis marched into Austria in 1938, Max had been working at the Austrian Chamber of Commerce. The Director of the Haus der Industrie had called an emergency meeting to discuss the dramatic developments and tabled a motion to record the Chamber's support for the Nazi occupation. Only three of the members present voted against it and refused the Nazi salute. Two of them were Jewish members of the legal department, the third was Max.

This opposition was quickly noted. At lunch in the Jockey Club a few hours later, two of the club's members came up to warn him that his act of defiance had already been reported to the Nazi paramilitaries who would surely only wait until they had complete control of the city before pouncing on all suspected opponents of the regime. Outside, attacks on Jewish shops had already begun and Vienna was entering its darkest night. When the Gestapo arrived a day later to take him, Max had already fled. Armed with a passport stamped with his credentials as a member of the Austrian Chamber of Commerce, he was saved by the counter-intuitive decision to drive towards Nazi Bavaria rather than towards Prague, like most other refugees. Max made it to Belgium, France and eventually a new life in Argentina for the duration of the war. Afterwards, he returned with his handsome Argentinian wife to rebuild his life in Austria, but he soon found that while those relatively few Austrians who had avoided conscription into the Nazi war machine were welcomed by the four Allied occupying powers, the reaction of his fellow Austrians was more mixed.

Applying for a job in the fledgling Second Republic Foreign Service, Max was interviewed by a thin man with a cold sharp-eyed countenance and Prussian manner. Max's hopes had been high: he was a scion of a great family and fluent in five languages. But the interviewer, after perusing the file for a few seconds, looked up at Max and asked, 'Dr Thurn, tell me, in which subject do you hold a doctorate?' Max thought this a strange question as it was plainly stated on his application form which the man had in front of him. 'I studied economics at the Queen's College, Oxford,' Max replied. At that moment his interviewer abruptly stood up and said, 'Candidates for the Austrian Foreign Service must have a doctorate in law. Good day, Dr Thurn.' The interview had lasted barely two minutes. Max took this brusque rejection philosophically – he was fond of saying that 'Nur Stubenmädchen sind beleidigt' (Only chambermaids are offended). In the event, a post in the Finance Ministry proved easier to come by. Years later Max still remembered the frosty encounter, and the name of his interviewer: Dr Kurt Waldheim.

When Waldheim began to be mentioned as a possible candidate for election to the Austrian presidency about two years into my time in Vienna, it was clear that the election would be bitterly contested. Waldheim's record between 1939 and 1945 did not label him a war criminal, but his reluctance to admit that he had been liaison officer in Salonika where Jews were being deported en masse was an error of judgement which, along with his other *piccoli difetti*, should have disqualified him from standing as a candidate. But as lack of self-awareness was one of these defects, it was perhaps hardly surprising that he continued to fight a campaign which sharply polarized his country.

As a result of Max's experience with Dr Waldheim, I had already been sceptical of his candidature. A year earlier, the President of the Republic, Dr Kirchschläger, had told me during a formal interview that as Ambassador in Prague in 1968 he had been instructed by Waldheim, then Austrian Foreign Minister, to withhold visas from Czechs seeking to flee the Warsaw Pact invasion. Kirchschläger had ignored this instruction on humanitarian grounds. As a piece of damning gossip from a head of state to the correspondent of a foreign newspaper this was unexpected.*

* I have always felt that my not using a tape-recorder or taking any notes (thanks to memory techniques honed a decade earlier in supervisions at Cambridge when generally it was considered bad form to distract the *rilassar* flow of 'conversation'

Irrespective of his wartime record, Waldheim was therefore a man with a history of faulty judgement. The world press tried in vain to find a smoking gun which would pin some Nazi atrocity on him, but it was clear from the beginning that such a discovery would prove elusive. Those who opposed him would have been better deployed focusing on his character faults rather than on his war record, which showed little sign of distinction in any field. Six years of war without advancing beyond the rank of lieutenant summed it up all too clearly.

As the spring of 1986 wore on, the campaign for and against Waldheim was on everyone's lips, creating bitter divisions even among the best of friends. For the small Jewish population of Vienna, a mere handful compared to their numbers before the war, the debate reignited Vienna's anti-Semitic traditions, and when the Waldheim camp began to put the old slogan 'Jetzt erst recht!' (Now more than ever!) on their posters, my friend Georg Eisler lamented that anti-Semitism had returned to Austrian political campaigning for the first time since the Anschluss of 1938. Eisler, the son of the composer (and Brecht's collaborator) Hanns Eisler, had one of the most original minds in Vienna. As well as being an accomplished artist – he had studied under Oskar Kokoschka – he was remarkably well informed and scathingly critical of his country's psychological and moral shortcomings. At the same time it would have been hard to find a more patriotic Austrian. Georg loved the best of Austria and surely would have agreed with Wittgenstein that 'the good things of Austria – Lenau, Bruckner, Grillparzer – are more subtle and diffi-cult to understand than anything else'.*

During the Waldheim crisis, Georg and I met regularly in the Café Prückel where, among the dusty pot-plants and 1950s furniture, my knowledge of Austrian history was constantly updated between snippets of political gossip. He knew perhaps better than most that the case against Waldheim was not one which would stop conservative

---

by writing anything down) partly encouraged this expansive indiscretion, although it cannot be excluded that Dr Kirchschläger was also preparing the ground for a future campaign against Dr Waldheim.

* 'Ich glaube dass beste von Oesterreich (Lenau, Bruckner, Grillparzer) ist viel schwieriger zu verstehen als alles andere' (quoted in Count Anton Wengersky's commonplace book, Elkhofen, 1985).

Austrians voting for him. They all saw it as a socialist plot to keep the presidency in left-wing hands. But it horrified him that his fellow Austrians could resort to wartime sentiments and resurrect the old phrases of Karl Lueger and Georg Schönerer, two notable Viennese anti-Semites from the turn of the nineteenth century. These repellent traditions certainly entered the campaign. There were also occasional examples of mild social anti-Semitism. One intellectually challenged Hungarian count thought he had unravelled the secret of the links between the press and 'international Jewry' when he seriously insisted that the London press was irrationally hostile to the Viennese. 'Think what the name of your paper means when spelt backwards.'

On the whole, however, most of the aristocracy was not hostile to the Jews and I rarely heard an anti-Semitic remark escape their lips. One exception was an absurd old Margrave, another Hungarian, whose palace had featured prominently in *The Third Man* movie. One afternoon, in the late summer of 1986, he invited me and a British diplomat *en poste* in Budapest to tea. When my companion asked whether the grand staircase with its magnificent tapestries was ever open to the public, our host replied gruffly that he did not open his rooms to the public 'as I do not want a crowd of New York Jews gawping at my possessions'. Tea did not last very long.

As the campaign came to its climax, the Dalai Lama, of all people, arrived on a visit to Vienna. In front of the entire political elite of the country he was to give a semi-public lecture on the fate of Tibetan monasteries under Chinese rule, and Dr Waldheim was to introduce him. The event was memorable as an indication of the breadth of Waldheim's following. Sitting between the representatives of two well-known wealthy Austrian Jewish families, I was struck by how supportive they were of Waldheim and how his war record seemed irrelevant to them. 'He is already our president,' insisted the glamorous red-haired lady on my right, summoning up the mood of the room.

The Dalai Lama's presence in Vienna that summer might have caused diplomats to scratch their heads over protocol, but within days of His Holiness's departure a new diplomatic challenge arose when the British embassy announced that the Prince and Princess of

Wales were about to descend on the Austrian capital for a visit, long planned by the ever-energetic Michael Alexander. The programme for the visit involved several dicey moments for the protocol departments. Both Dr Waldheim and the Prince were to attend the same concert at the Vienna Konzerthaus and it would require all the skill and discretion of the diplomatists to ensure that the two did not meet.

In the event they sat opposite each other in boxes divided by the wide expanse of the *Parterre* below, whose seats were filled with journalists eagerly craning their necks to see any telltale sign of some visual greeting. To the disappointment of the assembled press corps, the Prince of Wales showed not a flicker of acknowledgement, despite Waldheim's insistence on staring at him throughout the performance. The orchestra played Beethoven's Pastoral Symphony, the movement depicting a rustic thunderstorm appearing to express convincingly the tension inside the concert hall. As if this visit was not enough to keep the finest brains in the Metternichgasse occupied, a few days later Harold Pinter appeared at a performance of his *The Birthday Party*, in the English theatre in the Josefstadt. At the reception afterwards, who should appear yet again but Dr Waldheim. One could only be amazed by the tenacity of his efforts to greet the playwright, and by the consummate skill with which Pinter avoided the encounter, always showing his back to Waldheim as he approached.

As the election date in June neared, the media circus grew to an unprecedented size with hundreds of foreign journalists flocking to Vienna. Very few of these had any knowledge of Austrian conditions or indeed the Austrian mentality, so much of what appeared in the press was inaccurate and prejudiced. As a result, the voters closed ranks against what they considered to be external interference in their political affairs. When it came, the vote in favour of Waldheim was resounding but the victory struck many of us as pyrrhic. Even Waldheim's supporters began to wonder whether a president who was *persona non grata* in so many countries, including the USA, would really be a suitable figurehead for a small neutral country on the front line of the Cold War.

That evening, at the party celebrating Waldheim's victory in the headquarters of the ÖVP (Austrian People's Party) on the Ringstrasse,

I had my third encounter with Helga, the blonde photographer from the Café Landtmann. This time her plain dress from the Opera Ball was nowhere to be seen. It appeared that tonight under her short green-grey raincoat she was completely naked save for a bra, black leather gloves and stockings. In the heady atmosphere of raucous celebration, Helga homed in on one senior personality of the Austrian People's Party after another, all of whom she appeared to know. Yet again I attempted to make small talk and asked her where she was from. 'Czechoslovakia,' she answered, which I said surprised me for someone of such Germanic beauty. She icily shrugged off my comment with 'Where I come from, we all look like this' and glided into the crowd again. We had spoken long enough for me to discover that Helga's sense of humour was as dry as she was enigmatic.

The Waldheim campaign had obscured the other major event which occurred that spring, one whose repercussions I was reminded of a few weekends later when staying in the Wurmbrands' beautiful castle at Steyersberg, in the magical landscape south of Vienna known as the Bücklige Welt. As we sat at breakfast in front of a magnificent spread of different jams and fruits, we complimented the young housekeeper. She sighed and said, 'Of course next year this will not be possible.' This was a reminder that the pollution produced by the nuclear accident at Chernobyl had made its way across eastern Austria just a few miles to the south of where we were and it was assumed that all garden produce would be contaminated by radioactivity for years to come.

When the accident occurred, I was on the Waldheim campaign trail in Graz and the Foreign Desk of *The Times* asked me in a matter-of-fact way to 'go outdoors to see if anyone is dropping down from radioactivity', a request which expressed well the utilitarian dynamic between Foreign Desk and correspondent. Graz was looking as beautiful as ever and a brief thunderstorm forced me to take shelter under some trees in the Stadtpark. Although I recall it being rather quiet after the rain passed, there were plenty of healthy-looking people around, not least to hear Dr Waldheim. It is hard to judge today what the after-effects of Chernobyl were in Austria, and I cannot claim any symptoms arising from the accident. Others were not so fortunate. At least three younger women of my acquaintance in Vienna, including my delightful partner at the Opera Ball, sub-sequently died prematurely of various cancers.

That August, making an annual expedition to Salzburg to hear the Berlin Philharmonic under Karajan, I was met off the train by a new friend, Reinhold Gayer. Reinhold was a stalwart of the Salzburg scene. Eccentric and bookish, his Spitzweg-like frame and watery eyes belied razor-sharp powers of observation and a keen sense of fairness. A few weeks earlier, the well-known German-language writer Peter Handke had criticized one of Reinhold's colleagues in the Salzburg bookshop Höllrigl where Reinhold worked. The col-league had struggled to find a new edition of some obscure work Handke had sought. Shouting at her in stentorian tones, he had finally erupted, 'After all, we are in Salzburg's leading bookshop, not a shoe shop.' From the top of a nearby ladder Reinhold had come swiftly to his colleague's rescue and had quietly silenced the author with the words: 'Sagen Sie das Bitte nicht. Ein Paar gute Schuhe sind immer besser als ein schlechtes Buch' (Please don't say that. A pair of good shoes are always better than a bad book).

Reinhold's finger was always on the pulse of the city's social activ-ities. In fact it was said that as far as Salzburg's *Erste Gesellschaft* was concerned there was *Kein Feier ohne Gayer* (No celebration without Gayer). Reinhold was dressed in a much restored Styrian linen jacket which seemed made of a pre-1938 greenish cloth, and was accompanied by two handsome young women, both in crisp dirndls. With old-fashioned courtesy he escorted us into the magnifi-cent Salzburg railway-station restaurant which opened into a grand dining room with red-marble fountains and high ceilings, a legacy of imperial times and the days when all the great celebrities of the Salzburg Festival arrived by train. No Austrian railway interior had survived as well preserved as this one. It immediately transported the weary traveller into a vanished world of pre-war comfort and tran-quillity. Its walls were adorned with paintings from the 1920s, mostly Alpine scenes in the best *Heimat* style.*

A delicious glass of local Stiegl beer soon revivified me. Reinhold

* It was demolished in 2012.

insisted I enjoy 'the best of Austria' in this city, surrounded on virtually three sides by Germany but whose cultural independence from Germany is a psychological foundation of its existence. Few Salzburgers from Reinhold's circle had crossed the frontier to Bavaria even though it was less than two miles away. They were fond of pointing out with almost Viennese irony that although the Bavarians undoubtedly had their qualities they were *eine Mischung von Preussischen Charm und Oesterreischischen Gründlichkeit* (a blend of Prussian charm and Austrian reliability). Bavarians spoke a different dialect, ate different cakes and lacked that Salzburg finesse. When I suggested to Reinhold and his companions that we might visit the nearby Königssee in Bavaria, it was as if I was proposing to mount an expedition to the plateaux of Tibet requiring solemn precautions and elaborate preparations.

The one platform of the Salzburg station which was given over to German customs officials, in those pre-Schengen days, bristled with officious bureaucrats with strident voices and shiny uniforms. They may have lived less than a mile from Salzburg but, to my acquaintances, they were the dreaded *Piefke* who, most grating of all, spoke an ugly and unsubtle German which was dubbed *Piefkinesisch*.*

As I was regularly reminded in Salzburg, Austrian German had 60,000 words which were not found in standard German. But the vocabulary differences were only the start. Far more compelling were the differences in sensibility and *atteggiamento*. I was quickly given an example of this after my first glass of beer. The direct was banished in favour of the oblique, the transparent enveloped by the opaque. Would I not like to sit down and have supper with my friends? As I quickly realized, this was not a request but a fait accompli.

I was not in the least tired. Although I had planned to stay in my favourite hotel, the *kaisergelb* Oesterreichischer Hof, it was immediately indicated that I should consider other alternatives on offer. Reinhold had organized an entire three-day programme of events and it allowed little time for solitude or reflection. Would I not prefer

---

* Herr Piefke was a fictitious Prussian bandmaster of unimaginative, pedantic mindset. *Piefkinesisch* (lit. Prussianese) is a derogatory Austrian term still much *en vogue* in Austria for north German brogue.

to stay with his female companions in Nonntal, behind the Festung (Fortress) where there was going to be such a jolly dinner that evening at the Merans'? I gave up my reservation at the Oesterreischischer Hof and resigned myself to my itinerary being out of my hands and so I was taken to Nonntal where a beautiful seventeenth-century pebble-dashed villa with high oval-shaped windows awaited us. The rooms were cavernous with fine vaulted ceilings. A long staircase led through an old oak door into my bedroom which overlooked a garden full of venerable trees and, beyond, the glowering mass of the Untersberg and its neighbouring mountains. As I surveyed the view, the humidity was palpable. Battleship-grey clouds in the distance promised a storm.

At dinner the women were all in dirndls. Corks were dipped in candle flames and a flirtatious scene of mutual face-painting ensued. We stayed up until two in the morning when the distant rumble of thunder persuaded us to retire for the night. The storm, which broke half an hour later, brought a steady and noisy downpour.

The wind howled outside my window and the rain rattled the panes. I was about to switch off my light when there was a knock on the door. One of my companions from earlier tiptoed in and, resting herself on the edge of my bed, asked with a voice of sweet enquiry whether I was familiar with Goethe's 'Walpurgisnacht' which, with great solemnity, she proceeded to read to me. All the while, the lightning was illuminating the room in flickering bursts until a nearby strike cut the current and we were suddenly plunged into total darkness. Yet the words continued:

> Wie seltsam glimmert durch die Gründe
> Ein morgenrötlich trüber Schein!

> (How rarely flickers
> A dawn-red darkness!)

This combination of nocturnal Goethe and a beautiful young woman set against sublime natural events was novel. A candle was lit. Like a figure in an early romantic painting, the apparition in white with a thin blue ribbon in her hair appeared more tangible as my eyes became accustomed to the dark. She continued reciting with the rich vowels and soothing consonants that perhaps only the German language spoken by an Austrian woman of her background can ever provide. Joseph Roth in his magnificent novel *Radetzky Marsch* described this 'Austrian German' as recalling 'distant guitars in the night and the last delicate notes of a pealing bell'. 'Es war eine sanfte aber auch präzise Sprache, zärtlich und boshaft zugleich' (It was a gentle but also precise language, delicate and mischievous at the same time). It was Stendhal, a regular visitor to Salzburg, who best expressed its effects in his excellent analysis of 'seconde cristallisation' in the nearby saltmines: 'La cristallisation ne cesse presque jamais en amour . . .' (Crystallization continues almost without a break during love . . .).*

At breakfast, the sun was shining again and the grass had dried, so we all sat outside, the women once again in dirndls and with ribbons in their hair. At about 11.00, as we were still enjoying our *Kipfel* and *Kaffee*, a number of our hosts' nieces and cousins appeared, nearly all dressed in the uniforms and red-lined cloaks of nurses of the Order of Malta Volunteers. Some had their hair in long plaits. All were rosy-cheeked and attentive. The older ones smoked cigarettes drawn from elegant blue and white boxes.

After my experiences of the *Erste Gesellschaft* in Vienna, the Merans were refreshingly informal and had elevated the unconventional almost to an art form. They were descended from the romantic and brilliant nineteenth-century Archduke Johann and his wife Anna Plöchl, an Alpine postmaster's daughter from Aussee in the Styrian Salzkammergut. As the bride was a commoner and her consort the brother of the Emperor, the title of counts of Meran was created to bless this socially progressive union. The strong, characterful brow and enquiring eyes captured in so many of the Archduke's portraits were apparent in some of the breakfast guests, and the conversation was lively and amusing. Reinhold, who joined us still wearing his venerable *Tracht*, explained that Salzburg was really a city with a 'very thin upper crust' and that I could only understand it anthropologically if I thought of its surroundings in terms of 'agrarische demi-monde'. Humboldt, he insisted, had recognized these traits when he had visited Salzburg and described it as having,

* Stendhal, *De l'amour* (1822), ch. VI.

along with Constantinople and Naples, the most ravishing situation of any city he had seen.

I was invited to many houses over the following days. I was struck by the entirely different atmosphere of Salzburg compared to Graz or Vienna, both of which appeared to have their foundations in a culture more influenced by the east. Reinhold, however, personified the mentality of the sophisticated 'old Austrian'. He was accustomed to passing judgements with that obliquity and nuance inherited from centuries of living under various forms of ecclesiastical or monarchical enlightened despotism. One carefully pronounced word could sum up a person's character with an almost Counter-Reformation finality of judgement. Countess W was – the word purred from his lips – *discret*. Baroness F, on the other hand, was *penetrant*. The syllables grated like sandpaper. Countess W was also – here a beatific sigh – *verlässlich*, a word which was then repeated with Jesuitical solemnity. It denoted a quality rare in many parts of Central Europe but virtually unheard of during the endless rounds of festivities in Salzburg: total reliability.

There were several opportunities over the next few days to follow Osbert Lancaster's advice and enjoy the Café Bazar where, on sunny, early-autumn mornings, the view from the terrace epitomized the phrase *douceur de vivre*. The autumn light in Salzburg is much sharper than that which the city enjoys during its rather hotter and wetter summers. Reinhold with his usual pithiness summed up the relationship between the Bazar and Salzburg by saying, 'Salzburg ist ein Dorf und das Bazar ist der Dorfplatz' (Salzburg is a village and the Bazar is the village square). As one ate bread rolls with freshly grated horseradish and enjoyed the attentions of the *Tortenprinzessin* with her tray of cakes and strudels, one glimpsed many of those one knew as they threaded their daily routes unhurriedly across the city. In that pre-digital age, anyone trying to get in touch instinctively knew that the surest guarantee of success was to put a call through to the Bazar and leave a message.

There were of course other haunts which *Salisbourg profonde* valued as proof of discernment. By patronizing these one immediately demonstrated one's indifference to the regular invasion of (mostly German) tourists whose tastes were catered for by a host of other shops. These were excellent places, too, but they were not where the locals went. They reserved their attentions for the very fine Schatz Conditor (*patisseur*), with its magnificent *Traunkirchnertorte* and *Erdbeerroulade* (strawberry roulade), all displayed under fourteenth-century vaults. There was the impossibly grand outfitter Dschulnigg with photographs of its royal clientele and the more homely Trachten-atelier Jahn-Markl, both adept at making the authentic Styrian jacket, rather than its more gaudy imitations. These were the places to which the first families of Salzburg traditionally repaired, grumbling about the prices but never about the service or quality. As in all provincial societies, fastidiousness mattered, and its finer points were impressed upon the stranger.

On the penultimate afternoon of my stay, my nocturnal visitor of a few mornings earlier drove me from Salzburg to nearby Bad Ischl, some 35 miles east towards the Styrian Salzkammergut or Ausseerland. In July 1914, the imperial villa in this little town had been the scene of the Austrian Emperor's signing of the declaration of war. The Minister of War had turned as he was about to leave the imperial study and saw a pained expression on the Emperor's face. As the minister hesitated, Franz Josef said, 'Geh jetzt ... ich kann nicht anders' (Go now ... I can't do anything else).

The great discovery of Ischl that afternoon was not the Kaiser-villa, splendid as it is, but a more modest establishment called Zauner's. Given that Franz Josef spent his summers here, it is not surprising that Ischl has some fine buildings, but it is surely remarkable that a small town of barely 15,000 inhabitants can boast a *Conditorei* of world class. Zauner's can hold its own with any establishment in Paris, or even Vienna, and its survival in the globalized twenty-first century is testament to the Austrians' devotion to the cult of the *Mehlspeis* (pudding) and their great powers of improvisation. Every town in Austria has a *Conditorei*, but the mirrored interior of Zauner's is the ultimate refuge from the rain and wind which plague the Salzkammergut, even in summer. Gracing its elegant rooms are trays of Carlsbad wafers, Ischler florentines and, perhaps most mouth-wateringly of all, the unique *Zaunerschnitten*, a concoction of crushed almonds and hazelnuts encased in the finest dark chocolate.

My companion was keen to show me the Ausseerland and its dark, modest museum where a strange seventeenth-century painting depicts the characteristics of the then known races of the world. Did I conform to the qualities which the *Englisch* were supposed to enjoy? These were 'cautious, intelligent and stubborn'. This had a faint whiff of a 1930s analysis of the characteristics of the Aryan race, a discredited approach to nationality in the 1980s. The Ausseerland is the ultimate redoubt of the Styrian Alps and the Alpenvorland is a conservative place. It was perhaps unsurprising to encounter old-fashioned views even among the youngest and brightest of minds.

However, the Ausseerland has also long been a favourite haunt of many Viennese families, such as the Franckensteins, whose record of opposition to the Nazis was exemplary. Baron Georg Franckenstein was minister in the Austrian legation in Belgrave Square when the German Nazis took over Austria in 1938. The day after the Anschluss he loaded the secret archive of the legation into sacks and drove to Chelsea Bridge where he proceeded to hurl each sack into the Thames rather than allow a single document to be read by the Germans. He then instructed the chancery butler to lock every door in the legation and throw away the key.

The beauty of the landscape and clarity of the air here draw the eye upwards towards a glimpse of the distant Dachstein with its imposing glacier. Time and again these remote fastnesses have hidden the treasures of Central Europe. In 1945, many of Europe's greatest paintings were secured here while the Third Reich crumbled before the Soviet and Allied armies. Thanks to the local inhabitants, the paintings were not destroyed at the end of the war as per Hitler's orders. A local Austrian officer's disobedience similarly preserved Salzburg's heritage at about the same time. Despite repeated directives from a nearby Nazi general to defend Salzburg to the last brick, Hans Lepperdinger ordered the telephone lines to his German commanders to be cut while he made his way to the American lines to negotiate the city's peaceful surrender, narrowly avoiding the clutches of the SS on the way.

Nowhere is the mysterious beauty of the Ausseerland more potent than at the end of the path running along the foot of the Totesgebirge to the little Toplitz lake, known in local dialect as the *Dauplitzsee*. A solitary inn, the Fischerhuette, stands at one end. Inside, a small exhibition of Second World War German nautical experiments on the lake fills a glass cabinet, together with forged Bank of England notes found in submerged caskets. Undoubtedly, the Toplitzsee has many secrets. The gold for years thought to be hidden in its depths, and which even featured in the James Bond film *Goldfinger*, has never been found. As recently as the late 1990s, an Israeli mini-submarine was granted permission to look for submerged items, but nothing of interest emerged.

Back in Salzburg I was taken to a concert in the Grosses Festspiel-haus, part of the complex of buildings associated with the Festival set up by the Austrian producer and director Max Reinhardt after the First World War. In contrast to most London concert halls, the Grosses Festspielhaus, designed by Clemens Holzmeister, has an acoustic remarkable not only for the richness of the orchestral sound it produces but also because it enables those in the highest seats in the gallery to enjoy a sound which is immediate and convincing, never remote or muddy. This alone is sufficient to ensure that Holzmeister is remembered as one of the great concert-hall architects of the twentieth century.

The concert was traditional, but instead of Karajan and the Berlin Philharmonic we heard a memorable performance of Schubert performed by an Austrian quartet. I was reminded of a conversation I had once had with Ernst Gombrich in the Warburg Institute a few years earlier. He had suggested that music-making expressed national linguistic characteristics and claimed that he could usually tell whether an Austrian or German string quartet was playing a piece of Schubert or Mozart because the Viennese dialect somehow transposed itself into the Austrian quartet's phrasing. For Gombrich, Austria always had to be contrasted with Germany – sometimes negatively, sometimes positively. The two mentalities, cultures and ways of using the language were entirely different and he could be impatient with pupils who failed to take these nuances into account.

On the train journey back to Vienna, distracted perhaps after the excitements of Salzburg, I missed the connection at Linz and took refuge in the station restaurant, less elegant than that in Salzburg but with a monumental neo-classical saloon in the style of Troost or

Speer, complete with a dramatic staircase and niches filled with 1930s sculpture (it was demolished in 2010).

As the train renewed its journey alongside the Danube, the great monastery of Melk suddenly rose up in the evening twilight to announce the approaches to Vienna. Is it here that one crosses an invisible frontier between Western and Central Europe? In the 1980s, it certainly seemed so. Today, following the fall of the Berlin Wall, Vienna has become a more Western city and the contrast with Salzburg appears less marked. In any event, thanks to recent tunnelling designed to shorten the journey by fifteen minutes, this wonderful visual *coup de théâtre* is no longer granted to the traveller between Salzburg and Vienna.

From the Westbahnhof in Vienna to the city centre is a brisk fifteen-minute walk along the Mariahilferstrasse. In the 1980s, this thoroughfare was notable for the imposing palais housing the war archives and, on the opposite side of the road, the baroque Church of Mariahilf. High above one of the side altars is the most historic and striking paintings of the Madonna and Child still to be found in the city. A copy of Lucas Cranach's celebrated painting in Innsbruck, it was publicly displayed during the Great Siege of Vienna in 1683 when its miraculous powers were summoned in the defence of Christendom. Brought within the inner fortification walls, it was 'exposed' close to the present Kohlmarkt in order to grant comfort and solace to the beleaguered garrison's soldiers who daily faced their own possible annihilation with fortitude and equanimity, inspired in part by this simple canvas.

It is exemplary of the international traditions of the Habsburgs that opposite this church is a Jewish hat factory dating from the 1850s where the headdresses of the Spanish Riding School are manufactured. The present owner is the fifth generation of his family to make them. An orthodox Jew, Herr Szaszi refused, as many had advised him to do, to transfer his workshop out of Austria, despite all the horrors of the Anschluss. His presence underlines the trust in a future in Vienna that many Jews still share. Those who lost their families in the unique bestiality of the Holocaust are making a powerful gesture of confidence and reconciliation by returning to the scene of so much cruelty to their race

*

As autumn gave way to yet another winter, the cloudy grey days in Vienna were made bearable only by the never-ending sequence of invitations to parties, and the variety of cafés and *Conditorei* which offered consolation when the leaden winter skies cloaked all activities. Of these, the Café Eiles in the Josefstadt and the Café Prückel on the Karl Lueger Platz offered retreats where one could be alone and yet never feel solitary. Most of these cafés were relatively modest establishments, but at the centre of Vienna was the most opulent of them all, Demel's. Lunch at Demel's on Sunday with friends became a regular event, even though in those days the food was only a cold buffet and everything was generously wrapped in aspic. At that time, most of the cakes were made on the premises in quite primitive conditions and a heavy odour of cooking chocolate pervaded the air. A door at the rear of the ground floor revealed a group of aproned *Demelinerinnen* (as the waitresses immaculately attired in black silk were called) struggling with huge brass pots of chocolate, all smoking away while they carefully stacked trays of fragile *Spanische Windbäckerei* (meringues).

The *Demelinerinnen* were described by the pre-war Austrian writer Anton Kuh as the embodiment of the 'old Austria'. They united, in Kuh's phrase, 'die Allüre der Burgtheater-Grossmutter . . . mit der stillhuschenden Devotion einer Logenschliesserin' (the allure of a Burgtheater grandmother with the silent devotion of the keeper of the keys to an opera box).

Kuh continued: 'Sie tragen auf ihren schwarzen Blusen unsichtbare Erinnerungsmedaillions an Altoesterreich' (They bear on their black blouses the invisible decorations recalling old Austria). 'They were accustomed to the sight of hand-kisses (the most spontaneous and unassailable recognition of the old regime) and the so-called "Demel-Prosa", the aristocratic intonation of German where the simple question "Schon da?" (Already there?) was languidly pronounced "Chaudeau?" '

One Sunday, a group of us were tucking into some cold roast beef (in aspic) when the unmistakable thud of a distant explosion ripped through the air, and for a moment I thought the Cold War might be turning hot. Then at the rear of the saloon the door swung open to reveal extravagant scenes of disorder in the kitchen. One *Demel-inerin* appeared to have fainted while another two emerged with their faces covered in chocolate and fragments of meringue stuck in their hair. Evidently, a brass pot promising a future chocolate soufflé had been neglected on the fire with pyrotechnic results, showering the hapless *Demelinerinnen* with all the sweet shrapnel of Viennese confectionery.

As if these events were part of the everyday routine of a former Imperial and Royal *Hofconditor*, a tall and striking blonde *Demel-inerin* in a tight black dress confidently and calmly strode to the front of the interior salon where we were sitting and firmly drew the velvet curtains behind her. 'Just a little upset,' she smiled, as she walked purposefully on to marshal her staff. Within a minute, the *Demelinerinnen* had recovered their composure and were serving us again with brisk efficiency as though nothing untoward had happened. The Austrians could clearly be as cool under fire as the Prussians, although it needed a crisis to unleash their full reserves of discipline.

I thanked the tall blonde, whom I now finally looked in the eye and recognized. 'Helga?' I asked tentatively.

'Sssssh. Here I am called . . . Eleonore,' she purred.

I should have recognized 'Eleonore' immediately but her figure had been rather compressed by the elegant lines of the black and white Demel uniform. A few days later I returned to Demel's with a colleague from the *Daily Telegraph*, keen to share with him the qualities of the establishment and see whether 'Eleonore' was still working there. Indeed she was and with a brisk and detached manner she left to find the owner, the notorious Udo Proksch.

Proksch had a reputation in Vienna as a wild card. He was partnered with the Countess 'Kik' Salm, a handsome aristocrat in whose family the ownership of Demel's had long resided. But far from imitating the mannerisms of the high born, Proksch enjoyed provoking friends and acquaintances with sudden displays of bravado, including pulling a revolver from his tweed jacket.

In his limitless contacts with the Viennese beau monde, Georg Eisler had come across Proksch quite frequently. 'Unfortunately, you can never tell what is going to happen . . . and by the way, my friend, I remember from my school days in England during the war that a gun . . . is always loaded.'

That afternoon in the tranquil surroundings of Demel's, Proksch, attired in hunting tweeds, appeared, unarmed as far as one could tell. He shook our hands warmly and, after whispering something into Eleonore's ear, smiled radiantly at us and withdrew. We did not have to wait long to know what he had said. Within minutes we were being offered cognac, *Dobostorte* and even cigars by a brace of *Demelinerinnen*. This all seemed very amusing, but then we noticed that Eleonore had reappeared with a camera and was taking photographs of us from the corner of the room.

'Eleonore, my dear, why are you taking photographs of us?' I asked.

'It is for a very prestigious Italian magazine . . . who are doing an article about Demel's,' the husky voice whispered soothingly as the camera continued to click.

'Which magazine?' my colleague from the *Telegraph* asked sceptically. He had served his paper for many years in Moscow and was a hardened professional who had seen this sort of stuff before. But even he was nonplussed by Eleonore's reply.

'*Il Meglio* . . . The Best,' she replied confidently, adding, 'Some more cognac, gentlemen?' The word 'cognac' was pronounced slowly and deliberately from deep within her throat as if it was an arcane sexual rite rather than an alcoholic drink.

As it happened, my *Telegraph* colleague was in Venice the following weekend, and he looked in vain for *Il Meglio*. Of course it had never existed. We could only speculate as to why Eleonore would want to record two Western correspondents enjoying the hospitality of the house.

The top floor of Demel's was organized as a private political club along the lines of the Josephinian Enlightenment: Austrian cabinet meetings took place here, and many members of the Viennese political class spent their time in the 45 Club, so called because its membership was limited to that number, although it was rumoured by wilder imaginations that there might also have been an occult numerological significance to it.

It would be some months before Proksch's reputation and that of the 45 Club began to unravel. In 1986, he was arrested for sabotaging a ship nearly a decade earlier in the Indian Ocean and claiming the insurance. Inconveniently for him, several members of the crew had survived the explosion and the claim had been vigorously contested. Proksch was tried and imprisoned. Then, a few years later, it emerged that Demel's had been a front for operations run by East German intelligence. In retrospect the clues had been there: it had been noticeable how many of the *Demelinerinnen* spoke with strong East German accents. Eleonore's intonation was far more Sudetenland than Vienna. With Proksch's incarceration, she, like many of the *Demelinerinnen*, simply vanished and I never saw her again.

If this was Cold War espionage *à la Vienne*, it seemed to involve as much comedy as tragedy, but can there ever have been a sweeter cover for a 1980s Mata Hari than that of the efficient, discreet and beautiful *Demelinerin*? Eleonore's techniques were certainly old school. Her English targets were first lured into a false sense of security by the Union Flag pin she wore in the lapel of her long black coat. Then, once back in her rooms near the Theresianum, they were further lulled by a gramophone record playing a rather crackly version of Vera Lynn's 'White Cliffs of Dover', a strange accompaniment to the pursuits of the evening but one her victims no doubt found reassuring.

Even today, Vienna is a city where both East and West have rights. The Austrian State Treaty was signed in 1955 by Macmillan and Dulles but also by Molotov and Pinay. Russia and America have respected the fact that Vienna cannot become too much of a battleground without both sides losing; far better to continue the tradition whereby the Austrians tolerate Great Power espionage activities as long as no one really notices. Espionage is in one way simply a barometer of the relations between powers; spying scandals often illuminate the geopolitical landscape like forks of lightning before a thunderstorm.

No doubt the British played their role in such adventures in the 1980s and no doubt some people were being suborned, but little seemed to leak out. Occasionally one saw traces of the 'lightning' but it was distant. One Friday morning as I was walking past a bank near the Michaelerkirche, the revolving door spun out a British diplomat with a name well known even to Stalin's secret police. He emerged somewhat sheepishly with a rather heavy black attaché case. Was it stuffed full of banknotes to pay off some shadowy agent? Feigning even more habitual nonchalance than usual, he simply enquired after my plans for the weekend.

At the more exotic embassy receptions and Balkan national days it became apparent that we were inhabiting some sort of comfortable no man's land where temptations were being dangled by both sides. At one reception, a Romanian diplomat came up to me and asked if I would be interested in visiting his country and spending a few days in Bucharest. I thought nothing more of this until a week later, sitting in the Café Eiles, I read in the local newspaper that he had been fatally defenestrated in the suburb of Favoriten. 'Last seen alive talking to you,' quipped the diplomat from the bank at a reception the next day in honour of the Albanian National Day celebrations.

Predictably, the CIA presence in Vienna had a rather higher and more conventional profile. The Agency occupied an enormous building in the Josefstadt, a few minutes' walk from my apartment. Very occasionally, the press was invited to solitary briefings there. These were usually memorable because senior US officials indicated their reluctance to speak too loudly on sensitive topics and played a gramophone record which they were confident would obscure the conversation. These elaborate precautions appeared to confirm that Vienna was not as friendly to US interests as other Western European cities. Years later, courtesy of Wikileaks, we would read the US Ambassador to Vienna lamenting in a classified telegram that 'I have sadly no leverage here as there is nothing the Austrians seem to need from the US.'

The younger American diplomats and journalists conformed absolutely to type. At Cambridge in the 1970s, we had noted the presence of transatlantic 'scholars', clean-limbed and enthusiastic, who the colleges accepted to top up revenue. In Vienna similar young men displayed a touching faith in first appearances. One dressed in blazer and preppy tie reeled off irrelevant and mind-numbing statistics before he looked at a file and solemnly drawled, 'I see from your résumé that you also represent *Country Life* here in Vienna. Is that true?' When I admitted that I had from time to time written for that illustrious magazine, the attaché's eyes lit up so vividly I wondered whether some obscure indiscretion had been detected in my past. He gravely intoned: 'You know the entire Reagan administration is really big into *Country Life*.'

On the whole, movements and communications were not especially closely watched in Vienna. The technology still betrayed itself by telltale pings, what Graham Greene affectionately called 'tinkerbell'. One could usually discern when taps were deployed. Compared to the 'blanket coverage' of the twenty-first century which almost guarantees intelligence failure through its very non-selectivity, the warriors of the Cold War in Vienna usually focused their resources on each other.

Nevertheless there was a contrast in diplomatic styles. The Soviet embassy appeared to bristle with activity compared to its calm British neighbour in the Metternichgasse. Even its chancery seemed to be humming with uniformed staff rushing in various directions, files in hand. With the arrival of Gorbachev at the Kremlin in 1985, the younger diplomats who appeared in the Soviet embassies had ceased to be drawn from the stiff *nomenklatura* caste usually evident at Soviet diplomatic parties. Their press correspondents suddenly were no longer old, harassed and weary but dashing, handsome and young. They were all assumed to be 'spies'. No doubt they thought the same of us.

The Soviet Union's relationship with Vienna was symbolized by the imposing monument to the Soviet soldiery who had liberated Vienna from the Nazis in the spring of 1945. In the best traditions of Soviet realism, it blocked the view of the Schwarzenberg Palais from the Ringstrasse and, in the grey days of winter, appeared to sum up Vienna's proximity to the drab Eastern Europe of Soviet satellite states. Because no state can remain indifferent to the memory of its fallen, monuments to foreign military dead are among the more sensitive objects in international relations. Those who desecrate or seek to move them are virtually declaring war on the country whose soldiers are commemorated. After the Cold War, the Baltic states sought to remove several Soviet era monuments and found themselves facing trade sanctions and cyber-war reprisals – indeed in 2007 Estonia's entire banking system almost collapsed thanks to electronic viruses after it moved the Soviet-era 'Bronze Soldier of Tallinn'. It was therefore wise of the Viennese authorities to resist in the months following the end of the Cold War the popular clamour for the removal from the square of this period piece. Instead, by lavishing huge amounts of gold leaf on it, they improved an impressive reminder of more difficult times, now as much a part of the Vienna cityscape as the baroque palaces it interrupts. Perhaps the city planners recalled the old Emperor Francis I whose summer palace at Schönbrunn had been decorated during Napoleon's occupation with French eagles on the gateposts. When after Napoleon's defeat courtiers advised the Emperor to pull the eagles down, Francis turned to them saying, 'Auch das gehört zu unserer Geschichte' (That too belongs to our history).

Both the State Opera and the Musikverein offered civilized venues for spies to exchange messages in crowded rooms. At least one venerable intelligence officer has confessed in his memoirs to spending as much of his time in Vienna as possible in the State Opera House, not least because he could sit in the Chancellor's box with diplomats from 'the other side'.

As a political correspondent, I was not expected to review operas very often, but the great Vienna State Opera House soon demonstrated its ability to generate controversy over issues which went beyond simple musical standards. Shortly after I arrived in the city, the State Opera appointed the conductor Lorin Maazel as Director. At first it was difficult to gauge the Viennese response to this undoubtedly accomplished musician, but it was not long before a number of incidents suggested all was not well in the temple of Austrian opera. The truculent claque which felt itself the sole arbiter of good taste took to booing singers whom Maazel had engaged and who were new to the house, some of them Jews from New York. The claque could move from ecstatic applause to vociferous barracking as if at the flick of a switch. The scenes became increasingly ugly. There were rumours that the new Director wanted to dismantle the old repertory system by which the house played up to twenty different works a month and was closed only on Christmas Day, Easter Sunday and the night of the Opera Ball. Most opera houses enjoy a season of six or eight productions, but Vienna remained committed to the old system. On the one hand this certainly allowed for a rapid acquaintance with the repertoire; on the other, its critics felt it was a sausage factory of performances that were often dull and lifeless. Maazel understandably wanted to bring the house into line with other European houses, but the repertory system, like so many institutions in Vienna in those days, as in Ljubljana, was underpinned by a long-established consensus between artists, bureaucrats and trade unions, and these forces were against him.

Maazel's fate began to fill the pages of the local press. Having failed to organize an interview with the maestro through his secretary, I had resigned myself to this when the ever-dutiful Herr Magoni, who supplied the correspondents' tickets, politely took me aside. He said, 'You really should not put up with this. After all,' he added, glancing at my mid-twenties frame, 'you are hardly an insignificant boy.' This was a typically Viennese ploy, calculated to flatter and provoke a reaction from the unsuspecting foreigner. It worked. I sat down and with pen and paper embossed with the Sovereign's coat of arms (the old *Times* notepaper still carried the Reynolds Stone masthead) vented my frustration in a personal appeal to the conductor.

Within six hours of delivering this note, my request was granted and I was ushered into the maestro's presence in a large room at the side of the opera house. The room was thick with cigar smoke and, between long puffs, Maazel gave me an acidic *tour d'horizon* of his difficulties in trying to modernize the Vienna opera. His manner had undoubtedly been sharpened by the conflicts of the previous weeks and one could see the clash of two worlds in every gesture. Energetic, innovative and reformist, he had crossed swords with an establishment which was conservative, complacent and anti-American. Spearheading the attack was the redoubtable critic of the local Vienna newspaper, *Die Presse*, Franz Endler.

Endler saw himself as the heir to Eduard Hanslick, the nineteenth-century critic whose articles could make or destroy a musical career in a single edition. After hearing Bruckner's Eighth Symphony, Hanslick had famously written, 'No doubt these strange sounds have a place in the musical future of our world but it is not one that I can look forward to with any equanimity.' For decades afterwards the symphony was hardly ever played. A century later, Endler was deploying the same withering sarcasm in his 'appreciations' of Maazel's efforts.

By the time of our meeting, Maazel's fate had been sealed. Herr Endler had penned one hostile critique after another and Helmut Zilk (appropriately nicknamed 'Zilk Cut'), the Austrian minister responsible for the arts (and later Mayor of Vienna) had asked the critic to draft a letter firing the maestro. That the letter, a supposedly confidential ministry document, had been drafted at Endler's home soon became public knowledge, and indeed it was published soon afterwards in *Die Presse*. Nothing demonstrated the social cohesion of the Viennese political *Gesellschaft* more effectively than this episode.

Herr Endler met me for coffee at Sacher's a few days later. He seemed worn out by the battle he had fought and won, betraying only the slightest hint of triumph in his demeanour. Looking at this exhausted, wrinkled figure, a nervous, chain-smoking man who would be difficult to notice in a crowded room, I recalled the words of Kurt Vorhofer, the veteran and kind political editor of the Graz newspaper, the *Kleine Zeitung*: 'Journalism may be dirty [*schmutzig*] but cultural journalism? That my friend is filthy dirt [*dreckiger Schmutz*].'

The Vienna State Opera advertised discreetly for a new musical director to replace Maazel. A month later I was hastily summoned back from a weekend in Arezzo to interview Maazel's replacement, Claudio Abbado. The interview was scheduled for 8.30 a.m. The night express *Remus* which had departed from Florence at 8.33 p.m. arrived punctually at the Vienna Southern Railway Station at 8.05 a.m. and twenty-five minutes later I was being shown by Abbado himself into the penthouse of a block of flats just behind the Sacher Hotel on the corner of the Neuer Markt. He was diffident, boyish and strikingly low-key. The contrast between the Italian and his predecessor could not have been greater. And although both were superb musicians, Maazel had exuded the air of a man accustomed to command while Abbado appeared shy, hesitant and modest. It was hard to think of him as a person on whose every word a hundred of the finest (and most demanding) orchestral musicians in the world would hang.

I could not help wondering how this seemingly self-effacing maestro would deal with an orchestra as notoriously difficult as the Vienna Philharmonic. The great conductor Otto Klemperer, a protégé of Mahler's, had memorably said shortly before he died in 1973, 'I prefer the Vienna Philharmonic to any of the American orchestras and even to the Berlin Philharmonic. The sound, especially that of the strings, is magnificent, although individual members of the orchestra can be highly disagreeable.'

Other orchestral musicians, let alone members of the general public worldwide, have little idea of the extraordinary prestige, status and musicianship of the Vienna Philharmonic. The Philharmonic is like an extended family, entry to which is governed primarily but not exclusively by standards of the greatest musicianship. Family tradition also plays an important part in the recruitment process. The ensemble of the orchestra, the unique richness of its string sound, the magical timbre of its horn section; these are quantifiable and are demonstrated in countless performances and recordings. Less tangible is the idea that the Philharmonic really operates like a living organism linked with the past directly through performing works that are part of a tradition handed down from one generation of players to another. Especially where the greatest achievements of Brahms or Bruckner or Mahler are concerned, the collective memory of the orchestra can draw on the wisdom and experience of the very musicians who first performed these works.

The Viennese component is important in all kinds of ways. The members of the orchestra are predominantly Viennese and therefore, as Gombrich suggested, it makes music in a way which subconsciously reflects the intonation and cadences of their dialect. Its placing of chords and its lyricism add to its ability to play with the utmost crispness and precision. Nothing perhaps expresses this better than its unrivalled performances of the much underestimated but enormously demanding Johann Strauss canon each New Year's Day.

A conductor who attempts to impose too much of his own interpretation on these works is inevitably in for a difficult ride because the orchestra will always know the work better than he does. The musicians need a lot of persuading to play their beloved classics in ways that deviate from their established parameters. Without a very firm intellectual grasp of the score, a degree of charm mixed with authority and a seamless command of the German language, a new conductor faces a daunting task. If the conductor is Viennese it helps, but the players will nevertheless prefer a non-Viennese conductor who lets them sing (for example, Mehta) to a Viennese one who tries to get them to play everything according to his own, as they see it, 'misguided' views.

I write 'his' views because, even though the orchestra has admitted since 1997 some female members, the overwhelming majority of the players and all its conductors are male. Although I counted four female players last time I saw them perform in the Musikverein, I would not be surprised if at the end of this century it, along with the Vatican, remained one of the two great European institutions exclusively dominated by men. These two institutions, like the Brigade of Guards and the Treasury in the United Kingdom, bring only defeat and ruin to those who challenge their traditions. Harold Macmillan could have added the Vienna Philharmonic to his list of institutions 'one should never pick an argument with'.

As the flagship of Austria's status as a musical superpower, the orchestra – which also supplies the musicians for the orchestra of the Vienna State Opera – is financially unassailable. Its members enjoy a security and pension provision of which other musicians can only dream. To all intents and purposes they are civil servants with consonant privileges. To see them walk on to the stage of the Musikverein on Sunday mornings attired in 1950s diplomatic dress, or *Stresemann* as the Germans call the combination of pinstripe trousers, black coats with waistcoats and spongebag ties, is to witness the ritual of one of Europe's last but most enduring musical elites. Such concerts remain the highlights of the European orchestral calendar, yet in the 1980s any impoverished Viennese could attend at least the second half of the concert by simply wandering ticketless into the Musikverein during the interval and avoiding the not-too-discerning eye of the attendants, who even sometimes shepherded the newcomers to the best standing places at the rear of the stalls.

In the more competitive climate of the post-Cold War years, all these factors continued to ensure that the orchestra weathered the storms of globalization better than its rivals, notably the Berlin Philharmonic, which lost some of its unique tone quality and cohesion after the Cold War ended. Abbado, however, still found it no easy 'band' to conduct. He left as Director after barely two years, although not before he had introduced audiences to an account of Beethoven's Ninth Symphony which was of such lyrical beauty and unthreatening Latin grandeur that even die-hard German nationalists in the audience must have been transported. Like Abbado's later Bruckner readings, his Beethoven removed all vestiges of Teutonic martial interpretations. No one could level at Abbado the accusation, often aimed by the Viennese these days at Thielemann, 'Dass er macht unser Bruckner a bisserl zu Deutsch' (He makes our Bruckner a little too German).

After the departure of Maazel, the State Opera quickly settled down under Abbado – there were limits to the amount of cultural bloodletting permitted, even in Vienna – and guest conductors replaced the old guard of repertory conductors who had too often produced static performances of the classics. One of these newcomers electrified both the orchestra and the audience with his performances of Verdi's *Macbeth*. Giuseppe Sinopoli towered above the pit, and appeared literally to jolt the Vienna players out of any sense of apathy. Under his direction they played like men possessed. His performances easily ranked with Abbado's conducting of the same opera at La Scala in 1979.

Alongside such mesmerizing conducting, Vienna produced casts of exceptional quality: Lucia Popp, Edita Gruberová and Gundula Janowitz (then nearing the end of her career but unforgettable as the countess in *Figaro*), as well as Agnes Baltsa in *Carmen* and Hermann Prey in *Meistersinger* and Bernd Weikl in *Fledermaus*. Performances of Second Viennese School masterpieces such as *Lulu* and *Wozzeck* were played regularly and more conventional tastes were consoled by Pavarotti in *Rigoletto* or *Traviata*. Although the number of operas performed each year had been scaled back in the wake of Maazel's reforms, it was still possible to go to the opera twice every week for three months and see a different work performed each time. Productions remained conventional but inoffensive, in harmony rather than in competition with the music. The Regisseur in those days had not yet been gripped by the dead hand of the Dummes Deutsches Theater Regie (literally, Imbecilic German Theatre Production) set to destroy opera production at the Salzburg Festival for many years to come.

These public performances were complemented by chamber music in a variety of houses in the Vorstadt. Rare were the occasions wandering through the Josefstadt when one did not hear the sound, floating from a window, of a piano or other instrument in a room above. Classical music, increasingly peripheral in other European cities, still remains part of daily life in Vienna. Where else on the underground metro system does one find oneself sitting next to someone studying a score or reading Furtwängler's essays? The role of an orchestral musician is considered the highest calling, one that dwarfs in prestige any commercial activity. Even in the *Heurigen* of the Vienna woods, the *Schrammel* (Viennese popular music) – of course played live – remains a prized accompaniment to an evening otherwise devoted to food and wine. The songs sung by these musicians accompanied by violin and accordion have a bitter-sweet quality which is quintessentially Viennese. The zither, an instrument immortalized by *The Third Man*, is also often present. Its plucked chords conjure Central Europe in a way almost no other instrument can, just as the *Zymbalon* appears to embody the mysterious brooding character of the Hungarian plains and their gypsy inhabitants. It is often forgotten that the zither was a court instrument before the First World War and that Charles, the last Austrian Emperor, commissioned pieces from his resident zither composer. These haunting melodies continue to be played to this day.

In the mid-1980s, a picture of Austria's conservative musical taste was always available on Austrian Radio One, which was devoted to classical music. Coming from England, where Radio 3 in the 1970s was one of the glories of cultural life, I found the Austrian classical channel limited. There was no serious analysis to help one think about a complex symphony. Nor, ironically, was there a Hans Keller to engage the audience with deep knowledge and bold assertions[*] delivered in the only exception to received pronunciation then tolerated by the BBC: a thick Viennese émigré drawl. Instead, the Austrian channel simply announced, 'Beethoven. Symphonie Nummer Drei in Es dur, gespielt von der Wiener Philharmoniker unter Herbert von Karajan,' before a technical assistant placed the stylus

[*] For example, this from a Keller broadcast in 1971: 'Of course the Mendelssohn violin concerto is the greatest violin concerto ever written: I see some of you raise your eyebrows at this claim; but just ask any violinist which concerto they prefer playing.'

on the record and the music began. It was nearly always Beethoven, Brahms or Bruckner; very occasionally there was Mozart or Schubert. Apart from these announcements, delivered with the gravitas of an authority calling for immediate evacuation to the air-raid shelters, no words were spoken on this channel: no debate, no commentary, above all no unrushed introductions to the music we were about to hear. I took it for granted that this contrast was permanent.

In fact, in the 1990s, the Austrians moved on to the BBC's former intellectual high ground, more or less at the same time London abdicated it and introduced the spurious breeziness of the chat show to Radio 3.

It was inevitable that sooner or later this Viennese *douceur de vivre* would come to an end; London expected me to cross the 'Curtain' as a foreign correspondent. The arrival of Gorbachev in the Kremlin in March 1985 was widely seen as potentially shaking things up, but diplomats were sceptical about whether a man with strong KGB links would be in a position to change much in 'the evil empire'. Settling into a routine of providing regular correspondence, my days became more frequently punctuated by quick telephone exchanges with the Foreign Desk followed by the two hours of writing and telexing a dispatch. I was quickly encouraged to visit Prague and Budapest at the earliest opportunity. But here was a dilemma: if I were to go on a journalist's visa, I would almost certainly be monitored rather more closely than if I visited as a tourist.

Hungary had abolished visa restrictions for Austrians a year earlier and, with Moscow's blessing, appeared to be opening itself up to some Western influences. I thought it best to test these waters by visiting Budapest. Although I would have to call on the British Ambassador there for a briefing, I hoped it would not stir up too much fuss. It was generally thought that little notice was taken of a correspondent until the first article about a place behind the Iron Curtain had been published over a by-line. One morning in spring 1985, I waited at the Hungarian embassy in the Bankgasse in a long line of applicants for visas and presented my passport for stamping. The Hungarian officials were polite and correct with a formality bordering on the old-fashioned. A former Hungarian colleague from the Ljubljana opera corps de ballet arranged for me to stay in a family flat in Budapest.

Before setting off for the Westbahnhof to catch the afternoon train I had one important visit to make. My English journalist colleagues urged me to interview the dissidents in Budapest but, on closer questioning, none seemed prepared to give me their names, addresses or telephone numbers. Through the indefatigable and generous Georg Eisler, I was introduced to Barbara Coudenhove-Kalergi, who lived near the Franziskaner Platz, a few moments' walk away from the Stadtpark.

The Coudenhove-Kalergis are one of the most remarkable families of old Austria. Richard Coudenhove-Kalergi had been a friend of Churchill's and Leo Amery's, and had founded the Pan-Europa Movement after the Second World War. He had therefore been a progenitor of the idea of European unity and by extension of the European Community and European Union project. His ideas on European integration were radical and innovative at the time, although they have long since become mainstream. His father, the Austrian Ambassador to Tokyo before the First World War, had fallen in love with a Japanese lady-in-waiting. The resulting intermarriage of races from the *Abendland* (Occident) and *Morgenland* (Orient) had scandalized Vienna before 1914. One socially aloof member of the family had grandly asked the Japanese fiancée on her arrival, 'What does it feel like to be marrying into a family of 500 years of unbroken noble ancestry?' The Japanese girl had coolly responded, 'I do not know because my family is more than 2,000 years old.'

The Japanese genes invested the next generation of Coudenhoves with distinctive features. An elegant, intelligent lady smilingly motioned me towards a chair. On a table near where I was asked to sit, I noticed a fine black and white portrait of the older Austro-Hungarian-Japanese couple, he standing resplendent in Austrian uniform, she demure and fine-featured in a white kimono.

Barbara knew many of the dissidents and happily gave me their numbers. She kept referring to them as 'writers'. When I ineptly asked her, 'What about the dissidents?', she replied with a faint twinkle in her eye, 'But these *Schriftsteller* [writers] are they!' Thus prepared, I was ready to set off on my first official foray into the Communist Hungarian landscape. At nine the following morning I left the Westbahnhof and, after gliding slowly past Schönbrunn and its Gloriette, we soon reached the Hungarian border at Hegyeshalom, where the train waited for twenty minutes and our passports were politely checked.

The direct rail route from Vienna to Budapest still runs through the picturesque little town of Győr. As the train steamed in – there was still no electric locomotive – I was struck by the beauty of the railway station's 1930s architecture. Baedeker referred to a branch line which would take me from here to a Benedictine monastery and school, at Pannonhalma towards Veszprém. I was intrigued to see how the Roman Catholic Church and monastic life in particular coexisted with Communism, an ideology in theory dedicated to its extinction. How would Pannonhalma compare with Altenburg and Melk, or even Heiligenkreuz, the destinations of many a happy weekend in Austria?

We had completed passport and customs checks so I jumped off the train. Walking past the classical lines of the station's façade, I asked an official in German when the next train to Veszprém departed. The polite railway official in a red cap pointed to another steam locomotive across the platform which at that moment was loading up with Asiatic Soviet soldiery, their boots and astrakhan headdresses striking a note of exotic orientalism beneath the Ionic portico of the stationmaster's office. A high-ranking Soviet officer in a cape, attended by a military servant, gazed on impassively from one side of the platform.

I chose a compartment where three soldiers, all wearing the black collar patches and distinctions of a Soviet armoured regiment, had already taken seats, but as soon as I entered they stood up and left, marshalled by a junior officer down the corridor. For a moment I imagined their senior officer might join me in the empty compartment, but no such luck. Throwing me a scornful glance, he walked past and into an empty compartment further up the carriage. For a Soviet field officer I was a low form of life, a civilian and a foreigner.

The train moved at barely 20 miles an hour through picturesque country which might have been part of Eastern Styria had the fields not been so large. As Barbara had explained to me, the Communist collectivization of the Hungarian agricultural estates had been made easy by the stupendous size of the Magyar magnates' landed holdings, many of which were the size of a small English county. Certainly the landscape I beheld was of an almost feudal character, unrelieved by much building or even roads. Those roads which I did pick out seemed to be carrying horses and carts rather than cars.

The station for Pannonhalma, or St Martinsberg as it was known to the Austrians for centuries, lay about three miles from the monastery. With the sun low in the sky, I watched the train depart with its Soviet soldiery and turned to walk up the hill, a mile or so to the east, where the severe classical outlines of the monastery dominated the surrounding landscape.

It was about 5 p.m. when I arrived at the abbey church on the summit. The monks were gathering for Vespers. There was a powerful smell of polish mixed with incense as I entered the dark recesses of the choir to find a place on one of the rear benches. The cantor intoned the medieval chant. Around me was the architecture of the fourteenth century, more recent than the plainsong I was listening to. Hooded and dressed in black, the monastic community numbered barely a dozen souls, but they sang out confidently in two-part harmony. The unchanging ritual of the Benedictine order seemed to offer the traveller some respite from Marxist austerities.

By the time the service ended, it had grown rather late to continue the journey to Budapest. I sought out the Guest-Master who without hesitating showed me to a large vaulted room, empty of furniture save for a bed and a fine empire writing desk. On one of the walls hung an oil-painting of *The Temptation of St Benedict*, a theme I had come to know well as an undergraduate. Gorley Putt had had a sixteenth-century Italian version of the same subject on an easel opposite his Carolingian fireplace in the Fellows' Building in Christ's.*

In monotonic-accented German, the Guest-Master told me to wait because one of the younger monks, who spoke better German and even some English, would soon join us. Dom Valentine, probably in his early twenties, with cropped hair and an engaging manner, offered

* Now on permanent display in the Fitzwilliam Museum.

to give me a tour of the monastery library and its treasures the following morning. Breakfast would follow the first service of the day, shortly after 5.00 a.m.

Although too late for dinner, I was brought some sandwiches of salami and cheese and a flask of tea. By the time I had consumed them, darkness had fallen and with it a stillness and calm which only centuries of practised silence can create.

The following morning I awoke to find the sun streaming through my window and the abbey bell sounding. I was too late for the first order of the day – it was now just after 6 a.m. – but as I wandered down a staircase I was scooped up by a couple of smiling novices and ushered into the dining hall where a hot breakfast was served while one of the monks, standing at a small lectern, read an extract from the scriptures in Latin. On the walls hung two large portraits of Emperor Franz Josef, one in a glorious white hussar uniform surrounded by exotic Japanese blossom.

After warm goulash, Dom Valentine, dressed in an immaculately pressed black habit, took me to the library, a magnificent neo-classical interior whose columned shelves were crammed with, he told me, more than 100,000 volumes. Globes and writing desks bore witness to the spirit of the Josephinian Enlightenment but Dom Valentine insisted that however much Joseph II might be admired in the West by intellectuals, he had been no friend of the Church.

The Communists had simply restored that monarch's anti-clerical policies. Pannonhalma was allowed to exist only because it served a purpose: it had become the Ampleforth of Hungary and its boys' boarding school was ironically the most popular destination for the sons of the Communist Party leaders. 'Because we have a school we can pray,' Dom Valentine observed. 'Just as Joseph II said monasteries can only exist if they serve a practical purpose, so the Communists have revived this theme. We cannot devote ourselves to our traditional vocation of prayer unless we also fulfil a practical role for the state. This is not what St Benedict had in mind.'

I was visiting out of term time, so the school was closed, but Dom Valentine showed me round the classrooms. In its way Pannonhalma was testament to a peculiarly Hungarian sense of Magyar history and destiny. Because it had been founded by the father of St Stephen, the patron saint of Hungary, and because his cloak had been preserved in its vaults, this monastery had so far survived the worst excesses of Communism.*

Conversing with the monks in the beautiful orchard behind the abbey, I gleaned much about the Hungarian sensibility and the strength of character which was the hallmark of the patriotic Magyar. As I walked back down to the railway station after lunch, I felt I had been afforded an unusual glimpse of contemporary Hungary. The insights gained in those first twenty-four hours were to prove vital to my understanding of much that I later witnessed in the Hungarian capital. Beneath the verities of the Catholic faith, the sense of Magyar patriotism and Hungary's destiny at the heart of Central (not Eastern) Europe had been repeatedly and powerfully expressed.

Budapest was buzzing. The early 1980s were a time of optimism in that city which, in its liveliness and energy, still outstripped its more sleepy neighbours, Vienna and Prague. It was a curiosity of those days that the trains from the West arrived at the Eastern Railway Station, a veritable cathedral of nineteenth-century glass and iron. It was thronged with passengers running to catch their trains – an unheard-of occurrence in Vienna where nearly everyone arrived dutifully half an hour early for even a brief journey. Once established in the apartment I had been promised, I set about finding Barbara's 'writers' with the help of my Baedeker. As nearly every street had had its name changed since 1910, a modern map superimposed on the earlier one was essential.

Gáspár Miklós Tamás, László Rajk, Gábor Demszky were perhaps accustomed to meeting rather more informal representatives of the Western 'liberal press', but they quickly shared their views on the shortcomings of the regime. It was inspiring to see what faith they had in the British Prime Minister, Margaret Thatcher, who had visited Hungary a few months earlier.

It is hard to recall today how robust and energetic London was in the 1980s in standing up for the rights of Central European

---

* The monastery had a special significance for the Habsburgs, the heirs to the crown of St Stephen. When the last Habsburg heir to have been born into the empire, Crown Prince Otto, died in 2011, he left instructions for his heart to be taken and interred in Pannonhalma.

intellectuals who were largely ignored by the other European states. The West Germans did not wish to rock the boat of their relations with the East Germans. The French were reluctant to speak out in case it damaged their 'special relationship' with Moscow. The Italians and Spanish preferred to focus on commercial interests. In Europe, only London resolutely and consistently defended the human rights of the subject populations of the Soviet empire. In this cause, the Americans happily cooperated and offered a dazzling example of what Anglo-Saxon solidarity could achieve.

At that time, the British embassy in Budapest was staffed by several bright young men who seemed markedly less lethargic than their counterparts in some other Central European embassies. They eagerly supported any interest in the region showed by Western correspondents. Ably advised by Michael Alexander in Vienna, Mrs Thatcher had decided that Hungary was ripe for a more 'forward' British policy.

Official Hungary appeared to tolerate this and I found I was encouraged to explore further. A visa was quickly forthcoming to visit the state Tokay wine cooperative. Because this was an official visit, we were unfortunately obliged to use 'organized transport' from the moment we set foot on Hungarian soil, but the pretty village of Tokay, nestling in the folds of the hills east and north of Debrecen, appeared unchanged since feudal times. The former Imperial and Royal Hotel Adler also appeared at first glance intact, but inside it had suffered from its occupation by the Soviet army in 1956. The rooms were overlaid with plastic fittings, and the prevailing colour was brown.

In a pleasing counterpoint to this were the seemingly unaltered subterranean tasting rooms of the state cooperative cellars which were reached via a long stone staircase. The walls were lined with black tufts of mould which, we were assured, were the sign of a good Tokay cellar. Across a wooden table sat our hosts, unsmiling, polite and correct. The three men wore ill-fitting grey suits, red ties and white socks. As junior officials of the cooperative, they knew their position in the hierarchy perfectly. After a few initial courtesies, their silence heralded the arrival of more important figures.

The first of these was a grey-haired man in his early sixties whose suit and tie were covered by a white medical coat which invested him with a professorial air, although his rapid movements dispelled any hints of an introspective or reflective temperament. From his well-practised Magyar German, it was apparent he had entertained many of the East German *nomenklatura*. He rattled off at high speed a detailed analysis of the reasons why the wines we were about to taste were the finest dessert wines in the world. 'The king of wines, the wine of kings' was the summit of the wine-maker's art, but it owed its pre-eminence to the unique qualities of the Tokay soil, in particular the presence of disintegrated trachyte, commonly known as igneous volcanic rock.

After we had listened for nearly forty minutes to this scientific discourse delivered with the relentless and humourless pedantry of a political commissar, the moment finally arrived when footmen appeared, with great ceremony, carrying opened bottles of Tokay. Our glasses were filled repeatedly as the professor warmed to his theme. He urged us to sample the 1954 five *puttonyos* or degrees of richness (*Ausbruch*), then the 1937 Essenzia before attacking a horizontal tasting of eight wines from 1927 of ever increasing intensity. 'Tomorrow, you will have no hangover from this wine,' he promised, and he was right. The following day, as I passed over the frontier into Romania and the beautiful land of the seven castles, Transylvania, my head was crystal clear.

This clarity was just as well because it was apparent from the first moment that the easy-going ways of the Hungarians were not shared by the Ceauşescu regime which clearly felt more vulnerable to de-stabilization and ruled with a far heavier hand. Despite the most sophisticated of precautions, it was soon obvious that any attempts to meet with Romanians other than those designated to accompany me on the official programme would be thwarted. This crude and pervasive surveillance was symptomatic of the general atmosphere of suspicion which had descended on Romania after an attempted coup by some officers in the early 1980s. I had visited Transylvania a couple of summers before and found the Saxon inhabitants welcoming and trusting, so it came as a shock to find official Transylvania so claustrophobic. In Bucharest's eyes, a Western foreign correspondent was not the representative of a friendly state. He was at best a spy, at worst an agent provocateur.

After a few days of this oppressive treatment, and having failed to meet anyone who was not part of the state apparatus, I beat a hasty retreat to the comforts of Hungarian hospitality and the freedoms of Debrecen. Suddenly I could walk for an hour around the town without seeing the ubiquitous leather-jacketed 'escort' trailing a few yards behind. The Hungarians' distance from their Soviet masters was often demonstrated by their government in subtle ways. Back in Vienna, I found that my Hungarian friends among the *Erste Gesellschaft* quickly responded to my knowledge of their country with another flurry of invitations to parties. Their relationship with the representatives of official Hungary was also beginning to thaw. Communist Hungarian diplomats began to attend the annual Hungarian Ball in the Palais Auersperg, despite the presence of representatives of all the great exiled and dispossessed Hungarian magnates.

Hungarian courtesy towards the English was equally indicative of a certain reserve towards their Soviet brothers. This attitude took on exotic form when official Hungary began to lobby for some kind of British royal visit. Their diplomats began to make discreet enquiries about the health of the sovereign and her immediate family. I was therefore not entirely surprised to be told a few weeks later by a somewhat chagrined Foreign Desk that the editor, Charles Douglas-Home, had had a drink the evening before with one of Princess Margaret's equerries, a contemporary from Eton, and had been told that the Princess would be visiting Hungary for a few days later that month. Would I mind attending? the Foreign Editor asked. Apparently, I had made a reasonable impression at the lunch at the embassy a few months earlier, although the Foreign Editor, a staunch anti-monarchist, was unamused by this editorial démarche which appeared to him to be a total waste of his correspondent's time.

Arriving a few days later at the Budapest Hilton (at that time one of the most comfortable hotels in Eastern Europe, with rooms built into the medieval remains of Buda castle), I was handed a telex from London informing me that the *Daily Telegraph* was sending its court correspondent, Jenny Shields, to cover the Princess's visit. Miss Shields cut a dash very remote from the earnest, dishevelled colleagues of the Press Club in Vienna. Beneath her shimmering élan lay deep reservoirs of charm but also, as I soon discovered, steel. She was uncowed by any bureaucratic or diplomatic restriction. Unfailingly polite and impeccably dressed, she breezed effortlessly past uni-formed officials, generously allowing me to follow in her wake.

It said a lot about 'Communist' Hungary that Princess Margaret was received with wild cheers wherever she went and that at every corner the normally indifferently turned-out policemen were suddenly dressed in pressed uniforms and white gloves. At the opera, a white-gloved waiter was deputed to carry a silver ashtray discreetly behind her long black cigarette holder to catch each nonchalant flick of ash. I felt that the enthusiastic deference shown by the *nomenklatura* towards Her Royal Highness during this visit did not augur well for the longevity of socialism in the lands of the former Hungarian crown.

After an exhausting morning with her entourage looking at Buda-pest art treasures (including the symbol of Hungarian sovereignty, the famous crown of St Stephen with its crooked cross), we braced ourselves for the following day's visit to attractions outside the cap-ital. The first of these was the renowned Herend porcelain factory. Our ten-vehicle convoy set off, escorted by motorcycle outriders and the full panoply of security guards. We were soon racing across the deserted roads of the Hungarian plain. Carts and other traffic were halted while the cortège, lights flashing, sped to its destination. After about an hour, we were surprised to see a number of helicopter gun-ships above us and several squadrons of tanks trundling over the fields to right and left. Our route, agreed well in advance by the Hungarian authorities, had taken us through the principal Warsaw Pact military training ground at the height of a combined opera-tional exercise. Perhaps the Soviets had calculated that this would provide an awe-inspiring display of military might for Her Royal Highness. For the various British attachés in two of the cars behind us, such a close-up view of the latest Soviet equipment in action was no doubt the stuff of dreams. In the space of half an hour, we saw a good selection of the latest Soviet armoured vehicles as well as their helicopter gunships, then deployed all too effectively in Afghanistan. The timing of this journey was as remarkable as the route. Its signifi-cance was confirmed by the resolute insistence of all the British diplomats present that they had seen nothing unusual at all. No one else mentioned the incident, even obliquely, either.

At the Herend factory, Miss Shields and I, Princess Margaret's equerry and the Deputy Director of the factory, were siphoned off into a neighbouring room while the Director and HRH lunched in the principal guest salon. The equerry was a jovial pilot of enormous height, known to all as 'J.J.'. Once we had settled down to a long and formal lunch of several courses, he soon demonstrated his skills outside the cockpit. Our host, the Deputy Director, was less versed than his boss in the social niceties and from the moment the ubiquitous consommé arrived he displayed a stiff unyielding toeing of the Communist Party line. Fixing the blue-uniformed Group Captain in the eye, he proceeded in a sleep-inducing monotone to berate us all for the 'terrible events' in England and the 'awful difficulties' we were having with 'the miners'. The clashes between the government and parts of the National Union of Mineworkers were then reaching a violent climax. While our host intoned these criticisms, I found Miss Shields's eye expectantly meeting mine. The glance betrayed anticipation and excitement. She had seen J.J. in action before.

He now rose memorably to the occasion. Taking his cue from the Deputy Director, he began solemnly in an unemotional but fruity voice: 'Yes, you are quite right, Deputy Director. We have had some real problems with the miners, but do you know why that is, Deputy Director?' His voice became more earnest and confiding. 'You see, in England, we had a socialist government after the war which gave children free milk and orange juice so that now ... well ... they have all grown up so healthy and tall ... they simply cannot fit into the mines any more!'

I looked at the Deputy Director. He was seriously confused. J.J. continued to fix our host with a serious deadpan look while Miss Shields and I bit our lips and avoided looking at each other in an attempt not to betray the laughter desperately struggling to escape. There was not much room to develop our host's mining theme after this and the rest of the lunch moved on to discuss more tepid subjects, mostly connected with horses.

On the whole such ideological polemics were rare and Hungary always struck me as a country still eager for a restoration of the Habsburg monarchy, if only circumstances could permit it. A few months after Princess Margaret's visit, I found myself in a queue for a cinema in Budapest which was showing a recently filmed interview with the heir to the Habsburg throne, Archduke Otto von Habsburg. Otto spoke faultless Hungarian throughout and provided intelligent answers to probing questions about his family's relationship with Hungary and his views about Budapest's future. He arrested the audience's attention with his observation that the twentieth century had been dominated by two great movements, Nationalism and Socialism, and that these had reached their climax in the terrible symbiosis of National Socialism. Since then, he said, both movements had been in inexorable decline. This was strong stuff for a theoretically loyal Communist audience.

The film had another surprise up its sleeve. Otto was asked whether he could remember taking part as a child in the coronation ceremony of his parents in Budapest in 1916. He began to describe his vivid memories of the occasion. As he spoke, the screen switched to some original footage of the coronation, showing his father, Charles, the last Emperor and King, riding up the Budapest hill wearing the regalia of St Stephen, including the crown with its crooked cross. As Otto continued with his recollections, the film suddenly showed him as a four-year-old wearing his own Hungarian regalia and being lifted by unseen hands so that he could watch through the window of his carriage as his father pointed the Sword of Attila and vowed to defend the four corners of Hungarian territory. In a brilliant cinematographic effect, the film slowed down and the camera lingered on the child Otto. At that moment the frisson of the link Otto embodied across not only generations but different worlds produced an audible intake of breath throughout the cinema.

Such events were not isolated. A year later, in a gloriously retro display of military solidarity with the West, the Hungarian Ministry of Defence organized a 'festival of hussars' inviting officers from every hussar regiment in England to attend. Again, the pageant of an older order appeared to intoxicate the Hungarian population. I was reminded of Osbert Lancaster's wry description of the Corpus Christi processions of pre-war Budapest. Was Hungary really going to remain a loyal Communist satellite for much longer?

The Hungarians were not alone in Central and Eastern Europe in seeming ready to embrace change. To the north, across the Carpathians, another great nation was growing restive with Communism and hoping that the arrival of Gorbachev heralded bold new directions for Eastern Europe. As change began to gather speed and the words *glasnost* and *perestroika* were heard more frequently, an opportunity arose for me to relocate to Warsaw where *The Times* had an office which had become suddenly vacant. Five years spent in Vienna had been convivial but a period in Poland was essential if the entire picture of Moscow's European empire was to be understood. I was under no illusions that Poland would offer more bracing conditions than Vienna: even more than in Hungary or Czechoslovakia, progress in Poland had been severely curtailed by the Communist experiment. Huge tracts of the country had barely changed since the war. In Warsaw a few months later I felt that I had left the Edwardian summer world of 1914 and woken up to the cold realities of 1939 and the Molotov–Ribbentrop Pact.

The End of the Ancien Régime

Warsaw–Gdańsk–Cetinje–East Berlin–
Wolfenbüttel–Leipzig–Gera–Prague

The farewells to Vienna were long and sometimes tearful, but my friends promised to be there whenever I returned. Remarkably, they also arranged for the Hotel Bristol to allow me, for only a modest sum, to retain a second-floor suite, unchanged since the 1930s and much favoured by the Duke of Windsor who had come regularly to Vienna to consult his oculist. Further *douceurs* were promised by the local representative of Austrian Airlines in Warsaw, who was instructed by his colleagues in Vienna to 'look out for me'. Finally, Polish friends in Vienna gave me the telephone numbers of their cousins who would 'surely have a beautiful sister or two' to teach me Polish. Thus prepared, and after some happy days on the way in Bad Godesberg and Berlin, I boarded the train one day in late autumn for Warszawa Centralna.

The carriage was full of Poles who had been shopping in East Berlin and whose vivacity contrasted with the more stolid East Germans who occupied other parts of the train. The Poles' smiles and laughter halted immediately the East German customs officials and border police entered our compartment. The temperature seemed to plummet as the guttural Prussian accents echoed along the carriage corridor, a vivid example of the hostility these two nations still felt towards each other. An hour later there was palpable relief when the German guards departed to be replaced by the much less formal, green-uniformed Poles. An elderly Polish man in a suit sitting opposite winked at me, saying in heavily accented German as a tall blonde Polish girl in uniform passed by, 'Jetzt ist alles Scheiss egal!' (Now who the **** cares?). The train trundled slowly across the plains of

Pomerania. Outside the landscape was empty, flat and monotonous in the autumn sun. My eye searched in vain for any north German equivalent of the soft hills of the Alpenvorland or the craggy outcrops of rock on which so many Austrian castles were perched. Inside my compartment, an East German lady, in her early eighties, surveyed the landscape quizzically. Since her seventy-fifth birthday, she declared, she had been 'allowed to travel' and she was now preparing to leave the train at the Polish frontier to visit some friends. Her austerity and simplicity were impressive. She had grown up on the island of Rügen and had spent 'a little time' in Berlin before the war. She reminded me in a way of Blanka, a similar mien of self-discipline forged by life in a turbulent Europe. Like Blanka she also knew off by heart the old song immortalized by Mozart in *The Magic Flute*: 'Üb immer Treu und Redlichkeit bis an dein kühles Grab / Und weich keinen Finger breit von Gottes Wegen ab' (Be honest and loyal until your grave is cold / And never deviate by as much as a finger's width from God's merciful way). I remembered most of the words, sung to the tune of Papageno's first aria, and my new travelling companion filled in the rest which I quickly scribbled on my Thomas Cook's timetable.

After I had thanked her for reminding me of the words she added a detail which Blanka had omitted: this tune, at once so dutiful and cheerful and which I had imagined had been an integral part of a certain Viennese childhood, had in fact another dimension. It had also been rung out twenty-four times a day by the bells of the garrison church at Potsdam after each hour had been struck. This lady, in her simple woollen garments, invested the tune with an unfamiliar gravitas and I was once again struck by the seriousness of Northern Europe after the frivolity of the Danube basin. As we leant out of the windows of our carriage, my companion's face basked almost hedonistically in the setting sunlight for a few seconds. Then, suddenly, seeming to realize she was 'on parade', she stiffened and asked me if I had ever been to Edinburgh. 'I should like to go to Edinburgh. I have an old friend there but I don't suppose they will let me go.' Clearly there were limits to how far she was 'allowed to travel'. These few words epitomized the bureaucratic oppression of the East German state, the absence of the simple freedoms we took for granted in the West.

Bidding farewell to this unknown lady – the exchange of names could have implications in the German Democratic Republic – I settled back to enjoy the first glimpses of Poland or, as my recently departed companion would probably have called it, Pommern. At the end of the Second World War, Stalin had secured Western compliance in a colossal reordering of Central and Eastern Europe. Poland had been shunted 300 miles to the west. As a consequence, East Prussia around the historically German city of Königsberg, the old Galicia-Lodomeria to its south and large swathes of eastern Poland had been seized and occupied by the Russians. To compensate for these eastern losses, Poland was given areas which for centuries had been part of Germany: Danzig (Gdańsk), Posen (Poznań), Thorn (Toruń), Stettin (Szczecin). This brutal redrawing of the map, accompanied by huge population transfers and violence, contributed enormously to tension between Poles and East Germans. Today, more than thirty years since my first visit, that particular tension has largely dissipated and one can only wonder at the exemplary way in which the European Union, for all its faults, has succeeded in tending to these wounds.

By the time the train reached Warsaw a few hours later, I was beginning to understand something of the temperament of the Poles, which was at once brighter and more voluble than the Teutonic world we had left behind. Many of the women wore copious amounts of scent and had dyed their hair pink or blue. They had slim figures and an almost Latin vivacity but seemed wholly absorbed in their own lives and problems, which they discussed loudly in rapid-fire words of dazzling incomprehensibility. The men tended to be more taciturn, almost reluctant to engage with a stranger. The years of martial law in the early 1980s had left deep scars but, as I would discover, the Poles were largely united in their opposition to the state and the Communist system. They had bravely learnt how to hold on to their traditional character in their daily interactions with a godless, alien system determined to homogenize them into loyal creatures of the Soviet empire. There was no doubting the moral authority that in those days invested the Roman Catholic Church, which held sway over the minds and souls of most of the Polish population, thanks in part to the country's isolation. The millions who flocked devotedly to hear the Polish Pope, John Paul II, celebrate mass when he visited Poland in 1979 and subsequently were a powerful warning to the Communist authorities of the scale of civil disobedience which might await them if they pushed their luck.

I soon learnt, however, that the corrupt practices of the state were also potent forces. After nine hours, the train ran into a deep tunnel and emerged shortly before midnight in a dark and subterranean part of the main Warsaw station. When I tried to get off, a group crowded around me, pinning me against the interconnecting doors of the carriage. I could tell that something was wrong, but long hours of rail travel had blunted my acumen. Instead of using fists I simply raised my voice, without effect. Within two minutes the struggling mass of bodies vanished and I was suddenly alone. I collected my luggage and went up to the main floor of the station where the secretary of the *Times* office, Małgorzata, was standing with a large sign displaying my name. We went by taxi to the Hotel Europejski, where I was to stay because the office flat needed redecorating after the previous incumbent's tenure.

It was only when I reached for my wallet to hand over a credit card to the hotel receptionist that I realized what the rough theatre at the station had been about. For the first time in my life, I had been successfully pickpocketed. Fortunately I had come with travellers' cheques and had been carrying them separately from my wallet. Still, the loss was annoying and Małgorzata and I rushed off, despite the late hour, to report its theft to the police.

When I offered to give a description of my assailants, I soon understood that crime in the Communist system was the monopoly of the state and that my pickpocketing could easily have received official encouragement. The police were unhelpful and – a rarity in Poland – unfriendly. After studying mugshots of various criminals, I pointed to some that seemed familiar. The policewoman looked at me pityingly and pointed out that the people I had identified had been in prison for five years or were dead. She said that I should be grateful they had not taken my passport.

The following morning, I was woken at 7.00 (rather early in those days for a foreign correspondent), to be told by Małgorzata that I had been summoned to the Foreign Ministry for an appointment with the official responsible for the Western press. The meeting was not about my wallet and I could not reschedule the 'appointment' because this official had the authority to expel me without notice should I prove 'uncooperative' – he had already expelled several foreign correspondents in recent years. Małgorzata was clearly worried but was disinclined to tell me why. I was expected at the ministry within the hour.

It was still rather dark when I was ushered into a grey Stalinist building. After being kept waiting for fifteen minutes I was shown into a nondescript office where, behind a desk, a short and unsmiling man with glasses was smoking an acrid cigarette. He was dressed in a brown suit and his face was pale with watery eyes. His hands were thick and his nails unmanicured.

'Dzień dobry, Pan!' (Good day, Sir!), I ventured, practising one of the very few phrases of Polish I had so far mastered. But if I had expected some degree of Viennese politesse or Hungarian courtesy, I was to be disappointed. I suddenly felt like a small boy who had just returned to his school after a long and agreeable holiday to find new prefects in charge.

'Pan Bassett. You work for *The Times* do you not?' The official fixed me with a hostile stare. 'Is it honourable for a newspaper to call for the head of state of a country with which it has amicable relations to be executed? Is this a reasonable way of writing? I ask you, is this how you journalists of the West demonstrate your objectivity and integrity?'

Briefly I wondered if in an unbuttoned moment I had written something as extreme as this, but my interlocutor soon enlightened me. Handing me a copy of the previous morning's *Times* (how had it arrived so much earlier than my own?) he directed me to the centre page where the celebrated columnist Bernard Levin had indeed written that he hoped General Jaruzelski, who had imposed martial law and was the de facto Polish head of state, would be 'hanged as he deserved for treason to the Polish people'. I silently cursed the luck that had permitted this unfortunate coincidence.

'Pan Bassett, is this objective? Is this quality journalism? Is this your freedom of the press? You will agree that no country can permit its head of state to be insulted in such a crude and violent way. Please show me your accreditation.' This, even I dimly realized, was a sinister escalation and I silently handed over the black suede-covered document with which I had been issued a few weeks earlier by the Polish consulate in London. Remembering the pat phrases that had tripped off the tongues of countless Western officials at briefings in Vienna I began to point out that as a 'simple correspondent' I could hardly be held to blame for the emotional ramblings of a histrionic columnist. This unconvincing appeal made no impact.

I then tried to recover the moral high ground: the plurality of the Western media, in contrast to that of the Warsaw Pact, I insisted, allowed a very wide spectrum of views to be expressed. This platitude also made no impression. Finally, I recalled the lunch at the Herend factory a few months earlier and took a leaf out of the quick-thinking equerry's book. Striking a pose of contrition, I apologized unreservedly for any offence caused by my more emotional colleague and explained that Mr Levin had been through a difficult time in recent months. His very public unrequited love affair with a well-known soprano at the Royal Opera House, Covent Garden, had no doubt disrupted his emotional compass and affected his judgement. As I recounted these intimacies in a matter-of-fact way, referring *en passant* to various arias in *Rosenkavalier* and *Arabella*, the expression on my interrogator's face turned briefly to one of sullen astonishment. He impatiently indicated he had heard enough.

Throwing me another withering glance, he turned to a colleague who had been sitting silently in the corner of the room and said something which sounded uncomplimentary. For a moment, he menacingly fingered my small press pass as if uncertain whether to keep it. Then he slowly handed it back and stood up to indicate that the interview was at an end.

Stepping out into an icy wind beneath a leaden grey sky, I mused on the fact that I had been in Warsaw for rather less than twelve hours and, although I had not yet written a single word or even sat down at my desk, I had already been robbed, dragged from my bed to be given an official dressing down and threatened with expulsion. I had had some unpleasant experiences in Bucharest, but nothing in easy-going Vienna had prepared me for these new realities. I had been eager for challenges after the claustrophobic comforts of Austria and Hungary. But as I returned to my hotel in the half-gloom of an icy November morning, I began to wonder whether Warsaw might not prove a little too spartan.

In the event, over the following two years, Poland quickly demonstrated that it furnished the best education anyone trying to understand Eastern Europe could hope for. In the lull between 1987 and the storms of 1989 I soon learnt fluent Polish and I came to appreciate and admire the Poles. Once the decorators had moved out of the *Times* flat, I found myself the happy tenant of a generous suite of rooms on Rozbrat, an avenue overlooking the Arcadian approaches to Łazienki Park. Large windows encompassed a view of ancient trees and huge tracts of sky which turned blood-red at sunset. My apartment block was one of the very few buildings in Warsaw to have escaped complete destruction at the hands of Bach-Zelewski's SS troops in 1945. Because its bullet-holed façade still bore the scars of that terrible conflict, it was much in demand by Polish television companies making dramas of the Warsaw Uprising. Over the next two years, I often returned to the flat to find the courtyard bedecked in swastika flags and brutish actors dressed as SS stormtroopers, all of whom looked terrifyingly like the real thing, mowing down civilians with their faux machine guns for the sake of the cameras.

Otherwise this leafy suburb, barely twenty minutes' walk from the centre of Warsaw, was notable for its silence. Cars were rare, taxis even rarer. I was optimistically informed that there was a taxi rank just outside the house, but of this there was no sign. Eventually I realized that if you waited at a particular spot you might – after an interval of half an hour or so – pick up a passing cab. Life was too busy and fraught for the few Polish taxi drivers to hang around impoverished buildings. Gradually, I got used to walking the mile and a half into town for press conferences or hiring one of the American correspondents' drivers for longer journeys. The Americans were well represented, with almost every important US daily having a correspondent in the city. Apart from the *FT* and *The Times*, the British papers were conspicuous by their absence.

Today, in an era of instant communication, the isolation someone from the West might feel behind the Iron Curtain is hard to imagine. Telephone links between Warsaw and the outside world were at best intermittent, and communications generally relied on a large telex machine in my drawing room which now and then sprang into life. This pace of existence was not, however, entirely without its virtues. In the well-stocked library of the flat, there was time to immerse oneself for days on end in the substantial volumes of Adam Zamoyski and Norman Davies, then the essential foundations for any intelligent observer of Poland's condition. One of the pages torn off my telex machine's printer in those days remains evocative of the fragility yet richness of communication in a pre-digital age:

264971 times g
172345 exforeign

  1. thanks shipyard used inside page top tuesday above binyon file.

  1 a. general point: polish sub-editor-in-exile asks we remind you that Pilsudski was never a general but was a marshal.

  2. no rush about series on ordinary poles but glad to learn you have them in hand (if you see what i mean

  Regards
  Ends ib

'ib' stood for Ivan Barnes, the demanding but scrupulously fair Foreign News Editor. A stern critic of slovenly work, he always had the interests of his correspondents at the forefront of his thinking, with the result that they often produced high-quality work in the early 1980s which carried as much weight as a diplomatic dispatch. One of the most distinguished was the Moscow correspondent, Michael Binyon.

Sometimes days would pass without even these laconic messages. As I gazed out from my book-lined study at the red winter sun setting across Łazienki Park and at the lamp-lighter with his bicycle and ladder, laboriously illuminating each gas lantern by hand, it was hard not to imagine that the greater part of the post-war twentieth century had passed Poland by.

Thanks to the kindness of Adam Zamoyski, his cousins the Radziwiłłs took my formal Polish education in hand. As well as indeed providing a beautiful sister to give me regular Polish lessons, a dashing equestrian cousin, Ewa Dzeduszyńska, promised to take me riding in the Masurian Lake District. The Polish welcome was so embracing that I was even invited to join the Polish chapter of the Maltese Knights on their annual pilgrimage to Lourdes. This generous offer I had to decline 'for operational reasons', but I later learnt that as the Polish invalids' train drew in to the Gare de l'Est the flower of French aristocracy, both Bourbon and Napoleonic, welcomed their impoverished Polish cousins with crates of champagne, caviar and other delicacies before the more adventurous of the *malades* were taken up the Rue Pigalle in their wheelchairs to catch a glimpse of the more exotic side of the 9th arrondissement. The imminent departure of the night train for Lourdes prevented anything more than a glimpse of the professional ladies of the *environ*, but for the *malades*, men who had been deprived of the chance of travel to Western Europe for three and a half decades, it was enough.

One evening after I had been in Warsaw for a week, I went to hear the visiting Hallé Orchestra play in the Warsaw concert hall. They played Elgar, always a poignant experience for the Englishman abroad. It was deepest winter and as I waited near the Garderobe to pick up my coat I saw a pretty blonde woman quickly curtsey when an admirer briefly took her hand and kissed it. Such elegant manners were becoming rarer everywhere on the continent, but Warsaw still preserved what Paris and London had given up many decades before. The following morning I paid my first visit to the BBC office where, to my delighted surprise, I was let in by the very same blonde young lady I had glimpsed curtseying the night before.

Liliana was another product of those unusual times. Like several of her compatriots, she had become engaged to a British foreign correspondent at the height of the martial law crisis of 1982 but in this case the young man had been expelled, on the advice (so it was mischievously rumoured) of another British correspondent who at that time enjoyed intimate relations with a senior member of the Polish Foreign Ministry and was keen to eliminate a rival. Unable to travel to the West, and with her fiancé now banned from visiting Poland, Liliana had been the victim of this intrigue. She had quietly resigned herself to the long wait which might or might not lead to reunion with her beau. She was fond of quoting a Polish proverb with which her mother had comforted her: 'You do not need to own a brewery to enjoy a beer.'

I was to come to rely on Liliana in emergencies, and her selfless sense of duty and courage were never better displayed than during one spring weekend when cycling near Jabłonna, a few miles out of Warsaw, I was attacked by a dog which drew blood and sent me tumbling into a ditch. Cycling back to the city I found a bar still open in the deserted old town. In those days when people had no money to spend socializing outside the home, Saturday nights in Warsaw were very quiet, even quieter than in Vienna. Many of the inhabitants left to visit friends and family in the country. I asked the waiter for some brandy and went outside to clean the wound. After a few minutes, he came out to ask if he could help. I thanked him and recounted what had happened. He was much alarmed when I told him that I had been bitten by a dog and he said I should see a doctor immediately because rabies was widespread throughout the area beyond Warsaw's city boundaries. As if to underline the warning he pointed his hand at me, rapidly opening and closing it to give an unmistakable impression of imminent lunacy.

As it happened, the embassy in Warsaw had a British doctor on its staff, so I left a message with the duty officer to ask him to call me. When there was no reply after a couple of hours, it seemed best to find a local doctor. By happy chance Liliana was at home when I called and immediately offered to accompany me to the hospital, where a young doctor saw us within minutes. His response was not encouraging: 'If you have been bitten by a dog outside Warsaw, you have a big problem.' He urged us to track down the owner of the dog and find out for certain whether it was infected. We would have about twenty-four hours in which to do this before the symptoms of rabies would begin to manifest themselves. It was somehow characteristically Polish to regard this event as life-threatening but not desperately serious. At the crack of dawn, Liliana and I drove to where I had been bitten and immediately saw the dog and a man who appeared to be its owner. Completely undaunted by the fact that it might be infected and that it had an aggressive temperament, Liliana simply walked up to the dog and examined it before ordering the reluctant owner to take it to a clinic to have it put down. Dire threats were rained upon him if he did not comply. The dog was destroyed and, to my great relief, on examination of its remains was found not to be infected. On Monday morning, when the British embassy doctor finally got round to calling me, I was able to assure him that all was well, thanks to Communist Poland's state medical service.

During the spring of 1988 the political temperature in Poland began to rise. As in the past it was not in the capital but in Gdańsk on the Baltic coast where the escalating confrontation began to send tremors through the ruling elite. The weapon of a long and difficult strike in the shipyards had been tested to its extremes during the turbulent days before martial law. Would the authorities put up with a similar demonstration by Mr Wałęsa's Solidarity movement? What pressures might be brought to bear on the Jaruzelski regime from Moscow, where Gorbachev was making it abundantly clear that he expected the governments of Eastern Europe to follow the twin paths of *glasnost* and *perestroika* to reach a modus vivendi with their populations' more reformist elements?

We were about to find out. A renewed period of unrest at the shipyards began. The striking dockers were surrounded by heavily armoured riot police hoping to starve Wałęsa and his fellow shipyard workers into some kind of submission. It began to look as though we could be returning to the days of martial law. The small Polish press corps rushed up to the coast to watch the conflict develop. As journalists from outside Poland were denied entry visas for several days, the rest of the world had to rely on a handful of people for any information about events. In these circumstances, the foreign correspondent *en poste* had the advantage. In a few hours, a fast train brought me to Gdańsk, where the beautiful Grand Hotel at Sopot evoked the glories of the old Prussian Riviera. Built on the edge of the sea under German technical supervision, it commanded an unimpeded view across the Baltic.

Gazing out from the bedroom's ornate and decrepit balcony, I noticed that the sand in front of me seemed to have turned black. Suddenly the whole building shuddered. Deep in its bowels, a boiler of immense size and strength juddered into life to provide sixty rooms with heat and hot water. As the hum of the machinery grew louder I saw flakes of black coal float down on to the beach. In 1988, the Grand Hotel's plumbing had stood unchanged for the sixty-one years since it was built. This did not imply inefficiency. Drawing a bath a few minutes later, I was astounded to see the deep Prussian tub fill in less than half a minute, a tribute to an age of pioneering plumbing, even if the environmental consequences left something to be desired.

A few miles away, on the cobbled streets of the rebuilt old town of Gdańsk, a few journalists and camera crews, mostly from Scandinavian countries, sought ways of getting into the shipyard. The main herd of Western journalists had been kept waiting outside Poland's frontiers through rigid enforcement of the visa regime. Any local correspondent worth his salt would want to get into the shipyard before they arrived on the scene. Fortunately, the Poles rose to the occasion as they always have done. As I was turned away from the main entrance to the shipyard and walked back towards the old town, I was accosted by a teenage boy and girl who offered to smuggle me in. They were about to deliver supplies of food and water in their rucksacks to the striking shipyard workers. Throughout this strike these teenagers, often as young as fourteen, were the vital link between what was happening in the shipyard and the outside world. Patriotic Poles, they asked neither fee nor favour for their help.

The direct routes to the shipyard were blocked by lines of heavily equipped riot police, the infamous Zomo, with their shields, helmets and batons. The courier routes that these teenagers invited me to follow them along were an altogether more circuitous affair. First we took a tram in the direction of the city stadium, heading out of the town centre. From there we set off on foot, carefully passing under the stadium whose uppermost terraces had uniformed police posted at intervals to watch the ground below. By keeping close to the walls of the concrete stadium, we remained invisible because the line of sight of those watching above was obscured by the shape of the building, which bent inwards along its base.

Beyond the stadium, we paused in the long grass. Fifty yards ahead at a checkpoint more uniformed police were inspecting a vehicle. Keeping to the long grass, we slipped past these men who were preoccupied with the lorry they were searching. Another hundred yards across a stretch of industrial wasteland brought us to a railway track which we followed for twenty minutes until we spied a level crossing. In a shed near by, another two police officers appeared to be deep in their newspapers. One after another, discreetly and above all silently, we crept past this last checkpoint and reached a low wall over which we jumped, to be met on the other side by some shipyard workers who immediately offered to take us to Wałęsa.

I had met this most famous of electricians and union leaders a few months earlier on my first visit to Gdańsk when his rapid-fire Polish had appeared complacent, arrogant, almost unfriendly. He had warned then that the calm prevailing during those weeks was unlikely to endure. In the crisis now he seemed far more in his element, commanding his men with natural authority. He exhorted the demoralized to hold on for the sake of their country and not to be intimidated by the tactics of the surrounding riot police, who regularly staged feints and provocations in an attempt to undermine morale. When his men became disheartened – one even threatened suicide – Wałęsa was quickly able to restore confidence. He was, he insisted, answerable to God for the safety of his men and God would not let him or them or Poland down. This fine performance showed Wałęsa's mettle and went a long way towards persuading Western journalists to forgive his brittle attitude towards them.

Because there was no chance of returning to Sopot that evening, we prepared for a long night. To prevent anyone inside from sleeping, the Zomo pretended at frequent intervals to be massing for an attack. Sleep was at best intermittent, and in the early hours of the morning I slid away with the first couriers of the new day. As I said goodbye to a young lady writing for the *Chicago Tribune*, a paper with an important Polish readership, she quipped, 'I'm minded to write a story which will be headlined: How I spent the night with Lech Wałęsa.'

These politically charged events soon died down. Neither side was keen to push the confrontation to extremes. Both Wałęsa and the government claimed victory when the strike ended a few days later, just as the international press corps arrived in strength. Thanks to Polish officialdom, they were far too late to record anything of interest. Short-lived though the strike had been, it had furnished a vivid example of Polish courage and fortitude. The risk taken by the young teenage couriers was a reminder of the exceptional bravery which even the youngest Poles could display. Had they been caught, their fate would have been far more unpleasant than any punishment meted out to an officially accredited foreign correspondent.

Nineteen-eighty-nine began quietly. In Warsaw the snow fell with relentless monotony. As in previous years, my thoughts turned to the south and the Mediterranean. A year earlier, I had been present when Gorbachev visited Dalmatia during days of dazzling January sunshine. The few of us who had accompanied his entourage were especially struck by the affection he clearly felt for his wife, Raisa. She had even managed to persuade him to lose some of his minders one morning and deviate from the official programme to visit the city's Jesuit church. It was tempting to hope that a similar distraction this January might provide me with a visit to the clear blue skies of the Adriatic again. As I ruminated on how I might avoid the sub-zero Polish January, a telex message informed me that the remains of the last Montenegrin King, Nikola I, were going to be reburied in the family crypt, high in the mountains above the former royal capital, Cetinje.

Gorbachev's visit the previous year had highlighted some of the tensions which had been growing in the federal state of Yugoslavia since my days working there as a musician. Albanians in Kosovo, Croats and Slovenes, even Macedonians, were beginning to question the status quo which had kept the lid on the powerful centrifugal forces underlying the relatively calm exterior of Yugoslavian life. That winter, it was the turn of the Montenegrins to display some independent tendencies. In previous years there had been plenty of opportunities to travel down the coast to the former mountain kingdom and I had come to know it reasonably well. Fitzroy Maclean was fond of describing what the Montenegrins said were the origins of their rocky landscape: 'God, when he had finished creating the world, found some stones left over which he fashioned into Montenegro.' Certainly the Montenegrins appeared to possess unique characteristics, even among the endlessly fascinating peoples of the Balkans. Thanks to their traditional dependence on good marksmanship, they had the lowest incidence of myopia in the world. They were also the tallest people in Europe, and their women were renowned for their stature and dark-eyed beauty. The transferral of the remains of King Nikola to Montenegro from Italy, where he had been buried in 1921, seemed too good an opportunity to miss.

The land route to Montenegro from Warsaw ran through Vienna and the old Südbahn to Trieste. In Ljubljana, I dined with Professor Ravnikar, whose kindness had so enriched my life in the Slovene capital eight years earlier. Although the Professor insisted he was 'apolitical' in outlook, as usual he had his finger on the pulse of events. He predicted that Slovenia would soon redefine its relationship with the rest of Yugoslavia. The link with Belgrade would be broken. This prediction delivered one sunny morning in January 1989 was certainly more prescient than any from British diplomatic observers *en poste* in Yugoslavia at that time, but then the nearest they were to Ljubljana was Belgrade. Cuts to the Foreign Office budget had long eliminated even their token consular presence in Ljubljana and Zagreb.

In the studio of Ravnikar's pupil, Aleš Vodopivec, another 'apolitical' Slovene, a team of architects were busy designing a 'new' Slovene flag. If the generally law-abiding Slovenes were so keen to part company with Belgrade and Serbia, the break-up of Yugoslavia was inevitable. Both Vodopivec and Ravnikar gave the expected date of the rupture as June 1991. They were exceptionally intelligent.

The Slovene capital had been described in the Italian press as being in a state of *alta tensione* but of this there was little to be seen. The streets around Plečnik's Three Bridges were calm and I saw not a single policeman. My Italian colleagues, Benetazzo from *La Repubblica*, Altichieri from *Corriere delle Sera* and Rumiz from *Il Piccolo*, had taken up position in the foyer of the Union Hotel and we lunched at the nearby Opera Klet (cellar), one of my old haunts. After five minutes discussing the political situation, Altichieri took out a tin of shoe polish stamped with bold 1950s Eastern European lettering spelling out the word 'Illyria', the fabled kingdom of the Adriatic. Holding up the tin for us all to see, he asked in his fluent Milanese-accented Italian, 'Is it not a tragedy, gentlemen, that all that is left of Illyria in this modern world is a tin of Communist boot polish?' Benetazzo, a lion of a man, with a head straight out of the Roman Forum and a friendly disdain for the weaknesses of the Anglo-Saxon world, observed, 'In England *i posti prestigiati sono sempre malpagati*' (In England prestigious jobs are always badly paid), another piece of practical wisdom. These civilized men reflected the generally high level of education of the Italian press corps. Their insights were often sharper and more interesting than those of other colleagues, for whom a sense of history and irony had been replaced by ideology or political correctness.

That evening I continued the journey to Montenegro and took a wagon-lit to Belgrade. The carriage was a generation older than the Italian *carrozza-letto* and Austrian *Schlafwagen*. The space within each sleeping compartment was more generous, with a luggage stool, wood-panelled walls, a decanter of water, two glasses and starched linen. The cork of a small bottle of delicious Slovene Refošk was pulled by a tall Serb in the brown uniform of the Compagnie Internationale des Wagons-Lits. I slid between the immaculately crisp sheets and watched the landscape change while the train rattled into the defiles of Steinbrück (Zidani Most) towards the junction for Zagreb. Long before we reached the Croatian capital, I was fast asleep.

Some hours later Belgrade was waking up when the train crossed the last flat cornfields of the Voivodina and pulled into Beograd station. I had just finished shaving when a jolt sending brush and razor into the basin announced our arrival. A twenty-minute walk in the rain brought me to the Hotel Moskva with its spacious smoke-filled café, down-at-heel reception and gaudily decorated rooms, fitted out in the latest Marshal Tito revival style: vast ashtrays, hideous oil paintings in vulgar frames and a view across the concrete roofscape towards the brave new world of Novi Beograd (New Belgrade), shrouded in foggy pollution. All this seemed to match a strange sour smell in the air. On the table was a bottle of Dom Pérignon '82 with a card from *The Times* veteran Belgrade correspondent, Dessa Trevisan. The message on the reverse was terse: 'Welcome to ghastly Belgrade. Dinner 8 p.m. Writers' Club.'

The Writers' Club, like the PEN Club in Ljubljana, boasted the best restaurant in the city. Why writers throughout the Balkans deserved this gastronomic distinction puzzled me. In England, most writers could barely afford a sandwich. Perhaps it was a legacy from the late nineteenth century, when the written word proved as capable as the sword and rifle in inspiring the Balkan nations to liberty. In any event, the habitués of these restaurants had long ceased to be drawn exclusively from the literary world. In Belgrade, the club was run with dignified solicitude by Ivo, former footman to the last pre-war Papal Nuncio to be accredited to the court of the Regent Prince Michael.

Ivo, tall, dignified and taciturn, was as always benign and calm. There may have been an economic crisis in Yugoslavia with inflation running at over 100 per cent but somehow Ivo always secured the choicest delicacies: escargots from the Voivodina, foie gras from the Banat, sea bream from Dalmatia and veal from Bosnia. The wine was mostly from Montenegro with a sprinkling of Dalmatian whites. Each evening ambassadors, foreign correspondents and other actors on the Belgrade political stage gathered to sample these delights.

Resplendent in a 1950s Hermès scarf, Dessa held court, scattering scathing comments at colleagues and politicians. The rather eccentric new British Ambassador to Belgrade pricked up his ears when I was introduced as having just arrived from Slovenia. 'I am most concerned at the activities of Austrian military intelligence in Ljubljana,' he muttered in a conspiratorial hush. It was hard to stifle my mirth at this observation. Many Slovenes hated the Austrians almost as much as they did the Serbs. The idea that the military apparatus of the Second Austrian Republic was capable of staging anything more threatening than a spirited performance of *The Merry Widow* would have struck anyone familiar with modern Viennese capacities as completely risible. Yet here was one of our 'brightest and best' suggesting that Belgrade's problems with the truculent Slovenes were caused by the ghost of Marshal Radetzky. I tried to look suitably concerned. As an old friend who knew much about the art of secret analysis, Nicholas Elliott, once memorably insisted: 'The Foreign Office are generally always wrong on issues of critical importance and, rather helpfully, even publish a book of their documents every ten years or so setting out how wrong they were.'

The following morning, hitching a lift with the collegial *Guardian* correspondent, I set off for Montenegro. Travelling through a landscape as picturesque as any in the Balkans, we passed the ruins of an old narrow-gauge railway which the Austrians and then the

Germans had financed in the run-up to the First World War. After an hour of rocky defiles, the landscape opened into a vast plain studded with pine-trees set at intervals. We reached the old Austrian port of Herceg Novi (Castelnuovo) where Gottfried Banfield had been born in 1890, and wound our way up the dramatic Lovćen road to Cetinje.

I had long been captivated by the charm of this former royal capital, whose only principal buildings seem to be the palaces, consulates and legations long abandoned by the great powers in 1914. None of these exceeded two storeys in height. That evening I arrived to find them all candle-lit and echoing to the sound of merriment and the chink of glasses. In 1982, I had stayed with an English friend at Gospođja Marija's rooms above a chemist's, so I headed there to find the proprietor still in situ. The accommodation was simple, cheap and spotless, the bedrooms high up in the roof with a fine view towards the mountains. Mrs Marija remembered me and my 'beautiful companion' from seven years earlier. Marija's own granddaughter had now reached the age of sixteen and I was introduced to her smile and lively eyes. Both grandmother and granddaughter were excited at the prospect of the imminent festivities. As we talked about Cetinje, exploding fireworks began to fill the air from the direction of the Royal Palace. Anxious not to be late for the party, I hurried off.

Cetinje in those days possessed only one hotel and all its rooms had been taken by the extensive cousinhood of dispossessed Balkan royalty. Like long-lost family, the relics of the clans which had once held the peninsula in their grip greeted each other in the smoke-filled foyer with exaggerated gestures of affection and formality. In one corner sat the pretender to the Montenegrin throne, Prince Nikola, with his sultry dark-eyed Parisian wife, sketching with a silver-topped pencil the outline of the speech he hoped to make later that evening. His wife, attired in voluptuous deep-purple velvet, was enveloped in ever-widening circles of blue cigarette smoke as her black-gloved hands snapped shut an enamel and gold cigarette box upon whose lid the Royal Montenegrin cipher was emblazoned. A contingent of Austrian, Bavarian and Hungarian legitimists noisily exchanged 'Halli! Hallo!' greetings before rushing over to the royal couple to beg obsequiously for autographs. A distinguished Scot wearing a grey pinstripe suit and Brigade tie watched on. He was the British military attaché and told me he would be wearing trews the following day in a demonstration of Highland solidarity with the Montenegrins.

Outside, the entire town was filled with smiling crowds enjoying a nocturnal *Volksfest*. Every door was open and every house appeared to be at the disposal of any passer-by. Everywhere, the Montenegrins were eager to celebrate the return of their King's remains and the presence of his extended family. The sound of champagne corks popping, the sombre, melancholy notes of the one-stringed gusla and the ubiquitous candle-light utterly transformed the city into a romantic stage-set for some unwritten scene in a Lehár operetta. Wandering among the former consulates I soon found myself in front of the old palace. Even these doors were thrown open to passers-by. A young man in a bow tie asked if I required a tour, but I only had to say 'Novinar' (Journalist) to be allowed to wander by myself throughout the palace.

What events these rooms, unchanged since 1914, had witnessed: the stormy meetings of the Montenegrin sovereign with the representatives of the Great Powers in 1913, the arrival of the generals of the Austrian army after ascending Mount Lovćen in early 1916. When back in Vienna these officers had later tried to bully the old Emperor, Franz Josef, into annexing Montenegro, he had refused, apparently on the grounds that the fleeing Montenegrin sovereign had left a large portrait of the Habsburg Emperor prominently displayed in his bedroom. Such was monarchical solidarity even during war. Of that portrait there was alas now no trace, although a fine painting of Queen Victoria did adorn the green-walled bedroom, an atmospheric space of heavy black furniture and nineteenth-century gouaches of Vesuvius, perhaps a gift from King Vittorio Emanuele III of Italy, the last Montenegrin King's Italian son-in-law.

The following day, as the city emerged into the blinking sunlight as though nursing a collective hangover, the preparations for the reburial ceremony were in full swing. At midday, a muffled gun announced the imminent arrival of a long cortège and a band struck up Chopin's Funeral March. To capture a better view of the procession, I clambered up some steps at the back of the Atlas Tourist

Office where I found myself under the roof in a room with an enormous old bed and a balcony on which were squeezed two young women leaning over the railings. At first I tried to remain inconspicuous but this ruse failed. One of the women, with the blackest hair I have ever seen, turned round, seized my hand and dragged me to the railings where I was promptly sandwiched between her and her friend. They urged me to lean over more fully for a better view of the procession below. In this state of intimacy we gazed down at the cortège winding its way below us.

First came a unit of hand-picked Montenegrin guards attired in suitably picturesque uniforms of Ruritanian splendour, every one of them exceptionally tall. They advanced solemnly, sabres drawn. After them, still marching to the doleful tones of the Marche Funèbre, came a naval band, resplendent in white uniforms. Following them, twelve grey-haired men in dark suits, sunglasses, white shirts and Italian tricolour armbands advanced slowly as if in a Sicilian mafia epic. These men, all collateral descendants of the last King of Italy, Umberto II, whose mother, Elena, had been a Montenegrin princess, escorted the coffin containing King Nikola's remains. On their black ties was a single shield of the House of Savoy with the white cross on a red background. Between them, borne on a gun-carriage decorated with black crêpe, the coffin trundled past.

From our balcony, my companions felt compelled to cry 'Hurra!' I joined in with 'Avanti Savoia!' As the twelve solemn men passed by, this cry was taken up around us and the men, as if awoken from a trance, stirred slowly and turned their heads upwards, raising their arms to greet us. I tried to respond but my hand was still pressed too tightly to extricate itself from my neighbours.

After the coffin came representatives of the modern Montenegrin 'court' in grey suits except for the military attaché in his Highland trews. Behind them marched a throng of Montenegrins in national costume, looking as though they had just stepped out of the Vienna Volksoper, the sun glinting on the silver and gold decorations of their headdresses. Then the entire city appeared to be following the cortège towards the reburial ceremony. There was little sign of the late twentieth century: no cars, no modern music, indeed virtually no modern clothes. Even the cigarette packets on sale bore portraits of the last Montenegrin king. For a few hours it really did feel that we had stepped back into an earlier age.

Exhilarating though these days were I knew that I had to descend from the land of the Black Mountain to the coast and the modern world in order to find if not a telephone then at least a telex machine to file my story. An hour and a half's drive brought me to the 'pearl of the Adriatic', Dubrovnik, still one of the most beautiful cities in the eastern Mediterranean. In Dubrovnik I dined with the son of Ksenya Trescec-Branjski, a lady whose kindness to me in the early 1980s when I was studying Croatian here had cemented another life-long friendship. Ksenya had been born into a noble Croat family with origins along the Military Frontier of the Habsburgs which witnessed centuries of incessant warfare against the Ottomans. She was fond of saying that, as there was so much fighting, 'We all, if we survived, quickly became ennobled.' Her son was a man of similar temperament, clearly destined for high rank once Croatia freed itself of the shackles of Belgrade. The future Captain of the port of Dubrovnik, who had spent many years at sea, had all his mother's qualities of strong opinions and decisive thinking. The next generation of this family was under no illusions concerning the coming conflict. Even at this dinner, it was clear that the Croats were preparing for a showdown.

'You see, *Gospodin* [Sir],' the young man explained, 'to me Communism says I must put a million in the hat and they put nothing in but . . . we divide it equally! . . . My friend! Let's be serious here. This cannot continue.'

He was equally frank about Italian pretensions in the eastern Adriatic. 'The Italians believe they have rights here, but they were only in Dalmatia for three years, between 1941 and 1944,' he said. 'Yugoslavia is in a state of revolutionary chaos because certain people expect the same funds that they enjoyed for the last twenty years. Most of these people are Serbs.' Had the British embassy in Belgrade had access to this sort of thinking, perhaps much muddled policy in London before the break-up of Yugoslavia might have been avoided.

The spring of 1989 was dynamic. In Warsaw, the round-table talks between government and opposition brought the long-awaited political thaw. In Hungary a reformist government began introducing liberal economic and social measures. By the early summer, it was clear a transition to democracy in Poland was likely. In Hungary, the government began relaxing border controls, a move which encouraged East Germans to cross into Hungary and then seek political asylum at the West German embassy in Budapest. At the height of the summer holiday season, the pretender to the Habsburg throne, Otto von Habsburg, organized a Pan-Europa picnic along the Iron Curtain border between Austria and Hungary. In a move carefully choreographed in collaboration with reformist elements of the Hungarian Communist Party, the frontier was opened allowing hundreds of East Germans to flee to Austria. In a sensational, symbolic gesture, the Austrian Foreign Minister and his Hungarian counterpart cut open part of the wire beneath the shadow of the frontier watchtowers. The Hungarians, with Moscow's tacit approval, had decided to remove the Stalinist infrastructure separating them from Austria. It was a bold initiative which did not just affect bilateral Austrian–Hungarian relations. Because East Germans were allowed to travel to Hungary, and would now be able to move more easily on from there to the West, the East German regime of Erich Honecker began to be seriously destabilized.

More than anything else, these events hinted that Moscow under Gorbachev had decided to begin a careful Soviet retreat from Central and Eastern Europe. By exploiting the emerging progressive tendencies of the emerging Hungarian and Polish governments, pressure was relentlessly applied to the hard-line regimes of Czechoslovakia, East Germany and Romania. Every day, Gorbachev's antagonism towards the leaders of the governments in Prague, East Berlin and Bucharest became increasingly apparent. For several years Hungary had been used by Moscow as a kind of experimental station for tinkering with command economies. It was now being encouraged to adopt a new role as a kind of Trojan horse against the hard-line regimes of Eastern Europe. Even if the East German tourists who got to Hungary failed to make it to Austria, they could jump over the wall of the West German embassy in Budapest where, thanks to the articles of the West German constitution, they automatically became eligible for West German citizenship.

In Vienna that summer all the talk was of imminent change. 'Reform' was on everyone's lips and only the most cynical continued to imagine that the status quo in Eastern Europe was sustainable. The perceptive correspondent of the *Washington Post*, Jackson Diehl, summed it up neatly after a briefing at his embassy in June 1989 in Warsaw. 'It is impossible to imagine the cohesion of the eastern bloc prevailing once Poland and Hungary embrace western values.' The question arose as to how the hard-line regimes of Bucharest, Prague and East Berlin could be changed without violence. Each of their Communist elites had benefited from the deep corruption which had been their monopoly: they were unlikely to give up their wealth and privileges easily. Moreover, the Chinese massacre of the student demonstrators in Tiananmen Square in June 1989 showed that a determined government could *in extremis* retain power by mobilizing its army.

Were the hard-line regimes prepared to use force, as the Chinese had, to disperse their opponents? A few weeks before the Tiananmen Square massacre, Gorbachev had visited Peking where he had sealed a pact of Sino-Soviet friendship. He would have been left in no doubt that the Chinese regime was prepared to crush the opposition. It is tempting to think that he used the following months to devise a strategy which would cut the ground from beneath those of the Soviet satellites' leaders who might be tempted to deploy a similar approach.

At lunch at the Liechtensteins' in Vienna in early September, a former Japanese ambassador formulated an interesting theory that we might be about to see the end of the Cold War division of Europe, but that it could only become a reality with Soviet help. Success would depend on Moscow. As events were soon to show, he was absolutely right.

A few weeks later I flew to East Berlin on a half-empty Austrian Airlines flight. It was 6 October and I had little idea how busy the next few weeks were to become. The destruction of the old order in Prague and East Berlin were seismic events such as occur only once in most people's lifetimes. That such regimes could be gone by Christmas seemed unlikely. The dramatic events of Berlin and Prague over the coming months provided a conspicuous contrast to the lower-key transition by reform-inclined governments in Hungary and Poland. The riot police had surrounded the shipyards of Gdańsk for the last time, and in Hungary reforms were dominating the political agenda.

At Schönefeld Airport in East Berlin, these exciting events in Warsaw and Hungary appeared to have made no impression on the loyal *Deutsches Volk*. The border guards scrutinized passports with the same rigid faces I had encountered so often before. Flying from Vienna to East Berlin in fact was a ruse. In those days Austrian Airlines was (along with the Swiss) the only non-Communist European airline which flew to East Berlin Schönefeld. The advantage of landing 'behind the lines', rather than passing through one of the more rigidly controlled entry-posts such as Checkpoint Charlie, was that one was guaranteed a twenty-four-hour visa to traverse East Berlin and reach the West. Those twenty-four hours would be invaluable for gauging the mood and opinions of younger East Berliners and discovering what they thought of the changes occurring within neighbouring countries, and the increasing exodus of East Germans through Hungary. Gorbachev was due in East Berlin for a formal visit the following day. Some young friends in the Huszemann Allee thought it unlikely that the Soviet embrace would contain much warmth. More probably, they thought, it would be the proverbial 'kiss of death' for the East German leader.

Next morning, we were treated to a chilling demonstration of East German military power in the parade along the boulevard Unter den Linden to mark the fortieth anniversary of the German Democratic Republic (DDR). Goose-stepping, grey-uniformed infantry, the unhappy heirs to the Prussian martial tradition, seemed keen to demonstrate their superiority over any other European infantry. I retreated to a café after half an hour to write in my diary: 'When the Wall comes down, as it must, the thought of all this Prussian military tradition married to West German economic power is extremely disturbing' (7 October 1989). Happily, I was wrong: after reunification the quietude of the West German military quickly infected the former East German military; I had witnessed the last parade in my lifetime in which German soldiers would goose-step.

The speech given by the East German leader Erich Honecker was on every radio and television. He reminded me of the embattled

Austrian leader Schuschnigg in 1938. There was the same high-pitched voice and sense of desperation in the face of larger forces. When Honecker shouted 'Vorwärts immer! Rückwärts nimmer!' (Forward always! Backwards never!), he sounded like an old goat. But this particular goat had yet to be slaughtered and his military parade was a reminder that the DDR was neither Hungary nor Poland.

The following day I was back in West Berlin to have lunch with the Royal Welch Fusiliers, that 'astonishing infantry', as they had been dubbed by Wellington after their brave performance in the Peninsular War. They had subsequently fought gallantly in many of Britain's modern wars. The rear 'flash' on their uniforms, a legacy of having been at sea in the late eighteenth century when the regulations concerning powdered queues were abolished, reminded one of unbroken tradition. Yet barely a mile away, the modern world was moving forward rather quickly. That afternoon, with a gloriously autumnal light infusing the woods, some Fusiliers took me on 'wire patrol' along the electrified fence which divided the Soviet from the Allied Sector before I was granted an interview with a senior staff officer. He was adamant that little would alter over the coming months. 'For a start,' he began ponderously, 'the French wouldn't wear any change. Imagine if they suddenly were not allowed to march up the main Berlin axis playing the Marseillaise.' Who was I to break the news to these soldiers that the world was about to change? While the British army continued to discharge a major role in Germany, and while the only air corridor to West Berlin was controlled by the French, Americans and British, how could anyone suggest convincingly that the privileges enshrined in these ingrained protocols would soon vanish?

The imposing Olympic Stadium was once the monument to the Third Reich's sporting propaganda, but it had long since become the headquarters of the British military presence in Berlin. I was shown along a dark corridor to the office of the Chief of Staff who sat awkwardly alone, perhaps all too aware that someone not far away might be recording our conversation. The room was dimly lit. Outside, the sky was glowering in preparation for a full-blown Caspar David Friedrich thunderstorm. Just visible in the corner of the field beyond was a homely sign of British military occupation, a white cricket sightscreen.

The black buttons on the officer's tunic, indicating he belonged to a rifle regiment, made my host appear more saturnine than he probably merited. Our conversation was stilted, almost constipated. From the impassive expression on my face, he saw that the army Press Department's carefully rehearsed lines were not very convincing. Finally, he exclaimed in exasperation and in a rare moment of candour, 'Who in God's name knows what is going to happen here?' We parted with polite insincerities.

Luckily, thanks to an old friend who was now Adjutant of the 1st The Queen's Dragoon Guards (QDGs) I was able to see an altogether more relaxed side to the British army. The QDGs by happy coincidence were the only regiment left in the world to bear the Habsburg double-headed eagle, a link with the days when foreign monarchs were honorary colonels of British regiments and the old Emperor Franz Josef had accepted the colonelcy-in-chief of this distinguished cavalry unit. Captain Mark Ashley-Miller generously invited me for a few days R&R at the regiment's headquarters in a former Luftwaffe barracks on the outskirts of Wolfenbüttel.

It was one of the peculiarities of Berlin's special status among the victorious powers that rail transport between Berlin and the nearest West German railhead, in this case Brunswick, was the prerogative of a special British military train. This train left Charlottenburg at the relatively early hour of 8.00 a.m. A 'clean' passport, devoid of any East German visa stamps, was a strict requirement for boarding the train. Military protocols dictated that the train was passing not through the DDR but through the Soviet Zone. Even a single smudged DDR entry stamp on a passport ran the risk of compromising these requirements and would therefore automatically exclude the bearer of the document from travel.

Fortunately, a few weeks earlier, the obliging British Consul-General in Warsaw had provided a clean duplicate passport within minutes of my request and, thus equipped, I boarded the train. For the purposes of this daily British military train, Charlottenburg railway station, normally full of taciturn West Berliners pondering their commute, resounded for a few brief moments every morning to the accents and easy laughter normally associated with joining the London train somewhere in the Home Counties. Within seconds of departure, the British military police with their distinctive red caps vanished and the station became once again an insignificant point on the Berlin railway map. There was something faintly surreal about all this. The act of boarding a train gave the impression that West Berlin was a 'normal' German city, but the unquestioned nature of these exceptional if ephemeral procedures demonstrated that this was not the case.

'You'll find your seat in the third compartment of the second carriage,' the redcap had briskly informed me with a slightly quizzical look as he quickly examined the beautifully clean pages of my passport. Half asleep – there had been a foreign correspondents' dinner at the Paris Bar on the Kantstrasse the previous evening – I made my way to the dark, unlit and, as I thought, empty compartment.

I had just sat down, relieved to see my seat was next to the window, when I became aware that I was not alone. Opposite me, in the gloom, I made out silver RAF buttons attached to a dark-blue blazer. The thin man who wore it was staring at me intently. If I had thought I might be able to snooze off the night's excesses watching the East German countryside roll past my window, I was mistaken. I was a civilian guest on British military property. Long experience, no doubt at times bitter, had convinced my hosts that journalists on British military property, even someone as 'harmless' as a correspondent of *The Times*, were not to be left alone for a second. The Wing Commander introduced himself with a sardonic smile as 'a member of the vetting department of the BAOR [British Army of the Rhine]'. He attempted to put me at my ease by saying he 'just happened' to be taking the train and that he 'was delighted to have some company', but his eyes were unsmiling and cold. The rest of the carriage was empty. I felt general doziness was the best weapon to deploy with this no doubt well-meaning minder. With the paranoia of the hung-over I looked at the briefcase next to him. A tape-recorder? That I was truly caged became quickly apparent when, after fifteen minutes of his not very subtle interrogation about bank balances, sexual orientation and education, I tried nonchalantly to find the restaurant carriage and some tea. 'I'll come with you and show you where it is. I feel like a cuppa myself,' he said in tones of spurious chumminess.

I was used to this sort of clumsy minding in Ceauşescu's Romania, but it always came as a slight surprise to see such measures taken by my own side. A veteran correspondent of the *Daily Telegraph* with a sound grasp of le Carré had once assured me, 'The ideology may be different but the methodology is identical.' My minder's questions were so crude it was not difficult to deflect them with those tried and tested tools in any experienced correspondent's armoury: doziness and a façade of faint imbecility. By the time the train was safely on West German territory, I sensed my companion was in little doubt that I was an amiable halfwit.

After the train had pulled into the Soviet control point, there was some fine ceremonial with much stamping on gravel as the British commanding officer formally presented the train's documentation to the Soviet military. The salutes completed, the British officer, a young captain of a line regiment, disappeared into the Soviet officer's hut to exchange 'gifts' and drink vodka. These were obligatory parts of the ritual, off-limits to civilian passengers. 'Shall we go back to our compartment? . . . It's a bit boring waiting here,' my minder suggested in a distracted sort of way.

The train jolted back to life five minutes later and the rest of the journey passed relatively uneventfully. My interrogator's mood darkened visibly when I said I was looking for a few days' 'R&R with the cavalry', but no doubt he assumed one of his colleagues would be shadowing me all the time.

We bade each other a formal farewell at Brunswick railway station. He did not linger. Watching his spare figure vanish into the crowds on the platform, I mused that such work probably took the same mental toll on its practitioners in the West as it so clearly did in the East. He was not to blame, I suppose. He had been polite and had done his duty. Yet, while East and West pursued different causes, it was always a little depressing to note the symmetry in methodology.

As I came out of the station, a familiar Jack Russell poked its head out of a British military car, guiding me to my host. Immediately, in the exchange of greetings and friendship, the unpleasant interrogation of the previous hour was forgotten. I had first seen Bodger, a dutiful terrier, on the island of Colonsay, the previous Easter. He had since become a kind of unofficial regimental mascot of the Queen's Dragoon Guards and now rushed up to greet me.

After the rather stiff encounters with the military in Berlin, the QDGs transported one into another world. At Wolfenbüttel, no effort had been spared to recreate in the unpromising buildings of a former Luftwaffe barracks all the comforts of an English country house. The mess was approached via a formal panelled hall at the centre of which stood the regimental guidon, stiffly saluted by every officer who passed it. In glass cabinets on each wall, between military portraits, were items of regimental regalia: silver caskets, mementoes of Waterloo and the Zulu wars and even a letter penned in 1914 by the regiment's one-time Colonel-in-Chief, Emperor Franz Josef, in which he expressed regret that his regiment and his country were at war with each other, and added that in the event of any member of the regiment being captured, he would be treated as the Emperor's personal guest for the duration of hostilities.

Centuries of military history looked down upon me as I entered the mess where a wood fire was crackling and old copies of *Country Life* lay in neat piles on the table between chintz sofas. The mess waiter came up to me beaming a huge smile and the first words I heard – it was 12.15 p.m. – were 'Whisky and soda, Sir?' Everywhere exuded the spirit of St James's clubland or a well-appointed manor house rather than the sandy heathland of the German plain. Large glass bottles of Trumper's Eucris and Coronis adorned the marble basins in the lavatories. In my bedroom a tray with a decanter of whisky and a siphon of soda stood on the bedside table, flanked by two small anticipatory bottles of Underberg stomach bitters.

The family atmosphere was contagious. Tremendous warmth and bonhomie pervaded the entire barracks, thanks in no small part to the fact that many of the other ranks were drawn from Wales, combining that gentleness, sense of humour and practicality for which Welsh soldiers are renowned.

There was to be a formal dinner that evening but, before then, a party of thirty local CDU (Christian Democratic Union) politicians would be dropping in for drinks. The QDG commanding officer, Colonel Boissard, appeared and insisted that for the next few days

I was to consider myself a member of the QDG officers' mess and go wherever I pleased. (What would my travelling companion of a few hours earlier have said about that?) I would be welcomed as an interpreter, if required. 'Hardly any of these Germans speak much proper English, you know, even though one of them is the colonel of the local Landwehr or something in the reserve,' the Colonel remarked rather absent-mindedly. 'We really ought to know what the German is for *coup d'état*,' another officer cut in.

After a highly entertaining lunch I retired for a siesta and emerged a few hours later suitably refreshed. Taking up a position behind the Adjutant and a few officers attired in their scarlet mess kit, we awaited the arrival of the CDU delegation. They noisily swarmed into the mess hall without pausing for a moment to greet the reception party. Like a school outing let loose in the Science Museum they busily examined every portrait and display case on the walls. Finally their 'leader' appeared and introduced himself as the local Colonel. Dressed in a purple sweater and running shoes, this high-ranking officer provided unmistakable evidence that (in the later words of one of the QDG officers) 'all the aggression had long been bred out of the West German army.' A less military demeanour would have been hard to imagine.

His colleagues were largely retired older men. One, who confided to me in German that he had fought on the Eastern Front, openly lamented the absence of continuity in the West German army. Another, looking longingly at the guidon, could be heard saying to a colleague, 'Perhaps in a bit of time we shall have the old black and white Prussian standards back in the German barracks.' A third turned to his Colonel, unaware of a German-speaking Englishman near by, and said wistfully, 'We could have had all this once . . . if only . . .'

The mess waiters poured glasses of champagne for the guests. After some toasts and pleasantries, the party filed out, and I followed the Adjutant as he escorted them back to the main gate. The German Colonel looked at his watch and apologized for his staff car not being at the main entrance at seven sharp as ordered. While we waited, there was the usual chatter about what might or might not happen in Berlin over the coming days. These Germans clearly wanted change but were almost afraid of raising any hopes.

After ten minutes, the German Colonel's military car appeared, driven by a wimpish-looking young man in a rather untidy uniform who sported an earring and red spectacles. 'You are late,' the German officer said in an unconvincing display of authority. The driver was equally unimpressed. 'You told me to wait at the other gate!' he answered petulantly as he leant across to push the door of the passenger seat open towards the Colonel. Visibly exasperated, the German officer turned to us and said, 'I suppose in your army he would have apologized, called me "Sir" and jumped out of the car to open the door for me.' The Adjutant smiled, sharply brought his heels together and saluted. 'Absolutely right, Colonel. *Auf Wiedersehen.*'

Back in the mess, the regimental silver had all been carefully polished and laid out. The regiment was the result of a merger between the 1st King's Dragoon Guards and the 2nd Dragoon Guards (The Queen's Bays). This latter regiment had been exceptionally wealthy and its regimental silver was especially admired.

While we were gathering for dinner, the Colonel of the regiment introduced me to a distinguished Parachute Regiment brigadier who had served in the Falklands War a few years earlier. Both men insisted I sit between them and proceeded to lament the fact that the army was 'full of yes-men' rather than individuals. 'Why, only the other day some damn-fool officer from Staff Headquarters asked why I had not cleared the presence of a foreign correspondent in the barracks with the army Press Department. Is this my regiment or isn't it?' The Colonel threw me a knowing smile. My presence had clearly precipitated a blazing row with some military apparatchik in the Berlin headquarters, but the Queen's Dragoon Guards had fought my corner and put their opponents to flight. 'The thing about the cavalry, you have to realize, is that we have never had much appetite for red tape,' the Adjutant confided to me. He too had had 'some tiresome officer on the phone complaining'. The Colonel added, 'You see, the trouble with the army these days is too little money. In the old days if something was done badly, the officer could say, "Stuff that. I'm going back to my farm." These days, there are simply too many yes-men. As a result a lot of stupid things are done because no one bothers to question them.' The pudding was brought in and the regimental band entered to play the Radetzky March. Iced Sauterne was served before the port decanters and cigars arrived.

After the toasts we were just rising to withdraw to another part of the mess when an orderly quietly tapped the duty officer on the shoulder. The officer disappeared but shortly afterwards returned to whisper something in the Colonel's ear. The Colonel leant over to inform me that the IRA had just taken a shot at an RAF corporal a few miles up the road. Without missing a beat, the barracks was now on maximum security alert. Nonetheless, festivities continued. As a small knot of us gathered around a billiard table, a young subaltern was sent off for champagne. He reappeared a few minutes later reassuringly carrying a bottle in each hand and two under his arms. With great solemnity he placed them on a table and removed the wire around the bottles' necks. The junior subalterns then advanced with their unsheathed sabres and took it in turn to draw out the champagne corks with upward strokes of their blades. Each such sabering provoked wild cheers around the room. As the cigar smoke mixed with the sound of popping corks in the candle-lit interior, it was hard not to imagine oneself transported back generations. Indeed the soft light illuminating the silver and the scarlet mess uniforms invested the evening with a timeless quality. It could not have been much different the night before Omdurman or Balaclava. The British cavalry whose idiosyncrasy had so vexed Wellington was faithful to its traditions, and long years of peacetime soldiering had done nothing to cramp its style.

By 2.30 in the morning the party began to quieten down. A young subaltern fell asleep in an armchair, propping his head up on his hand. Before retiring, each officer carefully and silently placed another armchair around him until seven or eight chairs had been piled high to create a 'basket' which would no doubt disintegrate with an almighty crash once he woke up. When I returned a few hours later for breakfast, I was staggered to see this complicated arrangement intact. To the amusement but clearly not to the surprise of the mess orderlies, the hapless subaltern, fully attired in his mess kit, was still asleep in the armchair in the middle of his 'crib', his spurs poking out at the bottom and a flash of scarlet from his sleeve clearly visible. The mess staff moved efficiently around him, laying the tables for breakfast with the quiet industry of another normal day for the regiment.

It would have been agreeable to recover from these excesses at leisure but, encouraged by East German demonstrations in Leipzig, events were beginning to 'kick off in Prague' as an excitable message from the Foreign Desk put it. With great reluctance, I bade farewell to my hosts and took an early-morning train for West Berlin from where I passed quickly into East Berlin and caught the last direct flight to Prague. Apart from the novelty of the plane being full of East German prostitutes, who clearly did a roaring trade in Prague, this journey was uneventful.

Reaching the Alcron Hotel, then a faded art deco building with an excellent pianist who accompanied the diners with mournful renderings of 'Night and Day', I dined with the correspondent of *El País*, the resourceful Hermann Tertsch. The following day, 28 October, was a Czechoslovak national holiday and Tertsch believed that the military parade scheduled for the morning might provoke some demonstrations; but this struck me as out of the usual Czech character. It was the last Saturday in October and the parade, as suspected, turned out to be a half-hearted affair. On my leaving Wolfenbüttel, an officer of the Queen's Dragoon Guards had given me a regimental pullover as a souvenir. I donned this in the cold Prague morning and walked to the parade on Wenceslaus Square where I was mistaken for some kind of foreign military personage. One of the Czech military policemen saluted smartly and pointed to a podium where the military attachés were gathered for a ringside view.

In comparison with the one I had witnessed in Berlin a few weeks earlier, this parade was very unthreatening. It came to life only when the *Regimentsmusik* appeared playing the great Austrian marches of Fučík and Komzák – the Seyffertitz and Festetics marches, the Castaldo March and even 'Unter dem Doppeladler' (Under the Double Eagle) – which carried the troops past me. The Czechoslovak military bands played with vigour and a visible spring came into the soldiers' step as the drum-rolls announced these parade-ground classics. Was the use of so many old Habsburg marches a subtle sign of defiance?

No sooner had the parade ended, with the young conscripts

disappearing on the arms of their mothers like so many schoolchildren after the first day of term, than the mood on Wenceslaus Square began to turn confrontational. By 2.00 p.m. water cannon were sweeping across it and the riot police, rather quicker off the mark than usual, began clearing the protesters, a motley and not very numerous group.

Taking up a position between the art nouveau Hotel Europa and the Hotel Jalta, I was just in time to witness a baton charge fell a colleague from the BBC, a man who usually voiced strong left-wing views. Hastily withdrawing into the Hotel Jalta, I found myself with the British embassy's urbane and musical Chargé d'Affaires, John Macgregor. He seemed to be sheltering an imperious-looking older woman with black hair. He introduced her to me, somewhat implausibly I thought at first, as Shirley Temple. But Mrs Temple-Black, the US Ambassador, was indeed the once world-famous child star of Hollywood in the 1930s. The former lead actress of *Curly Top* and *The Little Colonel* had lost none of her charisma or authority. She demanded that the hotel porters open the doors for any demonstrators seeking shelter from the riot police. Her role as a six-year-old prima donna, capable of stamping her foot when she did not get what she wanted, still appeared to colour her personality more than half a century later.

In addition to these formidable personal qualities, Mrs Temple-Black was a political veteran. She had been in Prague in 1968 as part of a high-level US delegation and had been about to meet the Dubček government when the Warsaw Pact forces invaded Czechoslovakia. Very few diplomats in Prague in 1989 could boast such impressive credentials. As her presence in the hotel lobby became known, she found herself besieged by well-wishers asking for her autograph. By tea-time the demonstration had evaporated and we agreed it was about as unthreatening for the regime as the military parade might have been for NATO.

At dinner that evening a Czech friend summed up the generally prevailing sentiment rather well. 'The Western press think that a few thousand hippies in Wenceslaus Square can bring down a government.' It reminded me of a comment made by the outgoing British Ambassador who insisted that 'Change in Prague will be slower than anywhere else in the Eastern bloc.'

The following day the autumn light painted the city in its warmest colours. Along the Malá Strana island there was a richness in the yellow leaves I had not noticed before. As evening fell in the late afternoon, a mist began to form, enveloping the turreted skyline around us in a grey embrace. The few cars in the old town of Prague belonged to the police or to diplomats. The silence of the city in the autumnal air was haunting. Western visitors who were privileged to see the city at this time always had to balance disdain for the regime against the staggering beauty of the environment in which they found themselves. With American friends from Radio Free Europe, I had often posed the question of what would happen to the atmosphere and beauty of Prague and Bohemia once the energy and dynamism of Western capitalism penetrated the city. The brightest of these predicted an 'Austrianization' of Bohemia. Prague would become like Salzburg, its architecture beautifully restored and its restaurants and cafés open for business with a friendly smile. This was tempting to believe. We comforted ourselves with the thought, somewhat naive as it turned out, that the unique architectural heritage of Prague could be effectively protected only by the values and mechanisms of the West.

As darkness fell, I threaded my way through the deserted courtyards and passages leading to the Alcron Hotel. There was a poetry reading at the British embassy later that evening. I had met the new Ambassador, a novelist manqué, in Vienna where he had served as a junior diplomat. His handwritten note on chancery notepaper promised dinner and 'some excellent Moravian wine'. It proved an entertaining affair. I was placed next to the granddaughter of the founder of modern Czechoslovakia, Thomas Masaryk, a powerful woman with a shock of white hair which fell about her head like a sabre-cut. Thin and angular, she regarded me with some initial frost when I mentioned the infamous article in *The Times* in 1939 which had suggested, at the height of the Sudetenland crisis, that the Germans should be granted certain territorial concessions at the Czechoslovaks' expense. Fifty years later, unsurprisingly perhaps, this article still rankled. When I asked her why so few Czechs had demonstrated the day before, she replied that Czechs were 'not Germans, or indeed Poles or Hungarians. We always had difficulties with these peoples.' It was clear from her words that revolutionary nationalism would not be as easy to ignite in Czechoslovakia as in Poland, East Germany or Hungary. The revival of such sentiments in those countries would create all kinds of difficulties for Prague, but Madame Masaryk had left me in no doubt that the fire of Czechoslovak nationalism still burned brightly within her soul at least. How many Czechoslovaks could be persuaded to think as she did, and to make a stand? The groups of brave demonstrators I had encountered the day before were not enough.

As it did not seem that this situation would change over the coming week, the next day I boarded a train for Vienna, briefly stopping off at the Szaparys' in the Waldviertel for a night. My immediate schedule was demanding: the following day I would fly from Vienna to Rome and from there to London for consultations and thence, after the weekend, to Venice for two days to be a witness at an old friend's wedding. From there, a direct flight would bring me to Munich and then back to Berlin. Those who wonder how such an exhausting itinerary was possible forget that fewer people flew in those days, aeroplanes were often half empty, airline staff were unfailingly courteous and solicitous, and airports were places of relaxing calm where there were pleasantly few shops. Above all, security checks were non-existent for passengers with hand-luggage. It also helped that it was still a foreign correspondent's prerogative largely to dictate one's own itinerary.

The following Thursday, 9 November, having completed this five-country tour and reached Berlin, I set off for Leipzig by train. In the few days since my last visit, the internal pressure on the regime had grown noticeably. Each evening popular demonstrations took place in Leipzig, watched by the police who, somewhat to everyone's surprise, made no move to prevent them. Several prominent figures of the DDR took part in these marches. The conductor Kurt Masur, a cultural trophy of the East German regime, could be seen striding hands in pockets among the crowds. His presence gave the demonstrators courage: the police, they reckoned, would surely never turn their water cannon on Maestro Masur. With characteristic German discipline, the throng carefully avoided any provocative behaviour. They followed a pre-planned route around the main town square watched silently by hundreds of East German police. Masur was aloof and nervous. When I approached him and asked in my best high German if he would be prepared to speak to a correspondent of a Western newspaper, he immediately veered off in another direction. Many years later, finding ourselves sitting next to each other on a plane, we recalled the incident. 'At that stage I had nothing to say,' he admitted apologetically.

Returning to the railway station I fell in with some East Germans who had been marching in Leipzig but were now travelling on to Gera. They urged me to join them as I would see another demonstration. This one, they believed, would be more spontaneous than that in Leipzig. Sitting in the Mitropa restaurant carriage with these men, all computer programmers, I was confidently informed that great changes were ahead for East Germany's government and that Communism was finished. On the topic of reunification with West Germany, my travelling companions were however more circumspect. 'We will decide when and if that happens.'

We arrived at Gera just in time to see a mass of candles seal off the police station while thousands of demonstrators marched past the building, leaving their candles fluttering in the cool November night. Some of the banners the marchers were carrying called for a 'United Fatherland'. The houses around us all seemed deserted and unlit. Was the entire population of the city out on the street? 'You will see: when we Germans do a revolution, we do it thoroughly,' one of my new-found acquaintances insisted. We followed the demonstrators towards the magnificent Town Hall where we saw many candles being placed on different monuments commemorating Communism. As in Leipzig, the crowd was orderly and disciplined, although here there were no uniformed policemen to be seen. 'SED, das tut weh' (The Communist Party, that hurts) was chanted for a few minutes. My companion said, 'You see, the party has *nicht ein Pfennig kredit* [not a penny of credit].' A new cry, 'Stasi in der Volkswirtschaft!' (Secret police: work for the people!), was chanted even more enthusiastically.

Eventually the crowds arrived at the Palace of Culture where a huge monument in the best Soviet-realist style had blazoned across it a phrase which now looked rather forlorn under the circumstances:

'Communism begins here'. Whatever candles the demonstrators had left were relit, giving the concrete sculpture a menacing aspect. The old town centre seemed ablaze and wax dripped across all the symbols of Communist Party rule. Then, just as orderly as their arrival, the crowd suddenly and peacefully evaporated. My travelling friends invited me to a nearby 1930s hotel where they asked me to dine with some of their *Truppen*. The atmosphere in the restaurant was earnest and quiet. About a hundred men, mostly wearing check shirts, sat talking of politics in intense groups of five or six. It was well past 1.00 a.m. when my friend took me back to the small flat where his wife and family were fast asleep. He made up a bed for me on the sofa in his living room. For any Western correspondent to stay unannounced with an East German family would have been unheard of barely a week earlier: massive bureaucratic and other obstacles existed to prevent such unauthorized fraternization. This act of spontaneous kindness and hospitality was now lightly given. More than any other encounter I had experienced that week, it demonstrated to me that the regime had lost much of its capacity to terrorize the population. The most conformist and spied-upon population of the Warsaw Pact was now no longer petrified by the state.

I rose at 5.00 on the morning of the 10th to leave for Berlin. The family was already awake: their fourteen-year-old son was off to do his weekly six-hour stint in a factory. *Produktionsarbeit* from 6.00 a.m. to midday cannot have been a schoolchild's idea of fun, but here was this obedient young man quietly drinking his tea and eating some bread before heading off to his duties. Such mobilization of youth in the service of the state had a peculiarly old-fashioned feel to it, affording a glimpse of those traditional German qualities of self-discipline and austerity which continued to thrive, irrespective of the regime in power. The boy's mother offered anxious glances, as if fearful of the consequences of her husband's hospitality towards an English journalist. I offered to pay for the night's accommodation but my suggestion was spurned.

By 8.15 a.m., I was back in Berlin. The night before, my host in Gera and I had listened to a radio announcement by the Honecker government that all East Germans could now visit West Berlin through existing checkpoints if they wished. The regime was clearly panicking. My train was packed with East Germans heading west. When it passed Soviet military establishments, I could make out the soldiers standing in groups outside their barracks being briefed by their officers. Was the counter-revolution being prepared or were they to be confined to quarters, thus cutting the ground from beneath the East German government? One thing was certain: no crackdown on the population could take place without Soviet complicity. The military resources of the satellite Eastern European states were simply too weak to mount full-scale violent repression without Moscow's help.

In East Berlin, such was the volume of railway personnel who had abandoned their posts to catch a glimpse of the West that the S-Bahn had virtually ceased to work. As the afternoon wore on, new formal entry and exit offices along the Wall began to be opened up to make way for additional crossing points. At the Grand Hotel, where most of the correspondents were staying, the atmosphere was increasingly buoyant. One Sunday newspaper correspondent, a fluent German-speaker who had studied at Oxford, ordered two bottles of Dry Monopole and summed up the views of many of us when he said, 'You know, if this really is the end of the Berlin Wall, I am happy just to be here, without even having to write a word about it.' Another journalist quipped, 'Summer surprised us, coming over the Starnbergersee,' then another chinked glasses and continued the quotation from T. S. Eliot: 'stamm' aus Litauen, echt Deutsch' (I come from Lithuania. I am a real German). We laughed, a rare moment of solidarity among rivals. As night fell, the action moved to the Brandenburg Gate where thousands of young people had climbed on to the Wall and were chanting like Zulu warriors before battle, demanding the Wall be torn down. The strain on the East German border guards was visible, though some cheerfulness returned to their surly faces when the water cannon came into action and began knocking the protesters off the Wall. But this was to be the last act of violence by the authorities. Elsewhere along the Wall, they were permitting breaches to be made.

As news of these developments filtered out in West Berlin, Helmut Kohl, the West German Chancellor, appeared in front of the Wall to ask the young crowd to sing the West German national anthem to the famous tune by Haydn. To their credit, his young audience spurned this appeal to nationalist sentiments and drowned him out in a sea of catcalls, boos and whistles. With tears streaming down his cheeks, Kohl became more and more desperate as he realized that on this historic day, with the Berlin Wall falling, young Germans, the future of his country, held him in contempt. Rarely have I seen a politician in greater discomfiture. While this image of Kohl in Berlin was soon forgotten in the euphoria of reunification a few months later, it remains one of the abiding memories of those days for anyone who witnessed it, proof that much of West German youth had not only been successfully demilitarized during the Cold War but successfully denationalized as well. For them, the openings along the Wall heralded the end of a system and they were clear they did not want it replaced with Kohl's capitalist and conservative values.

The following morning was calm. At the nearby Potsdamer Platz, pre-war Berlin's answer to Piccadilly Circus, which the Wall had divided into two, there were rumours of a new opening. The small crowd that had gathered on the eastern side watched the rusty old tramlines being cleared to prepare for a new breach. An old man wheeling his bicycle looked on and recalled how the square, now a deserted wasteland, had been the glorious centre of the city's commercial life before Hitler. 'Large Jewish shops such as Herzog – wealth beyond all dreams,' he whispered to me. It seemed that despite the new checkpoints established along other parts of the Wall during the night, the Potsdamer Platz would not be opened that day. Everywhere crowds milled around, expecting new breaches in the Wall. The tempo of life in both East Berlin and West Berlin was changing rapidly. In the West, a taxi driver of Middle Eastern origin asked me, 'Can't you British stop this? The racist East Berliners will come and change everything here.'

The exodus to the West made it possible to get tickets for *Hochzeit des Figaro*, a new production, at the Komische Oper. Over the coming days, there were unforgettable performances of *Freischütz* as well as this memorable *Figaro* with a countess whose aria in Act II was sung with a haunting pianissimo. The Komische Oper is a small house, one of the gems originally designed by that nineteenth-century Austrian architectural duo Helmer and Fellner, whose buildings house opera from Vienna to Odessa. During the interval of *Figaro*, I wandered into the foyer. The public spaces here are grand but not extensive, so it was possible in twenty minutes to see everyone who was in the audience. While mounting the main staircase, I saw in front of me the newly appointed East German government spokesman, Wolfgang Meyer, standing with his wife in the foyer genially saying hello to various Party officials. These kinds of encounter always posed for me a momentary dilemma: should the correspondent exploit the coincidence, breezing up to the politician in hope of gleaning something of interest, or do good manners dictate that such unplanned interviews should always be avoided? That evening I decided that, in the middle of such sublime music, it would be a jolt to switch into investigative mode and ask another devotee of Mozart about politics. Act II beckoned; besides, it was doubtful whether Herr Meyer would have his job for very much longer, or have anything of value to say.

At dinner at the Grand afterwards two West German journalists wept into their glasses, overcome by the sentiments of the day. Like most of our German colleagues, over the last forty-eight hours they had become unrecognizable, transformed from clinical, dispassionate, humourless technocrats into emotional wrecks.

The following day, at 7 a.m., the Potsdamer Platz opened at last – the beginning of a process which would ensure that this square once again took its place among the great metropolitan centres of the world. But that morning, amid the barren concrete wasteland, such thoughts were still far away. When the new entry point was identified, the crowd surged forward and I found myself alongside a senior officer of the East German border guard. 'Wohin?' I asked. To my surprise, mistaking me for a German, he told me candidly that he just wanted to see inside the house on the other side of the border which he had been staring at from his checkpoint for the last fifteen years.

The crowd, becoming impatient, began chanting, 'We want to go to the Philharmonic!' A young officer appeared and climbed a temporary set of wooden steps. Talking through a loudspeaker, he said, 'You will shortly be permitted to pass through. But when you go, remember that these are your sons and brothers who are standing before you guarding this frontier, so pass forward in a disciplined

THE END OF THE ANCIEN RÉGIME

and German manner!' This calmed the crowd down, but as soon as the opening was completed they swept across. Having no wish to go to West Berlin, I detached myself and tried to return to the hotel in East Berlin, but it was too late. The East German guards, with predictable thoroughness, were setting up trestle tables with visa forms and rubber-stamps to check anyone wishing to enter. Because of the early hour, I had left my passport and accreditation in the hotel and I was now stranded between East and West Berlin. The East German guards became very bureaucratic and I had to insist, in my best authoritarian German, that they find an officer to whom I could explain my case. Five minutes later, a tired-looking officer whose badges of rank indicated that he was a full colonel appeared. At first he would not relent, but when I fixed him in the eye and addressed him in my most military Austrian as Herr Rittmeister (cavalry captain), his attitude changed immediately. He politely escorted me back to the East and saluted.

After their initial surprise, the East German authorities appeared to have the situation temporarily under control. Thanks to the new openings in the wall, Berlin seemed to be quietening down, but what was happening elsewhere in the country? I decided to return to Leipzig and Dresden. In Leipzig, I again saw Masur walking among the demonstrators, hands in his pockets. This time he looked even more distraught; indeed, he appeared on the verge of a nervous breakdown. As a beneficiary of the 'old system', its imminent collapse must have filled him with ambivalent feelings. The posters and placards around him bore mixed messages. Some, clearly planted by the authorities (they were too well made), carried the slogan 'What will happen to our money?' Others, less well constructed but more numerous, demanded *Rache* (revenge) for years of Communist mismanagement. Time was running out for the political elite which had supported Masur throughout his career. The opening of the Wall might have temporarily stabilized the situation in Berlin, but if the size of the crowd in Karl Marx Platz was anything to go by, tensions in Leipzig were still running high.

In Frankfurt a few months earlier, while waiting for a train connection for Munich, I had fallen into conversation with the stationmaster and had asked him which was the most interesting of Germany's railway stations to work in. He had paused for a few moments before saying that, if he had had a magic wand, he would have wanted to be stationmaster at Leipzig. 'The greatest job in the entire German railway network,' he had said in reverential tones. Curious to see if there was any truth in this, I made my way the following morning to a vast, almost completely deserted Leipzig railway station. Where hundreds of trains had rolled in and out of its platforms a few days earlier, there was now only an eerie silence beneath the huge steel and glass canopy of the station's roof.

With difficulty I found an official and asked if I could see the stationmaster. A few minutes later I was ushered into the office of the *Reichsbahnhauptrat*, a small tubby man with glasses called Paulusch. Despite being a long-standing and committed Communist Party member, he was friendly and informative. He neither regretted nor celebrated the dramatic political developments of the last few days. His life and duty was this station and the trains which normally occupied its many platforms. He conceded that his workforce had evaporated, but he was confident he could maintain a 'skeleton network' for the next two days with the help of reservists and pensioners. 'It is important that the young are satisfied at this particular moment. We can help them,' he said, adding that he expected 'normality' to be restored by the end of the week, 'or perhaps a little later'.

I returned to the hotel hoping to find a *Times* photographer who might capture Leipzig railway station for posterity: the grandest and most important junction in mainland Northern Europe, virtually empty and ground to a halt. This would be a haunting black and white image but there was little sign of my colleagues. On the way back to my room, I bumped into another photographer, Brian Harris, a former *Times* man, who had transferred over to the *Independent*. I had admired his work for *The Times* when I first wrote for the paper and I knew that he could be relied upon to take a hint from a former colleague. When he asked me if I had seen anything interesting to photograph, I said, 'Go to the railway station and you will capture the atmosphere of this entire revolution.' Harris's photograph of the empty Leipzig railway station that morning is still one of the defining images of those days.

To find another enduring image, I decided to move on from Leipzig to visit those giants of German literature, Goethe and Schiller, both buried in nearby Weimar. A few hours later, a tram took me from Weimar railway station to the Hotel Elephant where another crowd had gathered with candles. Appropriately in a university city, their placards were more sophisticated and internationalist: 'Freedom to the Czech Chartists!', 'Down with the tyranny of Ceauşescu!' – refreshingly unprovincial sentiments which a few days earlier would have been unheard of in a country loyal to the brotherhood of Warsaw Pact nations. The crowd heckled a few visiting West German CDU politicians as they tried to address the demonstrators in front of the equestrian statue of the Kurfürst of Weimar.

All this made for sparkling material, but the challenge of telephoning a story to London from provincial East German cities was proving immense. Pressures of deadlines had made the telex inadequate. For several weeks I had come increasingly to rely on the newspaper's team of excellent copy-takers, an unsung group of heroes and heroines without whom the foreign correspondent in a hurry stood little chance of getting his story to London. But in Weimar this lifeline depended on an underdeveloped and primitive network. The lines to the West from East Germany were overstretched and overused, and even the prestigious Hotel Elephant could not cope. A tall blonde telephonist stiffly informed me that she could not help for at least an hour but – her eyes flashed across the room behind me to check no one was listening as she imparted some information transgressing decades of unhesitating obedience – I 'might have better luck' at the Hotel Russischer Hof across the street.

At the Russischer Hof, another team of tall blonde telephonists proceeded to dial away remorselessly for about thirty minutes without complaining before finding me a line to London. In the half-light, in their crisp white blouses and waistcoats, and with their hair cut and neatly dressed in an almost pre-war style, these young women seemed to be straight out of a Marlene Dietrich film. They were calm, patient and unperturbed by the technical difficulties. The stoical qualities of the stereotyped German Fräulein appeared to be embodied in these helpful, studiously polite damsels of the analogue world. Once connected, the seemingly harmless question, thrown back at the correspondent after a few dictated paragraphs, 'Is there much more of this?', reminded one that the *Times*'s copy-takers were always the severest judges of one's efforts.

By the time the obligatory 850 words had been dispatched, it was well past midnight. A delicious spinach soup and a bottle of beer sent me to sleep instantly, but I was woken around 5.00 a.m. by a pungent smell of pollution such as I had experienced only once before, in Belgrade. The foul-smelling air was coming from thousands of fires burning lignite coal and other non-smokeless fuels. Even with the windows closed, the pollution penetrated every corner of the room. Outside, a yellow haze hung about the soft street lamps. A few hours later, a taxi driver explained that the air quality in Weimar was sometimes so bad that children were advised to stay at home for days on end. A winter before, a month of this foul air had destroyed a beautiful avenue of 300-year-old horse chestnut trees. As we sped towards the cemetery housing the Goethe and Schiller mausoleum, we passed rows of beautiful late nineteenth-century villas coated in black soot and dust. They all appeared to be deserted. Indeed, we were virtually the only car on the road. Weimar, my taxi driver informed me, had 'moved west'. Who knew how many would be coming back?

At the gates to the cemetery, an elderly attendant responded to my ringing for attention. After paying a few pfennigs for entry, I was escorted to a small classical pavilion at the corner of the graveyard. Beyond the cemetery gates, peeling stucco pilasters and crumbling gables appeared to afflict every building. There was no one else to be seen anywhere. Having opened the mausoleum with a large key, the attendant returned to his office. Alone I entered a space lit only by the open door and a large grille in the ceiling which revealed the grey November sky. This gentle light illuminated two classical sarcophagi below. With no railings surrounding them, I knelt for a few moments at the side of these giants of German literature, placing a hand on each sarcophagus in turn. To be left alone with the remains of these men would be a privilege at any time. To be with them on the 14 November 1989 imparted an unforgettable frisson.

How well they would have captured the drama unfolding now across Germany!

Deutschland? Aber wo liegt es?
Wo das gelehrte beginnt, hört das politisch auf.

(Germany? But where does it lie?
Where the educated begins, the political ceases.)*

From Weimar I travelled that afternoon to Erfurt where there was yet another demonstration. But it was a sorry affair compared to Leipzig, Gera or even Weimar. In a shop, I heard an old lady berating a friend with the words, 'I do not believe the world any longer. Everyone queuing for money to go and spend in the West. It's madness. They are only helping inflation. They should stay here and go to church!'

Dotting the route between Weimar and Erfurt were Soviet bases packed with helicopter gunships and tanks. Both these cities were Soviet garrison towns, but the thought that the Russians might soon return to the Soviet Union had not really crossed the minds of the demonstrators. 'I suppose if they go we shall finally have enough apartments for ourselves' was a common response.

That Germany might finally be free of Soviet occupation and even reunified still seemed to be a remote prospect. At a hotel in the old part of the city, rich in picturesque gables and late Renaissance strapwork, another team of dedicated female telephonists struggled to establish a line with London. One of them dialled continuously without response for about fifty minutes, and I apologized for putting them to such trouble. She simply turned and said that she had been so 'marvellously treated' on her first visit to West Berlin the other day, the least she could do was help me. As she said this, her colleague, another exceptionally tall blonde woman, popped out from a nearby room, gazed at me wistfully and added, 'We'd also like to visit England one day.'

Suddenly, the quiet politesse of their efforts was interrupted by loud chants. I saw a large demonstration taking place outside the hotel, this time of 'artists' protesting at the opening of an official fortieth-anniversary Communist exhibition. 'Täter vor Gericht!' (Criminals on trial!) they chanted. This outburst of popular feeling

* Schiller, *Xenien* (1797).

appeared less choreographed than others and more threatening. A worried Party secretary, who was identified by a passer-by as 'Frau Loman', overweight, heavily made-up and wearing a grey trouser suit, demanded that the crowd back away. An art historian joined her, but the sight of these two well-fed officials seemed only to spur the crowd on and they began shaking their fists, forcing Frau Loman and her colleague to beat a hasty retreat. 'Es wird abgerechnet!' (There will be a reckoning!), a demonstrator shouted at her venomously. It was hard to see how these emotions could be kept under control, yet, throughout this time, I never witnessed a single act of violence – a tribute to German self-discipline, even at a time of *Umbruch* (upheaval).

By 16 November, this excitement had died down. Back in Berlin, I walked through a much reduced Checkpoint Charlie where, only a few weeks before, a young East German border guard had shouted at me, 'Nothing will change here.' This time the guards waved me through with no more than a perfunctory look at my papers, and I reached Tegel without delay to catch the next BA flight to London. The West German airline Lufthansa was not permitted to operate any flights along the highly profitable Berlin route. I wondered how much longer the Allied powers would retain their monopoly over civilian flights in and out of Berlin. Strict protocols governed the height and path of all British, French and American air-traffic on this route. As my plane flew at low altitude over the Warsaw Pact training grounds in East Germany, it seemed it would not be long before these artificial constraints on German sovereignty would be lifted.

I had gone to London to recuperate for the weekend but then decided to return to Eastern Europe barely twenty-four hours later when the political temperature again began to rise in Prague. The BBC described a large student demonstration being baton-charged by riot police with considerable violence; there were reports of scores of young Czechoslovaks being hospitalized. That was on Friday, but no Czechoslovak visa could be procured until Monday when the Czechoslovak embassy in London reopened.

First thing that morning I found myself in the dark softly lit concrete bunker of the Czechoslovak embassy visa office where a smiling but uncooperative apparatchik asked me when I hoped to fly to Prague and took my passport. After fifteen minutes he reappeared and asked me to sit down and have a coffee. I struggled hard to suppress my impatience. I was booked on a flight to Prague at midday and the time was now 10.15. I knew that to vent my frustration would be counter-productive, so I settled down to answer a series of banal questions about where I thought Eastern Europe was heading and what I thought might happen in Prague. The minutes ticked by until I had no chance of making the midday flight. I looked at my watch and asked gingerly if my visa was ready. As though he had suddenly remembered something, the diplomat put his hand in his pocket. Smiling, he brought out my passport and visa. 'You should have asked earlier. It has been ready for some time.' If the old order was about to end in Prague, his job would disappear with it and he was clearly determined to make the most of the little pleasures he could still command.

I rushed out of the grim concrete building on Notting Hill Gate, then a partly dilapidated district of west London, and jumped in a cab, but the flight had left a good fifteen minutes before I arrived. Wondering how on earth I could reach Prague that afternoon, I was about to go to the British Airways desk when I bumped into a familiar face from my days in Warsaw. The British Airways office manager in the Polish capital was now in charge of Heathrow Terminal 1. 'In a hurry again?' he asked nonchalantly. I asked how I could get to Prague and he swiftly escorted me to an office where a flight was found via Zurich leaving in half an hour. Within five minutes the paperwork was complete and the boarding gate was waiting for me.

By 6.30 p.m. I was in Prague, following a crowd of demonstrating students marching towards the Charles Bridge. I failed to notice the ranks of red-bereted police blocking our path until it was almost too late. The crowd surged over the bridge and the familiar sound of truncheons on shields heralding an imminent charge began. The police charged, the crowd turned and I was swept back over the bridge towards the tower on the Old Town square, where I tripped and placed my hands over my head as the demonstrators rushed by, desperate to escape their pursuers. For a few seconds I thought I was unlikely to emerge unscathed, but the police never appeared – they had charged only halfway towards us, which was enough to send the students scuttling for cover.

I picked myself up and examined some superficial tears to my clothes. A pretty young woman with her hair in plaits asked me in Hungarian-accented English if I was all right. I was dazed and must have looked rather helpless. Taking my arm she escorted me to the next bridge. She was a Slovak and in Prague for the celebration of the canonization of St Agnes, the patron saint of Bohemia, to be held later that week.

John Paul II had canonized St Agnes of Bohemia in Rome on 12 November. Unable to travel to Italy, Czechoslovaks were preparing for their own ceremony in Prague two weeks later. Thousands of pilgrims would be in attendance and the commemoration was now also set to become a demonstration of anti-Communist sentiment. My Slovak guardian angel told me that the Communist government had that morning summoned the Cardinal Archbishop of Prague, František Tomášek, and tried to bully him into postponing the St Agnes celebrations. He had apparently countered with the words, 'The canonization of St Agnes is a celebration of God, not the Communist Party. I am not answerable to you for it.'

The Slovak girl guided me through some back streets to Štěpánská and the dimly lit Alcron Hotel. I hauled myself up to my room on the fifth floor, past the stained glass and panelling of the dining room where the life-size 1930s statue of a silver naked beauty with outstretched arms permanently beckoned the hungry diner. I collapsed on to my bed and fell asleep, only to be woken at 11.30 p.m. by the telephone and the remote voice of the night editor on the Foreign Desk, commanding me to file 1,500 words by 2.00 a.m. This accomplished, I wandered early the following morning into Wenceslaus Square. It was full of young women, most of them apparently medical students, sweeping the streets with broomsticks. 'We want to show that we are good citizens and will clean up after the mess of our demonstrations,' one of them explained. She sported a badge on her tracksuit proclaiming membership of the International Women's Lacrosse Association; her aquiline nose and square jaw suggested a formidable presence on the playing field. She told me that she was a member of the students' committee and that I could come and see them in their nearby headquarters, borrowed from the grammar school just beyond the Alcron. In this room, a dozen Amazonian women (I assumed the rest of the lacrosse team) were busily engaged in what can only be described as enthusiastic anarchy. Some were typing and copying slogans. Banners were being painted with the words 'Resign! Resign!' On a classroom blackboard was written in giant chalk letters, 'If not us, who? If not now, when?'

A demonstration of musicians and artists was to take place later that afternoon. To find out more, I set off to visit a friend who had a studio near by in the former Dominican convent. On reaching his medieval quarters, I found everything shuttered and closed and was about to return up a side street to the hotel when a car beeped me and I saw another old Czech friend with whom I had spent the previous Easter in western Bohemia. 'Get in,' he shouted. 'You need to see the tanks.' We drove off towards the Janáček Embankment where forty-six armoured riot police vehicles were parked near three larger more heavily armoured trucks. Would this be another 1968 moment? But my friend was undismayed by the presence of all this 'hardware'. 'Everyone has been waiting for the authorities to make a mistake. When they attacked the students on Friday, they only showed how stupid they really are,' he said. Back at the Alcron, there were unprecedented scenes of quasi-revolutionary activity. The normally sedate hotel staff were gathered around a television set volubly watching the 7 o'clock news. As the Communist Party chief of Prague, Štěpán, appeared on the screen, the staff, including the usually politically reliable receptionists and meek telephonists, suddenly began to boo. When Adamec, the Prime Minister, appeared, even the usually placid lobby porter shook his fist. 'They are trying to make everyone believe it is just students, but that is not so,' he insisted.

Later, crowds began to queue outside the hotel for the evening newspapers. What had occurred to bring about this dramatic change in mood? Within a couple of days, the Czechs had thrown off their apathy and had become determined on upheaval. One of the catalysts was the widely disseminated news earlier that day that a young student, Martin Šmid, had been so badly beaten on the previous Friday that he had died. While the political authorities half-heartedly attempted to correct this rumour – a clever invention – the news of

Šmid's 'brutal treatment and death' spread across the city like wildfire. Another Czech student, Petr Payne, dressed in an English-looking Barbour, said in an interview that he had witnessed the murder. The ruling hard-line elite fell straight into the trap. They no longer had a monopoly of news and their lack of credibility meant that the rumours of their wrongdoing significantly overwhelmed their official denials. As it happened, Šmid was found a few days after the revolution, healthy and unharmed, but on that Monday the reports of his death had served their purpose. For the first time in decades, the Prague Czechs threw off their caution and became collectively incensed, openly venting their anger. They now began to swell the ranks of the student demonstrators and huge crowds began to gather in Wenceslaus Square.

Despite his high profile among the Western media, Václav Havel, the dissident playwright, had never commanded a particularly wide following in Prague. Cardinal Tomášek probably attracted many more supporters through his sermons than Havel ever had, but in the new mood of resentment and anger gripping Prague, Havel now emerged as a focus for political change. He was ably supported by another prominent dissident, Jiří Dienstbier. Both were removed from the Czechoslovak mainstream, but if these avowedly atheist dissidents could link arms with the Czechoslovak Catholic Church over a sea of Communist outrages, the opposition movement would be immeasurably strengthened. Thanks to the happy coincidence of the canonization of St Agnes, Prague was more and more packed with anti-Communist Slovak Catholic pilgrims, who were also taking to the streets. The 'revolution of students and playwrights' had found some powerful allies.

Crowds with a voracious appetite for news began to gather outside the Alcron. They struggled to see messages typed and pinned to windows and walls or even the windscreens of cars. This was the most news-hungry population I had ever seen; it was as if war had suddenly broken out. As in East Germany, the people had clearly lost their fear of the state apparatus. That night, I wrote in my diary that the government must have been terrified. The following morning, Wednesday 22 November, I was woken by a Czech friend who said she had important news but could not speak over the telephone.

Could I come over and see her at 2.00 p.m.? After a breakfast of scrambled eggs with raw onions, a Bohemian speciality, I set off for the university where a student called Lucy was pinning a news bulletin to one of the walls. Lucy was bright and clear-eyed and I began to ask her the usual questions about where she thought events were leading. On hearing I was a journalist, she suggested I should meet her father, the editor of one of Prague's most prestigious papers. He had just returned from Namibia. He was a Communist ('He could not have got a job without being a member of the Party'), but Lucy thought he would be pleased to meet me.

After a phone call, she walked me round the corner to a nineteenth-century building which housed the editorial offices of *Mladá Fronta*. A rather bemused secretary showed us into a small office where a jovial grey-haired man rose to his feet. After his daughter had effected the introductions, he smilingly asked me one simple question. Did I know Neal Ascherson, the Eastern Europe Correspondent for the *Observer*? When I replied that we had been friends for some years, he visibly relaxed and offered me a cigarette. His daughter left us alone and from that moment I was granted almost unlimited access to this intelligent editor's time and thoughts. This was to prove of immense value in the days to come. 'Ottokar' was certainly part of the Communist reformist apparatus, a man well connected to the Communist *nomenklatura* and intelligence services. As the days wore on, it quickly became apparent that 'Ottokar' also had intimate links with Moscow.

During my final architectural history supervisions at Cambridge, I had been introduced by Professor David Watkin to the idea that political revolutions were usually organized from above, not from below. (It was a sign of the intellectual breadth of a Cambridge education of those days that one did not need to be reading History or Politics to discuss such ideas with the dons of other faculties.) Theories which had lodged in the deepest recesses of the mind a dozen years earlier now sprang back as it suddenly dawned on me that a reformist wing of the Communist Party was driving parts of this revolution, and was driving it with the conscious backing of Moscow. At this stage 'Ottokar' was cautious, pessimistic even. The Party chief of Prague, Štěpán, was 'one of those people who would stop at nothing to hold on to power', he explained. 'Do not under-estimate the support for the Party. The army, the militia, the police and all the factory workers are in favour of the status quo.' He urged me to keep in touch. 'The situation could change at any moment.'

I reflected on his words and the pensive expression of a man whose world (and privileges) could be coming to an end. I returned to the hotel, filed a 'holding' piece and then went off in search of my Czech friend who had wanted to contact me so urgently first thing in the morning. Agnieska, a dark-haired medical student, was keen to take me to a hospital where those who were not Party members were treated and where some of those wounded during the demonstrations of the previous days were recovering. In contrast to Czechoslovak hospitals reserved for Party members (there was a gleaming example next door), this building was squalid. Cigarette butts were strewn all over the corridors. The wounded students were in a sorry state. Many of them had head injuries but they were adamant they would be back on the streets as soon as they had recovered: they were not giving up now 'blood had been drawn'. The medical staff treating them appeared to be made up largely of volunteers. From here we descended to the suburb of Smíchov and back to Wenceslaus Square, where vast crowds were gathering again. Half an hour later I was making my way out of the Alcron when a woman with the femme-fatale features of an Alfons Mucha painting appeared.

Her name was Daniela. She was another member of the lacrosse team and had been instructed to bring me to the Laterna Magika Theatre in a warren of underground spaces constructed not far from the Alcron in the 1920s. There I listened to the student dissidents and their unknown mentors spell out their demands for the government's resignation. When a representative of one of the biggest factories in Prague took to the stage and pledged support for the students, the applause was ecstatic. The constellation of anti-government forces was growing. Daniela sat next to me whispering an English translation; her soft melodic cadences reinforced the atmosphere of subterranean complicity.

It snowed that afternoon and the demonstrators dispersed peace-fully. The police had looked on but not intervened. However, their presence in nearby side streets suggested a build-up of force was being prepared. The following morning was icy but sunny. The momentum for change appeared to be stalling. Communist militia occupied the TV studios; the television crews had gone on strike in protest at not being allowed to broadcast events in Wenceslaus Square. 'Ottokar' appeared distracted by this turn of events but promised 'full details tomorrow' if I 'remained silent' today. 'Today is the decisive day. The Politburo will meet at 5.30 p.m. and there will be an attempt by three of its members to unseat President Husák and General Secretary Jakeš. If this does not happen the situation will become critical.' He had lunched with 'two of the men in this drama and they are still hesitating to play their hand'.

He gave a vivid description of the uncertainties plaguing the decision-making at the apex of the Communist power pyramid. 'The moment may not be quite right, but if they do not move now, there will be no chance for Communism in this country. Then, because no one imagines how we can leave the Warsaw Pact, it could become very dangerous.' It seemed that even among the best-informed elements of the Party, no one had the slightest inkling of how radical the imminent changes would be and how even 'reformist' Communism and the Warsaw Pact would be swept away. I was back at the Alcron and halfway through a bowl of pea soup when I was paged by the reception who said London was on the phone. The Foreign Desk had picked up a Reuters story predicting military intervention and quoting a senior Czech officer who said that the army would defend socialism 'to the end'. But according to my source the Politburo was still meeting and the Central Committee would meet the following day so I did my best to calm my colleagues in London. I optimistically promised 'sunshine and roses' soon, imploring them to keep their nerve and to dismiss any rumours of a military coup for what they were: provocations.

The afternoon and evening passed without event. The following day I awoke to find the sky white with snow. The rumours of military intervention had seized the BBC. Another Czech journalist contact, briefing me that morning on the night's events, had to break off to take a call from his wife asking if the militia had occupied his office. But as 'Ottokar' had predicted, the last twenty-four hours had been decisive: matters were now slowly relaxing ahead of the Central

Committee's meeting. The militia had withdrawn from the TV studios and the crews had returned to beam images of the demonstrations across the world and, more importantly, into the hundreds of thousands of Slovak homes which had recently acquired colour television. As the provinces were being won over by these broadcasts it was suddenly announced that Alexander Dubček, the leader of the Prague Spring in 1968, would be making his first appearance in Prague in public since then on a balcony in Wenceslaus Square. I called an English friend who had lived in Prague since the 1970s and urged her to come to Wenceslaus Square at 3 p.m. for 'an historic moment'. She was only persuaded with the greatest of difficulty because her mother had phoned her from London to tell her that the BBC had spent the day predicting another Tiananmen Square. She agreed to come but ordered her daughters to stay at home.

By 3 p.m., the crowds in Wenceslaus Square had swelled to hundreds of thousands. Together my friend and I made our way out of the Alcron and down the crowded 50 yards into the square. Scores of chimneysweeps, with soot-covered faces and large coiled pipe cleaners around their shoulders, stood dressed in black and white, an old symbol of Enlightenment Prague. Some of them had clambered on to the art nouveau roof of the Hotel Europa. Thanks to the chimneysweeps, hundreds had accessed long-forgotten stairways and climbed through lanterns and domes to emerge watching silently from the roofs of nearby buildings. It was as if every fire escape, hidden ladder and roof passage had been reopened to allow as many people as possible to catch a glimpse of the man who had been forced into silence for twenty-one years. Then the old familiar voice rang out across the square. As Dubček spoke, his melancholy vowels seemed to turn the sky an extraordinary hue: white, grey, a hint of orange in the snow-filled clouds. The silhouettes of every building suddenly appeared sharper as if we were protagonists in a black and white pre-war postcard. When Dubček spoke of 'Socialism with a human face', the slogan of his 1968 reform programme, the crowd sensed the moment and as in Trieste in 1914 a *silenzio assoluto* reigned.

After Dubček came the equally familiar if more grating voice of Havel, ripping the air and promising a new era for Czechoslovakia, but I could listen to barely five minutes of this. Looking at my watch

I realized that the deadline for the first edition meant I would have to file within the next twenty-five minutes. Hastily scribbling some notes, literally on the back of an envelope, I left my friend and squeezed my way slowly through the crowds to the Alcron. So crammed with people was the road back to the hotel that the 50-yard journey took almost fifteen minutes. On entering the hotel I found beaming smiles on all the faces of the usually melancholy receptionists. They immediately set about connecting me with London and while I sat in a corner to file my report, the wing-collared head waiter approached to ask whether he should keep me some food if I were working late again and missing dinner. Bowing with a formal but sincere courtesy, he promised to keep the kitchen open until 2.00 a.m., an unprecedented favour.

Fifteen minutes later, just as I had put the phone down to London, my English friend burst into the hotel, this time with a ticket for the Czech Philharmonic at the nearby Smetana Hall. 'You have to hear this!' she insisted. We headed off, arriving just in time for the concert which was to begin at 6.30. To my surprise I saw 'Ottokar' in the front row. He waved me to my seat with a look that said, 'Things are moving.'

The orchestra had sat down and was about to play when the leader stood up unexpectedly. Taking a crumpled piece of paper from his pocket, he read out what amounted to a manifesto, pledging the orchestra's support 'to the cause of democracy'. After he had sat down, the conductor turned to the crowd and gave the 'V for Victory' sign which sent the audience into a paroxysm of cheering. Without waiting for this near-hysteria to die down, the conductor raised his baton and brought the orchestra in for a rousing performance of Smetana's 'Ma Vlast' (My Homeland), the unofficial Czech national anthem. The musicians played with visible passion. When it ended and the ecstatic applause had died away, the leader stood up and was again handed a piece of paper by one of his colleagues. He read out a text that said the entire Central Committee had resigned, and once again the audience burst into delirious cheering. I immediately went to find a telephone in the nearby Hotel Paris, but the telephonists were adamant that every line was 'taken', so I made my way quickly back to the Alcron where the staff immediately connected me to London.

The new Central Committee leader was Karel Urbánek, but 'Ottokar', whom I found a little later that evening, thought this was unlikely to last. Urbánek was 'the worst possible solution'. Another 1,500 words made their way to London just before 2.00 a.m., courtesy of the Alcron telephonists. Ten minutes later I demolished the spinach soup and beer which the loyal head waiter had kept for me at a table in the deserted stained-glass-decorated dining room.

The following day the thermometer outside the window of my fifth-floor balcony read minus 5 °C, but it was a bright morning. The canonization of St Agnes was set to be celebrated in St Vitus' Cathedral so I made my way across the Charles Bridge and joined the thousands of Slovaks, many of them in national costume and their women in bright-red headscarves, walking up to the castle. As I neared the castle entrance, I saw thousands of the pilgrims gather outside Cardinal Tomášek's palace, where they awaited a glimpse of the only Czech they unequivocally loved and admired. To tremendous cheers he appeared on the balcony with a broad smile. After the service, the crowds milled around singing hymns and Marian anthems. It was a scene of Catholic fervour such as I had previously witnessed only in Warsaw. In the Černý Orel (Black Eagle) pub opposite the Palais Czernin (Foreign Ministry), I joined some of the pilgrims sitting next to Czechoslovak conscript soldiers, now sporting the Czech tricolour on their drab uniforms. The beer here was the finest in Prague. Long years of slaking the thirst of exhausted bureaucrats, whether under the rule of Maria Theresa or the Communists, had given the Black Eagle a reputation unequalled anywhere in Prague.

That evening I dined with some Czechs celebrating the release from prison of our mutual friend Moriz, a devout Catholic who was overjoyed to be free in time to celebrate St Agnes's canonization. Moriz had been thrown into prison after a demonstration a month earlier during which he had distributed some Catholic leaflets. His wife, an elegant woman in a crisp white-collared Black Watch tartan suit, said she had lost kilos worrying about him in prison. Moriz, however, insisted he had enjoyed it because it was the closest he had ever got to living in a monastic cell (monasteries being banned in Czechoslovakia). There was plenty of time to think and pray, a 'real luxury' in a Communist state. Also at the dinner were the musical Chargé d'Affaires and his wife who soon lost their chancery stiffness when I produced two bottles of champagne, courtesy of the head waiter at the Alcron. We sang our way through various *Lieder* until three in the morning.

A few hours later, London woke me up with the usual barrage of questions (What's happening now? Can you see any soldiers? etc. etc.). I promised to give them an update at midday and once again urged them not to believe the 'rumours' about an imminent military coup. Their confusion and anxiety were understandable. It required nerve to listen to your man on the spot when everyone else was giving a different story. The unhesitating confidence in the correspondent in the field which had been the hallmark of the Douglas-Home regime had undoubtedly been undermined by the relentless carousel of editorial appointments.

Outside the temperature was now minus 12°C and it was snowing again. I walked to the Church of St Jakob where the announcements board at the main entrance provided a witty reminder that reform was not yet a 'done deal'. It stated that the music for that morning was to be the Coronation Mass by Mozart but this had been hastily crossed out and replaced with Haydn, 'Missa in tempore belli' (Mass in time of war).

The Haydn was performed vigorously to a packed church. When the music was not being performed, the old Latin ritual marked the liturgy of the Universal Church. After mass, I met some Czech friends who invited me to lunch, dispatching their six-year-old son to the nearest pub with a large jug to get some beer. On his return, three generations sat down to Sunday lunch. The eldest, a lady in her late seventies, told us, 'Twenty-one years ago, it was just the same. We had ten days of euphoria and then ... the Russians.' She was right. Everything now depended on the Russians rather than the Czechs. To what extent were they prepared to support the reforms and how far would they allow those reforms to run?

After lunch I again visited 'Ottokar' in his offices, which were now picketed by guards 'to prevent provocations'. Despite all the optimism of the previous evening at the Czech Philharmonic, he now echoed the old lady's words: 'Twenty-one years ago in 1968 I was a young man and I stood here in this very room watching NBC make the first satellite broadcast about the Prague Spring. I told them that there was no chance of the Russians coming in! Now I am very cautious.'

There were still many dangers. 'The Party is split,' he warned me. 'Those who are passive at the moment may become active.' The situation in Moravia was not very comforting. The workers there were reluctant to join the strikes. They were putting up posters in their factories saying, 'We want to eat, not strike.' It also had not helped that the crowds had shouted 'Resign' at the local Party leader, Adamec. He still had power and the hard-line Communists were still capable of regaining the ascendancy. If that happened, 'Ottokar' warned me, it would be immediately apparent on television because the studios, which had now resumed normal service, would be the first target of those wishing to organize a counter-revolution. Early that evening after filing another long story, I fell asleep only to be awoken by a telephone call from 'Ottokar' urging me to get to the International Press Centre, recently set up in the Intercontinental Hotel, to hear the 'latest developments'.

When I arrived at the hotel around 8.30 p.m. I found about 300 of my media colleagues milling around. Then just as I was resigning myself to yet another long and trying night, I spied 'Ottokar' in the corner of the room. With delightful skill, he wandered past the row of seats where all we British journalists were sitting and through the most fleeting of eye contacts indicated the queue for coffee where I gingerly strolled to join him. Although I tried to walk nonchalantly across the room, I felt the eyes of several colleagues following me. A few minutes later, once their attention had receded, we walked separately out of the room into the dark concrete foyer beyond.

'Ottokar' had a fascinating tale to tell. An hour earlier, the new Central Committee had voted almost unanimously to send in the army the following morning to restore order. But they had no sooner taken this vote than a 'gentleman from the Soviet embassy' had appeared with a 'personal message from Comrade Gorbachev'. This had read simply: 'The Central Committee of the Czechoslovak Socialist Party is entitled to take whatever steps are necessary to restore public order in Prague but it may be helpful for you to know that as of midnight tonight I have ordered all Soviet military personnel stationed in Czechoslovakia to remain confined to their barracks and other installations.'

When asked for clarification, the Soviet diplomat had added, off the cuff, that the message was clear: the present crisis was not a situation which would be resolved by resorting to the old methods. He seemed to be telling them, my Czech friend said, that 'the ship is sinking.'

The implications of the 'gentleman's message' were obvious. Any military or police crackdown in Prague and elsewhere in the country would be unsupported by the Soviet military. We both knew that the Czech authorities would never orchestrate a violent crackdown on their own population unsupported by the Soviets. What he had told me would in itself make a sensational story, but in true Czech style my friend saved the best until the end. 'The interesting thing was', he began almost absent-mindedly, 'the Soviet diplomat who delivered this message was the son of the Soviet official in the Prague embassy who called Moscow in 1968 to advise Brezhnev to send in the tanks.' My friend's eye met mine. He was savouring the moment.

Thanking him as discreetly as possible, I gently broke away to move towards the telephone booths to file an update to London, but to reach the telephone booths I had to pass again through the room where my colleagues were gathered. Two of the more alert among them began to follow me. I fell into a booth, got through to the copy-takers immediately and started to dictate a 'new top' to my earlier story, including the emergency meeting of the new Central Committee, and the outcome of its deliberations both before and after the Soviet démarche. I took a childish, arrogant delight in seeing one after another of my colleagues walk casually past my telephone booth and linger for a few seconds hoping to catch the gist of what I was saying sotto voce to London.

Once I had dictated my piece, there was nothing else to do. After the long, intense days of the last few weeks, exhaustion was taking hold. I no longer cared whether the paper used my story or not. I had filed what I knew. If they decided it did not carry weight and pre-ferred to follow the conventional narrative, so be it. It was time to set off back to the Alcron where, after more filing for later editions, I went to bed at around 3.00 a.m.

Then, as now, foreign pieces for a newspaper always ran the risk of domestic events knocking them off the page, so it was with a philo-sophical attitude that I listened the following morning, Monday 27

November, when the desk woke me up at 8.30 a.m. to inform me that the paper was holding the piece. Two days later I was told that 'unfortunately' my old friend and mentor at Cambridge, Norman Stone, had pushed me off the page with a large feature about Lord Aldington's victorious libel claim against Nikolai Tolstoy. Tolstoy had alleged that Aldington had been instrumental in the repatriation of thousands of Cossacks and non-Communist Yugoslavs to what he knew would be certain death in May 1945, an obvious war crime. Aldington's victory, accompanied as it was by a successfully upheld award of millions of pounds in damages and legal fees and the unprecedented destruction of every copy of Tolstoy's book in British public libraries, was undoubtedly an exciting piece of news and I could hardly resent a former Cambridge mentor.

In Prague meanwhile a general strike was called for the afternoon of the 27th. The staff of the Alcron made great efforts to keep our lines of communication with London flowing while putting on a strong demonstration of solidarity with their striking countrymen. Bells and car horns sounded at midday. The waiters at the hotel, immaculately turned out in their lunchtime uniform of white jacket and bow tie, gathered in the hotel foyer to shake hands with each other and congratulate the excellent pianist who normally accompanied our dinners, and who now struck up Czech national songs in place of his usual Cole Porter medley. Even the formidable manageress, Mrs Charvátová, whose opinion and 'protection' decided whether one got a room or not, appeared in rather smart Western clothes with a Czechoslovak tricolour flag pinned to her lapel. She had been a hard-line Communist of the old school just a few days earlier, so I congratulated her on her 'conversion' to a more enlightened cause. She affected not to notice my thinly veiled sarcasm and fixed me with a steely glare, snapping her fingers at an underling. 'A flag for this gentleman! Mr Bassett is one of us!'

I set off to visit 'Ottokar' who by now agreed that the battle was more or less won and that the danger of counter-revolution had probably passed, although he predicted that in Slovakia it would require another few days to 'subdue' the Communist leadership. In that struggle the detested President Husák might be able to play a role before he too departed the scene. In this way 'one's enemies could help one's friends,' he explained.

The news of progress on all fronts tallied with that most eccentric of political barometers in Prague, one which always had struck me as quintessentially Czech: the modest art deco Modêva ladies' hat shop on the right-hand side of Wenceslaus Square. This small shop, which boasted an unrestored 1920s interior, had long tailored its window to political events. When Gorbachev had visited Prague in 1988 its window had sported eighteen hats, all of them a bright Soviet red. During the weekend after the first November beatings of the demonstrators, all the hats in the window were stark black and white. A week later the window had borne hats of the three Czech national colours: blue, white and red. Today, on the eleventh day of the so-called Velvet Revolution, Modêva was displaying a window of exclusively blue hats. Communist red had been banished for good.

There were other characteristically Czech signs of change. As I made my way to see a contact whose offices took me past the memorial to Egon Erwin Kisch, the greatest of the twentieth-century *rasende* (rushing) reporters in whose shadow all we latter-day correspondents worked, I noticed that invisible hands had scratched the rendering away from the corners of the Biedermeier buildings near by to reveal the old street names in German and Czech script. This was a powerful symbol of the city's long overdue reconnection with its historical links with the rest of German-speaking Central Europe.

A press conference on the castle hill given by the newly constituted dissident-led political group Civic Forum illuminated the lack of political experience of the men who had had greatness thrust upon them. Father Maly, a handsome Catholic priest and the Forum's spokesman, asked us all to make the sign of the cross – a courageous gesture but one unlikely to win him friends among the atheist and Hussite men now taking over the levers of political power. One of these, Jiří Dienstbier, was clearly uncomfortable with any signs of overt Christianity. I had seen him, the ardent Communist of the 1950s, the dissident of the 1970s and the 'we are not anti-Communists' of the late 1980s, only a few weeks earlier, clad in pyjamas in his western Bohemian dacha, unshaven and with the long unwashed hair of a 1960s Central European beatnik. Through an act of stupendous self-improvement, his appearance had been transformed. His hair was cut, he had shaved and he was wearing a suit. I have often wondered at what point he decided to break the habits of a lifetime and join the well-groomed political elite. Whenever it was, I think future historians might date the success of the Velvet Revolution to that moment.

Because he seemed keen to overshadow the more modest Fr Maly, I wondered whether he was manoeuvring to take over the priest's position as Civic Forum spokesman. His demand that Husák, the Czech President, should resign by 10 December was imprudent as well as naive. Husák's wide-ranging legal powers were intact, so it would be far better to force him to deploy them to dismantle as much of the Communist architecture as possible. And the news from Slovakia was still disquieting.

At the same time, rumours about the army's role a few days earlier were circulating among the more imaginative news agencies. Did the army mutiny? Was there a split in the General Staff? People forgot that although the Czechs have a martial tradition which runs deeper than the amusing superficialities of *The Good Soldier Schweik*, they are one of the least aggressive nations in the world. In 1939 and in 1968, Czechoslovak troops remained in their barracks at times of national crisis. Twenty-one years later, true to form, there was no appetite among their senior military men to become involved in the latest upheaval. Perhaps in similar situations in Poland or Serbia, the army would have played a more active role, but those who wanted to imagine there might be a Czech military component to the Velvet Revolution were disregarding history.

The next day brought confirmation that some Communist elements were still resisting. 'The conservatives are mobilizing,' a Czech friend said as we strolled past the printing works which housed the insurance office where Kafka had worked. But Moscow was still involved, facilitating the reinsertion of one of the major figures of 1968, Zdeněk Mlynář, who now, at their bidding, after long years in Vienna, moved to Prague. The key to Mlynář's reappearance was Gorbachev's desire to re-evaluate publicly the Warsaw Pact invasion of 1968. He was expected to do so the following day at a press conference in Rome, but to prepare the ground Czech television was to interview Mlynář about 1968 that very evening.

This intimacy between Moscow and the reformist elements in the Communist apparatus had long ceased to surprise me, but when we met later that day I was unprepared for 'Ottokar's' next revelation: he had been summoned to Moscow the following morning to meet the Soviet Foreign Minister, Shevardnadze, and to give him a detailed briefing on the situation in Prague. 'The Russians think we are bunglers!' he said, describing the apparent verdict of the Gorbachev circle. My friend was confident that Mlynář would eventually appear on television at 10.30 that night. If he did not appear, it would show that the 'conservatives' were making progress.

That evening, a farewell concert for John Macgregor, the outgoing Chargé d'Affaires, in the British embassy included a poignant performance of Schubert's Quintet in which he gamely took the cello part. The able Chargé had held the embassy together for three years, coping with one ambassador being in hospital for weeks, another being *en poste* in Vienna for half the year and a clutch of expulsions which had left him often running things single-handedly. This he had done with great humour, sangfroid and bonhomie. The newly arrived Consul and Chargé replacements had pitched up the week before and were both running to catch their breath. In the course of the first forty-eight hours they had had to discard everything they had been told for months in briefings in London, notably the idea, current in Whitehall, that Communist reforms were 'running into the sands'.

The following day, 1 December, was, appropriately enough, Campion Day, the Jesuit feast dedicated to the martyr Edmund Campion, who after studying at Oxford had taught in Prague during the 1570s. Along with John Dee and Philip Sidney, Campion had been one of the great English figures to visit the city in its most glorious period. But if Campion's spirit glided along the frosty ice of the Malá Strana squares that morning it was becoming clearer by the hour that the new order in Prague was taking a secular direction. The Civic Forum held another press conference where it was immediately apparent that Dienstbier had replaced Fr Maly as spokesman.

Mlynář meanwhile, a day later than expected, had finally given his interview, enabling Gorbachev to pay lip-service to the fiction of Czechoslovak 'independence' and revisit in turn the subject of 1968 in his press conference in Rome later the same day. Mlynář had been cautious in talking about 1968, preferring to dwell on the 'dreadful consequences' that might arise should the 'current experiments' fail. That night, alarm sirens sounded in the city. Although they were only to warn of smog so that the elderly and children could stay at home, they gave everyone an uneasy feeling. Sleep in any case was becoming an increasingly rare luxury. For several weeks I had been living on my nerves and painful stomach cramps implied imminent exhaustion.

On 3 December, the government announced that it would be holding an extraordinary press conference which was expected to include a formal request to the Soviet Union to withdraw its military infrastructure from the Czechoslovak Republic.

Meanwhile at a summit in Malta Gorbachev and President George H. W. Bush of the United States were discussing the possibility of recasting Central Europe as a demilitarized buffer zone between NATO and the Warsaw Pact. The Czechoslovak Republic, together with Hungary and Austria, might constitute this neutralized zone. Soviet troops might even leave Czechoslovakia within two years. My Czech friends wondered what quid pro quo the West might make for this concession. The press conference in the Foreign Ministry building along the river duly announced a new government, but only six of its members were non-Communists. The 'conservatives' were ceding power reluctantly. The large conference room was packed with scores of journalists listening with interest to the new government's agenda and its comments on the continued presence of Soviet troops on Czechoslovak soil.

All eyes were on the officials on the podium as one of them began reading a long statement in Czech. Through years of habit, I turned towards the back of the room where I noticed an upper door quietly open and two figures emerge on to a small 'private' dais behind and above us. One, a thin white-haired man in his seventies, looked familiar. I realized I had seen him several times in the Palais Czernin where he had escorted me to meetings with Foreign Ministry officials. Then, as now, he wore the faded blue uniform of a ministry beadle. He had spoken neither English nor much German, but we had exchanged some pleasantries in Russian. He was obviously an educated man but apparently of no significance in the hierarchy of the ministry. As I looked at him now it was his companion who arrested my attention: a stocky man in his late forties, wearing a coat and trilby hat, as if he had only dropped in for a few minutes to check things were running smoothly and would not be staying long. This man silently watched the men on the stage while the Czech official deferentially bent and whispered into his ear.

There were simultaneous French, German and English versions of what the podium politicians were saying in Czech. The Foreign Ministry official was therefore clearly translating into another language: Russian? I asked myself, who kept their Soviet-style trilby hats on their heads indoors in 1989? Who commanded this kind of special treatment from the old hands of the Czechoslovak Ministry of Foreign Affairs? Everything about this man's clothes and demeanour suggested a senior Russian official. I was almost certainly looking up at the Soviet 'diplomat' who had delivered Gorbachev's 'greeting' to the Central Committee a few days earlier. If this was right I was also looking at the son of the Soviet diplomat who in 1968 had been directly responsible for urging Moscow to snuff out the Prague Spring. At the very least, here was proof that Moscow was carefully watching the progress of political events. 'Ottokar' had as usual been well informed; Moscow was leaving nothing to chance with these 'Czech bunglers'.

In East Berlin, Politburo members were being threatened with arrest. Would Prague go the East German route or would it go the more conciliatory Hungarian route, or, as 'Ottokar' put it when we next met, the German route in a Hungarian way? Would Prague's evaluation of 1968 give the Soviets the window of opportunity to 'deprive the West of an enemy'? As the press conference drew to an end, the two unnoticed observers discreetly retired through their private door. A system was falling, an ideology was being buried and the map of Central Europe was about to be remade, but the head of the KGB in Prague still possessed certain privileges. He vanished as silently and unobtrusively as he had appeared.

Walking back to the Alcron Hotel I saw for the first time in ten days a policeman in Wenceslaus Square. Fog sealed the side streets and the air was again heavy with the unmistakable, almost incense-like smell of burning brown coal. For the first time in many days I was asleep before 3.00 a.m. The following morning I read in *Rudé*

Právo that 'Ottokar' had been promoted to be head of Četeka, the national news agency. His trip to Moscow had obviously been successful. The following day when I visited him it was in the opulent panelled room on the fifth floor of the news agency's headquarters. A large portrait of Lenin still hung on the wall above his desk. He was at the heart of what colleagues called 'the nuclear forces of the Czechoslovak media'. That morning, he had called his 1,700-strong workforce together and told them that he wanted to make the news agency 'open, independent and above all free from government interference'. They had stared at him in amazement and disbelief.

That afternoon I stopped at the Franciscan church and watched a painter high up under the dome swing on a rope across the sanctuary, trying to recover a brush that had fallen 20 feet below him and lodged behind a statue of a Madonna. The reformist Czechs would have to engage in similar acrobatics to navigate the new world they were now entering. Already in the Alcron Hotel, the Czech national tricolours were vanishing from the waiters' jackets and, even though Christmas decorations were being put up, the cameras which had covered every corner of the foyer were still firmly in place, a vivid symbol of the totalitarian state. We fondly imagined they would soon be dismantled along with the rest of the state apparatus of repression and surveillance, not knowing that within a generation such cameras would become de rigueur throughout many parts of the West.

The following day I took a train for Berlin and that same evening wandered under a full moon through the deserted gardens of Sanssouci in Potsdam with only a single swan and some ducks for company. That idol of Victorian England, Frederick II of Prussia, cast a long shadow over the events of these days. Would it be long before the spirit of the Prussian hegemony stirred again? A nearby market in the centre of Potsdam conjured up a harmless picture of an almost fairy-tale Germany. Lantern-lit stalls were selling tin soldiers and wooden toys while a group of young children chanted, 'Einheit, Einheit: wir wollen Einheit' (Unity, unity: we want unity), with a sweetness that only eight-year-old girls in plaits can produce.

That these sentiments did not meet with universal approval beyond Germany's borders was brought home to me a few days later when I was asked to file a story on the meeting in Berlin of the British, French, Soviet and American ambassadors to West Germany. The story was really nothing more than a caption to a photograph of these diplomats in front of the Four Powers' Kontrollratsgebäude (Control Commission Building). Yet this meeting was fraught with symbolism. The photo-opportunity on 11 December was a visual *coup de théâtre*, warning the Germans that reunification and the dramatic de facto changes to West and East Germany's sovereignty were as yet neither legal nor permanent. Despite the euphoria and the public demonstrations of the previous weeks, the four victorious powers of the Second World War were still legally in control of Berlin.

This seemingly harmless meeting was a shot across German populist bows, an unambiguous call for a pause in the momentum which was building up towards reunification in West German political circles. In his memoirs, West Germany's Foreign Minister, Hans-Dietrich Genscher, recalled this event with thinly veiled fury:

> The ambassadors felt it correct to organize a photo-opportunity recording their meeting together at this time. What did they intend by this démarche? A warning to the Germans? ... How had it come to this photographic recording of their meeting? ... Was this the Allies' answer to the peaceful revolution of the DDR and the wishes of all Germans for freedom, democracy and unity? ... I was deeply perturbed.*

A few days later he angrily protested to the NATO foreign ministers that London and Washington would have to choose whether 'they wish to speak to Germany directly or discuss Germany with Moscow'.

Oblivious to these controversies I took a train to the Rhineland to catch a flight back to London for a few days' rest before heading off to Bucharest. In Romania, Moscow was clearly beginning to lay the charges for the demolition of the Ceauşescu tyranny and yet another seismic change.

As the train sped south across Germany in the winter dusk, its compartments were empty; even the Mitropa restaurant car was

---

* Hans-Dietrich Genscher, *Erinnerungen* (Berlin, 1996).

deserted. Outside, a countryside rushed past in which people seemed equally absent. Within a few years, bright lights, modern infrastructure and above all cars would completely transform this landscape.

Two days later, when the bustle and noise of London appeared remote in time and space from everything I had experienced, I headed off to a routine examination at St Thomas's Hospital. I dropped into the Duchy Arms for a drink. A group of retired Buckingham Palace retainers who lived on the nearby Duchy of Cornwall estate were discussing the events in Berlin of the previous weeks. They were all in their late seventies and veterans of the Second World War. They, too, had followed the dramas with interest.

'You can't tell me that there isn't something wrong with a country like Germany,' one of them ponderously argued. 'One moment they are shooting each other for crossing the Wall; the next they are all crying and hugging each other. It just isn't normal, is it?' Here was a practical counterpoint to the elation of the last few weeks. Anglo-Saxon prejudice, or cold realism in the light of bitter experience? Who was I to question the views of those who had also lived through some of Germany's dramas? I hoped they were wrong, but only time would tell.

A few hours later my exhausted enthusiasm for the events I had witnessed was given a check of a more enduring nature. Two doctors at St Thomas's carefully examined my weary body and immediately diagnosed acute appendicitis. The revolution in Bucharest would be one I would miss. For me too, the Cold War was over.

Afterword

In the aftermath of the Soviet withdrawal in 1989 from *Mitteleuropa*, the map of Europe was remade. Two important creations of the 1919 post-Great War settlements, Czechoslovakia and Yugoslavia, were dismantled – the former peacefully, the latter violently. It was the nineteenth-century Czech historian František Palacký who sagely predicted that once the Habsburgs left Central Europe their place would be taken by competing Russian and German influence. The experience of the Warsaw Pact countries in the twentieth century and more recent events in Ukraine in the twenty-first have underlined the truth of Palacký's prediction. In that sense the Cold War was just a phase in the life of a part of the continent which continues to be shaped by historical and geographical constants. When the cost of the Cold War arms race threatened to cripple the Soviet Union, its leadership realized it had no choice but to withdraw from its defensive glacis in Central Europe, but it would be a mistake to imagine Moscow's influence in these parts ceased at the moment its formal power retreated.

Within Palacký's geopolitical parameters, material progress in Central Europe has been enormous since 1989. Warsaw embraced Anglo-Saxon capitalism and flourished, becoming in the space of a few years a prosperous European capital. Berlin followed a similar path and began (tacitly) positioning itself once again to become the rival of Paris and London. Even Prague demonstrated that it was no slouch when it came to the heady new world of private equity and venture capital. The Alcron Hotel, whose faded charms were home for so many correspondents during the Cold War, survived for barely three months after the Velvet Revolution. When it reopened after radical refurbishment a year later, we looked in vain for the stained-glass and faded art deco charm which had given the hotel its unique atmosphere. The Alcron's interiors had survived intact the Nazi occupation in 1939, the arrival of the Red Army in 1945 and the Warsaw Pact invasion in 1968, but against the armoury of 'turbo-capitalism' following the 1989 Velvet Revolution it had proved utterly defenceless. Its bland interiors today could be equally appropriate in Hong Kong or Los Angeles; any hint of the connection with the pre-war world of Masaryk's Prague has been erased.

Very few elements of daily life in Central Europe were impervious to these types of changes. Continuity, however, did not entirely vanish: the duties of a professional musician for example remained more or less unaltered. Passing through the Slovene capital in 2005, I lunched with former colleagues and was pleasantly surprised to be offered back my old job at the Ljubljana Opera House, as if nothing had changed in the intervening twenty-five years. The next season's performances of *La Bohème* still required a first horn player. Despite the violent break-up of Yugoslavia, most of the orchestra were those with whom I had made music a quarter of a century earlier.

But if the life of a professional musician had not changed significantly since the end of the Cold War, the former *douceur de vivre* of the foreign correspondent's world was shattered once developments in modern communication took hold. Paradoxically, while logistics became easier, the burden of competition and costs increased. The small band of British foreign correspondents behind the Iron Curtain may have competed with each other almost as much as we tried to outwit the ideological enemy, but at least we fought alone, untroubled by the imperatives of the digital age with its blogosphere, tweet-decks and demands for instant response. We may have had a pistol pointed at our heads each afternoon as we struggled with deadlines, but we rarely spent more than an hour or two a day at our 'desks'. In the two and a half decades since I last penned a dispatch, the internet and smartphone with camera have undoubtedly changed all that.

As a consequence the modern foreign correspondent faces challenges which were not even part of my generation's worst nightmares.

We could not have imagined our 'authoritative' newspapers changing out of all visual (and intellectual) recognition or indeed in some cases ceasing to exist. The modern foreign correspondent can perhaps take only slight consolation from the fact that our old sparring partners, and sometime allies, the diplomatists, have been rendered possibly even more obsolescent by advances in modern technology.

My professional life in Central Europe began in Trieste in 1979, and Trieste has remained ever since a refuge and inspiration. Whenever, perhaps sometimes to the chagrin of colleagues, I adopted Blanka's mantra 'Ich verschwind mich gern' (I enjoy disappearing), it has usually been to Trieste. I kept in contact with friends there for many years, although gradually, one by one, each has passed away.

Sometimes death brought significant changes. It was to be more than fifteen years after my first visit to the beautiful Torre e Tasso castle beyond Trieste before I stood in the *salotto dell'imperatore* at Duino again, gazing out on to the *Felsen*. Inevitably the wind was blowing under a bright, cloudless sky and once more Rilke's words came to mind:

> *und gesetzt selbst, es nähme*
> *einer mich plötzlich ans Herz: ich verginge von seinem*
> *stärkeren Dasein. Denn das Schöne ist nichts*
> *als des Schrecklichen Anfang*

> (And even if one of them pressed me suddenly against his heart
> I should be consumed in that overwhelming existence
> For beauty is nothing but the beginning of terror)*

This time I was alone, standing in a forlorn and empty room. Large squares of brighter paint revealed where the pictures of Venice, Bohemia and Austria had hung. All the Viennese blue-upholstered furniture had been carried away, along with the fine bust of the Archduke Johann and the exquisite portrait of Maria Theresa, all dispersed by the auctioneer's hammer. Of the sparkling kindness of *Durchlaucht* Raimondo, there was no longer any sign. An almost French iciness seemed to invest the space.

---

* *Duino Elegies* (Leipzig, 1923).

The old Prince had died in 1986 and his descendants had apparently given up the idea of continuing the eclectic old Austrian style accumulated over several earlier generations. These rooms which had resounded to our laughter and happy *Tratsch* were now cold and deserted, the treasures of several hundred years scattered. Where was the desk Rilke had written on? Where were the books the Empress Elisabeth had carefully read, sitting in the old library above the Palladio staircase?

As I walked between Duino and the nearby village of Sistiana, I stumbled across a small plaque announcing the recent dedication of a newly constructed public square, the Piazza Goffredo Banfield, a modest tribute to the 'Eagle of Trieste'.

Banfield had also died in 1986, though not before he had written his memoirs and had been fêted in Vienna. At the reception for its launch, he had cut a dashing figure, dressed in a grey double-breasted suit, cream shirt and midnight-blue tie. He seemed like a sepia photograph in which the only splash of colour was the small red-white-red ribbon of his buttonhole, emblem of the chivalric military brotherhood of which he was the last surviving member.

Apart from the effervescent Salmona, the habitués of the Bar Danubio had also all departed: Giorgio Voghera, Lina Galli and Piero Kern, as well as their friend Alma Morpurgo. Today, some two decades after Voghera's death, his writings are finally receiving the critical praise they merit from a wider international audience, although his books still remain unknown to English-language readers. As for Blanka and Gianpaolo Tamaro, whose lives had become intertwined thirty years before I got to know them, they met a poignant end together when Tamaro's Alfa Romeo crashed in dense fog one winter's evening near Zagreb. The car had been pulverized by an oncoming lorry less than half a mile from the village of Samobor where Blanka had spent her holidays as a child with her *Feldmarschalleutnant* grandfather.

Perhaps it was Marcus Aurelius, writing in Vienna nearly 2,000 years ago, who best described the curious symmetries in our lives: 'All things are interwoven with one another; a sacred bond unites them; there is scarcely one thing that is isolated from another.

Everything is coordinated, everything works together in giving form to the one universe.'*

I like to think that from the Molo Audace, the Triestine sky remains unfailingly the bluest in the Adriatic, but if its infinite horizon tells us anything it is surely that it is not time which passes but we, the fleeting protagonists of our own modest epics, who, etching out the patterns of our lives, move swiftly on.

* *Meditations*, Book VII, 9 (trans. Maxwell Staniforth, Penguin Classics, 1964).

Index

ALLEN LANE
an imprint of
PENGUIN BOOKS

Also Published

Ivan Krastev and Stephen Holmes, *The Light that Failed: A Reckoning*

Alexander Watson, *The Fortress: The Great Siege of Przemysl*

Thomas Penn, *The Brothers York: An English Tragedy*

David Abulafia, *The Boundless Sea: A Human History of the Oceans*

Dominic Sandbrook, *Who Dares Wins: Britain, 1979-1982*

Charles Moore, *Margaret Thatcher: The Authorized Biography, Volume Three: Herself Alone*

Orlando Figes, *The Europeans: Three Lives and the Making of a Cosmopolitan Culture*

Naomi Klein, *On Fire: The Burning Case for a Green New Deal*

Hassan Damluji, *The Responsible Globalist: What Citizens of the World Can Learn from Nationalism*

John Sellars, *Lessons in Stoicism: What Ancient Philosophers Teach Us about How to Live*

Peter Hennessy, *Winds of Change: Britain in the Early Sixties*

Brendan Simms, *Hitler: Only the World Was Enough*

Justin Marozzi, *Islamic Empires: Fifteen Cities that Define a Civilization*

Bruce Hood, *Possessed: Why We Want More Than We Need*

Frank Close, *Trinity: The Treachery and Pursuit of the Most Dangerous Spy in History*

Janet L. Nelson, *King and Emperor: A New Life of Charlemagne*

Richard M. Eaton, *India in the Persianate Age: 1000-1765*

Philip Mansel, *King of the World: The Life of Louis XIV*

James Lovelock, *Novacene: The Coming Age of Hyperintelligence*

Mark B. Smith, *The Russia Anxiety: And How History Can Resolve It*

Stella Tillyard, *George IV: King in Waiting*

Donald Sassoon, *The Anxious Triumph: A Global History of Capitalism, 1860-1914*

Elliot Ackerman, *Places and Names: On War, Revolution and Returning*

Johny Pits, *Afropean: Notes from Black Europe*

Jonathan Aldred, *Licence to be Bad: How Economics Corrupted Us*

Walt Odets, *Out of the Shadows: Reimagining Gay Men's Lives*

Jonathan Rée, *Witcraft: The Invention of Philosophy in English*

Jared Diamond, *Upheaval: How Nations Cope with Crisis and Change*

Emma Dabiri, *Don't Touch My Hair*

Srecko Horvat, *Poetry from the Future: Why a Global Liberation Movement Is Our Civilisation's Last Chance*

Paul Mason, *Clear Bright Future: A Radical Defence of the Human Being*